# Effects of the Second Language on the First

**SECOND LANGUAGE ACQUISITION**
**Series Editor:** Professor David Singleton, *Trinity College, Dublin, Ireland*

This new series will bring together titles dealing with a variety of aspects of language acquisition and processing in situations where a language or languages other than the native language is involved. Second language will thus be interpreted in its broadest possible sense. The volumes included in the series will all in their different ways offer, on the one hand, exposition and discussion of empirical findings and, on the other, some degree of theoretical reflection. In this latter connection, no particular theoretical stance will be privileged in the series; nor will any relevant perspective – sociolinguistic, psycholinguistic, neurolinguistic, etc. – be deemed out of place. The intended readership of the series will be final-year undergraduates working on second language acquisition projects, postgraduate students involved in second language acquisition research, and researchers and teachers in general whose interests include a second language acquisition component.

**Other Books in the Series**
Portraits of the L2 User
    *Vivian Cook (ed.)*
Learning to Request in a Second Language: A Study of Child Interlanguage Pragmatics
    *Machiko Achiba*

**Other Books of Interest**
Cross-linguistic Influence in Third Language Acquisition
    *J. Cenoz, B. Hufeisen and U. Jessner (eds)*
English in Europe: The Acquisition of a Third Language
    *Jasone Cenoz and Ulrike Jessner (eds)*
Foreign Language and Culture Learning from a Dialogic Perspective
    *Carol Morgan and Albane Cain*
The Good Language Learner
    *N. Naiman, M. Fröhlich, H.H. Stern and A. Todesco*
Language Learners as Ethnographers
    *Celia Roberts, Michael Byram, Ana Barro, Shirley Jordan and Brian Street*
Language Revitalization Processes and Prospects
    *Kendall A. King*
Language Use in Interlingual Families: A Japanese-English Sociolinguistic Study
    *Masayo Yamamoto*
The Languages of Israel: Policy, Ideology and Practice
    *Bernard Spolsky and Elana Shohamy*
Motivating Language Learners
    *Gary N. Chambers*
Reflections on Multiliterate Lives
    *Diane Belcher and Ulla Connor (eds)*
The Sociopolitics of English Language Teaching
    *Joan Kelly Hall and William G. Eggington (eds)*
World English: A Study of Its Development
    *Janina Brutt-Griffler*

**Please contact us for the latest book information:**
**Multilingual Matters, Frankfurt Lodge, Clevedon Hall,**
**Victoria Road, Clevedon, BS21 7HH, England**
**http://www.multilingual-matters.com**

**SECOND LANGUAGE ACQUISITION 3**
Series Editor: David Singleton, *Trinity College, Dublin, Ireland*

# Effects of the Second Language on the First

Edited by
Vivian Cook

**MULTILINGUAL MATTERS LTD**
Clevedon • Buffalo • Toronto • Sydney

**Library of Congress Cataloging in Publication Data**
Effects of the Second Language on the First/Edited by Vivian Cook.
Second Language Acquisition: 3
Includes bibliographical references and index.
1. Language and languages–Study and teaching–Psychological aspects.
I. Cook, V.J. (Vivian James). II. Second language acquisition
P53.7 .E37 2003
418–dc21                    2002015681

**British Library Cataloguing in Publication Data**
A catalogue entry for this book is available from the British Library.

ISBN 1-85359-633-7 (hbk)
ISBN 1-85359-632-9 (pbk)

**Multilingual Matters Ltd**
*UK*: Frankfurt Lodge, Clevedon Hall, Victoria Road, Clevedon BS21 7HH.
*USA*: UTP, 2250 Military Road, Tonawanda, NY 14150, USA.
*Canada*: UTP, 5201 Dufferin Street, North York, Ontario M3H 5T8, Canada.
*Australia*: Footprint Books, PO Box 418, Church Point, NSW 2103, Australia.

Typeset by Wordworks Ltd.
Printed and bound in Great Britain by the Cromwell Press Ltd.

# Contents

# *Acknowledgements*

I am grateful to the contributors who gave their time and support, first to the workshop out of which this volume arose, then to the preparation and writing of their chapters. I would like to thank the following who helped me by looking at various parts of the book: Panos Athanasopoulos, Jean-Marc Dewaele, Roger Hawkins, Batia Laufer and Andrew Radford. And finally no book of mine would get written if not for the music of people such as Wayne Shorter, Django Bates and Max Roach.

# Contributors

**Pat Balcom:** Université de Moncton: balcomp@UMoncton.ca

**Jasone Cenoz:** University of the Basque Country: fipceirj@vc.ehu.es

**Vivian Cook:** University of Essex, England: vcook@essex.ac.uk

**Jean-Marc Dewaele:** Birkbeck College, England: j.dewaele@french.bbk.ac.uk

**Elisabet Iarossi:** eiarossi@lycos.com

**Scott Jarvis:** Ohio University: jarvis@ohiou.edu

**Ulrike Jessner:** University of Innsbruck: ulrike.jessner@t-online.de

**Istvan Kecskes:** SUNY at Albany: istvank@nycap.rr.com

**Batia Laufer:** University of Haifa: batialau@hotmail.com

**Victoria Murphy:** University of Herts: V.A.Murphy@herts.ac.uk

**Tunde Papp:** SUNY at Albany: tundep@nycap.rr.com

**Aneta Pavlenko:** Temple University, USA: apavlenk@astro.ocis.temple.edu

**Karen Pine:** University of Herts: psyrkjp@herts.ac.uk

**Graeme Porte:** Universidad de Granada: gporte@ugr.es

**Teresa Satterfield:** University of Michigan: tsatter@umich.edu

**Nektarios Stellakis:** nstellakis@yahoo.com

**Yuki Tokumaru:** University of Essex: ytokum@essex.ac.uk

Chapter 1

# Introduction: The Changing L1 in the L2 User's Mind

VIVIAN COOK

In 1953 Ulrich Weinreich talked about interference as 'those instances of deviation from the norms of either language which occur in the speech of bilinguals as a result of their familiarity with more than one language' (Weinreich, 1953: 1). This fits with everybody's common-sense belief that your first language (L1) has an effect on your second language (L2). The foreign accents we hear confirm this every day; an English speaker can tell whether someone is French or Japanese after a few words of English. In the fifty years since Weinreich's book, there has been extensive research into how the learning and use of a second language is affected by the first language, whether conceived as Contrastive Analysis, transfer, cross-linguistic influence, resetting of parameters or in many other ways.

Yet few people seemed to notice that Weinreich's definition concerned deviation from *either* language. As well as the first language influencing the second, the second language influences the first. Perhaps this effect is less detectable in our everyday experience: only complex instrumental analysis of a Spanish speaker's accent in Spanish will reveal whether the speaker also knows English. It becomes blatant only when the first language starts to disappear, for instance when a speaker brings more and more L2 words into his or her first language.

This volume is perhaps the first book to be devoted only to the effects of the second language on the first, sometimes called 'reverse' or 'backward' transfer. It arose out of an invitational workshop held in Wivenhoe House in 2001, at which all the papers included in this volume were delivered, apart from two (Porte, Chapter 6; Cook *et al.*, Chapter 10). By using a variety of perspectives, methodologies and languages, the research reported here shows that the first language of people who know other languages differs from that of their monolingual peers in diverse ways, with consequences for second language acquisition research, linguistics and language teaching. The range of contributions shows the extent to which this question impinges not only on all the areas of language from vocabulary to pragmatics, but also on a variety of contemporary approaches currently being developed by second language acquisition (SLA) researchers.

The book is intended for researchers in second language acquisition research and bilingualism, students and teachers around the world. The breadth of the contributions in terms of countries, languages, aspects of language and theories means that it relates to most SLA courses at some point, whether at undergraduate or postgraduate level.

This introduction provides some background to the different contributions in this volume. It tries not to steal their thunder by anticipating their arguments and conclusions, but provides a more personal overview, with which of course not all of the writers will be in complete accord. It relies in part on a summary overview of issues provided to the writers by Batia Laufer after the conference. It does not attempt to deal with the vast areas of language transfer from L1 to L2 or with the field of language attrition, covered in such classic texts as Odlin (1989) or Weltens *et al.* (1986).

## Multi-competence

For me, and for many of the contributors, the question of L2 effects on the L1 arose out of the notion of multi-competence. Initially the term was used almost as a convenience. While 'interlanguage' had become the standard term for the speaker's knowledge of a second language, no word existed that encompassed their knowledge of *both* the second language *and* their first: on the one hand the L1, on the other the interlanguage, but nothing that included both. Hence 'multi-competence' was introduced to mean 'knowledge of two or more languages in one mind' (Cook, 1991). For convenience we will mostly talk about 'second language' and bilingualism here, but this does not preclude multiple languages and multilingualism.

Since the first language and the other language or languages are in the same mind, they must form a language super-system at some level rather than be completely isolated systems. Multi-competence then raised questions about the relationship between the different languages in use. How do people code-switch fluently from one language to another? How do they 'gate out' one language while using the other (Lambert, 1990)? How do they manage more than one pragmatic and phonological system? Multi-competence also raised questions about cognition. Does an L2 user have a single set of ideas in the mind, more than one set of ideas, a merged set from different languages, or a new set of ideas unlike the sum of its parts? And multi-competence also led inevitably to questions about acquisition. What roles do the first language and the other language or languages play in the creation of knowledge of the second or later languages? Multi-competence led me in particular to a re-valuing of the concept of the native speaker (Cook, 1999). While the concept of interlanguage had seemed to establish the second language as an independent language system, in effect SLA research still treated the L2 system in an L2 user as an approximation to an L1 system in someone else (i.e. a monolingual L1 user). SLA research methods compared knowledge of L2 syntax against the knowledge of native speakers (Cook, 1997). Whether L2 learners had access to Universal Grammar (UG) was seen as a matter of whether they learnt the same grammars as monolingual native speakers – 'slightly over half of the non-native speakers typically exhibit the correct UG-based judgements on any given UG effect' (Bley-Vroman *et al.*, 1988: 24). Whether age affected L2 learning was seen in terms of how close people came to monolingual native speakers – 'whether the very best learners actually have native-like competence' (Long, 1990: 281). Whether they had an accent was a matter of how native-like they were – 'the ultimate goal – perhaps unattainable for some – is, nonetheless, to "sound like a native speaker" in all aspects of the language' (González-Nueno, 1997: 261). The independence of inter-language was largely illusory, since the norm against which the L2 user was compared was almost universally the native speaker, whether overtly or covertly.

The arguments against the native-speaker standard have been mounting over the past ten years. Let us first define the native speaker as 'a mono-lingual person who still speaks the language they learnt in childhood' (Cook, 1999). This combines the priority of the language in the development of the individual and the continuity of use by the individual with the usual simplifying assumption in linguistics that native speakers are mono-lingual. It does not preclude the possibility of a person being a native speaker of more than one language, if he or she acquired them simulta-neously while a child. By this definition, however, it is impossible for an L2 user to become a native speaker – one reason why so many L2 users think of themselves as 'failures' and so many SLA researchers treat them in the same way: 'learner's language is deficient by definition' (Kasper & Kellerman, 1997: 5).

The main arguments against the use of native speakers as the norm against which L2 users should be measured are as follows:

## The rights of L2 users

One group of human beings should not judge other people as failures for not belonging to their group, whether in terms of race, class, sex or language. People should be measured by their success at being L2 users, not by their failure to speak like native speakers. The object of acquiring a second language should be to become an L2 user, not to pass for a native speaker. SLA research has to do justice to its constituency – people who know two languages – not subordinate them to people who know only one language. The L2 user is a person in his or her own right (Cook, 1997; Grosjean, 1989), not an imitation of someone else.

## The numbers of L2 users

It is hard to arrive at precise figures about the numbers of monolingual native speakers in the world. It is slightly easier in reverse to find some numbers for people who are learning or using second languages. Taking English as an example, the British Council (1999) claims that a billion people are studying English in the world, including all children over 12 in Japan. English is used everywhere for certain purposes (such as academic journals and the Internet); many people communicate with each other through English who have never met a native speaker (for example business people doing international deals). Some countries where English is hardly spoken at all natively (such as Singapore) deliberately use it as a 'first language'; others (such as Nigeria, Cameroon, India and Pakistan) employ it as an official language. Turning away from English, most people in, say, Cape Town, Islamabad or Brussels switch from one language to one or more other languages in their daily lives. Monolingual native speakers are far from typical of human beings and are increasingly hard to find in the world (as we shall see in some of the contributions here), even in the highlands of Papua New Guinea. While it may be hard to prove that L2 users actually make up the majority of human beings, they at least form a very substantial group.

The usual resort in SLA and bilingualism research is to see the L2 standard in terms of the balanced bilingual or 'ambilingual'. Toribio (2001: 215), for instance, defines a balanced bilingual as 'a speaker who has native-like ability in two languages' and sees the standard against which an L2 user is measured as being 'an idealised bilingual's native speaker competence'. While the construct of native-speaker competence may be appropriate in first language acquisition as all human beings attain it, the concept of idealised bilingual competence can be extremely misleading since so few L2 users attain it. How many people have native-like skills in both languages in a reasonable range of their contexts of language use? They are the exception rather than the norm among L2 users, defined by their ability to function like native speakers in two languages not by their whole language ability to use two languages. The use of a native-speaker measure that is virtually impossible to achieve, even when disguised as the double-monolingual native speaker of the balanced bilingual, will blind us in the future (as it has done in the past) to the overwhelming majority of L2 users who are far from native-like across two languages. First language acquisition research is about what most people achieve, not about the abilities of monolingual Shakespeares. Second language acquisition research should equally be about what typical L2 users achieve, not about bilingual Nabokovs. Hence I now try to avoid the word 'bilingual' in discussing people who know two languages, not only because of the plethora of confusing definitions, but also because they usually invoke a Platonic ideal of the perfect bilingual rather than the reality of the average person who uses a second language for the needs of his or her everyday life.

## The distinctive characteristics of L2 users

If L2 users are different kinds of people, the interest of SLA research lies in discovering their characteristics, not their deficiencies compared with native speakers. In Cook (2002a: 4–8) the characteristics of L2 users are stated as four propositions:

(1)   the L2 user has other uses for language than the monolingual;
(2)   the L2 user's knowledge of the second language is typically not identical to that of a native speaker;
(3)   the L2 user's knowledge of his or her first language is in some respects not the same as that of a monolingual;
(4)   L2 users have different minds from those of monolinguals.

This book is thus primarily an expansion and justification of proposition (3) that L2 users differ from monolingual native speakers in their knowledge of their first languages. Inevitably it simultaneously provides further information about the distinctive nature of the L2 users' uses for language, their knowledge of their second language, and their minds.

Multi-competence led to seeing the L2 user as a person in his or her own right, not as an approximation to a monolingual native speaker. This is why I prefer the term 'L2 user' to 'L2 learner' in recognition of the person's ability to use the language rather than remaining a learner in perpetuity, always recognising that the same person may be both 'learner' and 'user' in different aspects of his or her language identity.

The belief in the native-speaker standard is one reason why the effects of the L2 on the L1 were so little studied. If the L1 of the L2 user were different from that of monolingual native speakers, SLA research that used the native speaker as the target would be based on shifting sand. As argued in Cook (2002a), a comparison of the L2 user with the native speaker may be legitimate provided any difference that is discovered is not treated as a matter of deficiency. Persistent use of this comparison prevents any unique features of the L2 user's language being observed, since only those that occur in natives will be searched for. For many years this led, for example, to a view that code-switching in adults or children was to be deplored rather than commended; Genesee (2002), for instance discusses how young children's code-switching was interpreted as a sign of confusion rather than as skilful L2 use.

While this argument has been couched in terms of multi-competence, this is not the only approach for dealing with the effects of the L2 on the L1. In this volume we find general models such as the dynamic model of multilingualism of Jessner (Chapter 12), the Common Underlying Conceptual Base (CUCB) of Kesckes and Papp (Chapter 13), Karmiloff-Smith's Representational Redescription Model, and Bialystok's Analysis/Control Model (Murphy and Pine, Chapter 8), and variants on the Chomskyan Minimalist Program used by Balcom (Chapter 9) and Satterfield (Chapter 11). Most of these share the assumption that at some level the L2 user's mind is a whole that balances elements of the first and second language within it. Furthermore, as Satterfield argues, this is essentially the normal state that all human beings can reach, and so must form the basis for *any* account of human language. If monolingualism is taken as the normal condition of humanity, L2 users can be treated as footnotes to the linguistics of monolingualism. With most people in the world learners or users of second languages, however, monolinguals can be considered the exception, not only statistically but also in terms of human potential.

## The Relationship of the First and Second Languages in the Mind: The Integration Continuum

What could the logical relationships actually be between the two or more languages in the mind? One possibility is that the languages are in watertight compartments, seen in the separation model in Figure 1.1, akin to the idea of coordinate bilingualism associated with Weinreich (1953); the L2 user speaks either one language or the other, with no connection between the different languages in the mind. The early SLA research controversies about the natural order of acquisition asserted a separation model in which the L2 interlanguage developed without drawing on the L1 to any great extent (e.g. Dulay & Burt, 1980). The separation model forms the basis for much language teaching methodology that teaches without reference to the first language and discourages its use in the classroom, hoping that the students will build up a new language system with no links

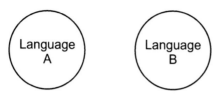

**Figure 1.1** Separation model

to the first. This model sees no point to discussing the effects of the L2 on the L1, as they do not exist. Separation does not, by the way, imply anything one way or the other about universals of language whether language design (Hockett, 1960) or innate properties of the mind (Chomsky, 2000). Both separate languages might be similar because they are governed by the same constraints and potentials as any other language acquired by a human being.

The opposite possibility is that the languages form a single system, shown in the integration model in Figure 1.2. In the area of vocabulary some people have claimed that, rather than two separate mental lexicons, the L2 user has a single lexicon where words from one language are stored alongside words from the other (Caramazza & Brones, 1980). In terms of phonology some have found that L2 users have a single merged system for producing speech, neither L1 nor L2 (Williams, 1977). Integration does not say that L2 users are unable to control what they do; they can still choose which language to use in a given context, just as a monolingual can choose which style or register to adopt in a particular situation. In this model, the discussion is not about the influence of L2 on L1, but about the balance between elements of a single language system. Indeed there is little point to counting 'languages' in a single mind – L1, L2, L3, L*n* – as they form a single system.

Clearly neither of these two models can be absolutely true: total separation is impossible since both languages are in the same mind; total integration is impossible since L2 users can keep the languages apart. These

**Figure 1.2** Integration model

possibilities represent the endpoints on the integration continuum (Cook, 2002a; Francis, 1999). In between these two extreme, and probably untenable, positions of total separation and total integration, there are many different degrees and types of interconnection, two of which are shown in Figure 1.3.

The linked languages model A in Figure 1.3 captures the idea of influence between two essentially separate language systems in the same mind, i.e. it is a variant of the separation model in which the two separate language components interact with each other. This is perhaps the typical model assumed in much SLA research; development and use of the L2 is affected by the already-existing L1, as surveyed say in Odlin (1989). Studies of language 'transfer' or 'influence' have assumed an interconnection model by seeing how the development of interlanguage (the L2 element in multi-competence) takes advantage of the first language (the L1 element in multi-competence). The linked languages model does, however, allow the links to go in both directions: the Revised Hierarchical Model of the lexicon (Kroll & Tokowicz, 2001) for instance assigns unequal strengths to the links between L1 and L2 according to direction and stage of acquisition.

The variant called the partial integration model (B in Figure 1.3) captures the idea of partial overlapping of the two language systems in the same mind; i.e. it is a limited version of the integration model. Inevitably this is bi-directional in a particular area since, like the integration model, it does not distinguish between languages in the areas of overlap but shows how the single conjoined system differs from monolingual versions of either language. There may be shared or overlapping vocabulary, syntax, or other aspects of language knowledge. Van Hell and Djikstra (2002: 1), for example, show that 'the multilingual's processing system is profoundly non-selective with respect to language' and that the lexicon of the language that is not overtly in use is nevertheless still active.

One question is whether the differences between the two concep-

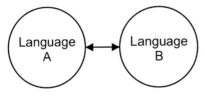 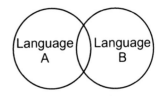

A: Linked languages                      B: Partial integration

**Figure 1.3** Interconnection models

tualisations of interconnection (linked languages and partial integration) are alternative wordings of the same idea, as implied in Cook (2002a), or represent different types of relationship. Is there a difference between saying that the languages in the mind are merged towards the integration end of the continuum, or that the links between them are stronger? This may partly be settled by the research in this volume, or indeed by neurolinguistic approaches such as that of Fabbro (2002).

Figure 1.4 displays the integration continuum as a whole, and is equivalent to the figure in Cook (2002a: 11). The continuum does not necessarily imply a direction of movement. It may be that some people start with separation and move towards integration or vice versa, or the languages might stay permanently separate. Paradis and Genesee (1996), for example, see bilingual children as having 'autonomous' languages from early on rather than 'interdependent' languages.

The integration continuum does not necessarily apply to the whole language system (Cook, 2002a); a person's lexicon might be integrated, but the phonology separate. Nor does it necessarily affect all individuals in the same way; some may be more integrated, some not, a factor of individual variation subsuming Weinreich's types of bilingualism. The point on the continuum may also vary from moment to moment in the individual according to his or her perception of language mode (Grosjean, 2001), level of tiredness and other personal factors; or indeed, as Porte suggests in

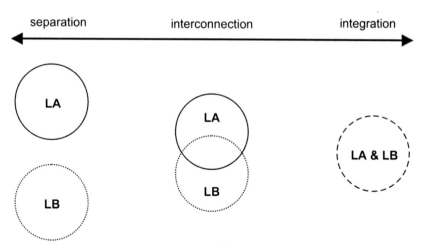

**Figure 1.4** The integration continuum of possible relationships in multi-competence

Chapter 6, because of fondness for language play by L2 users. The continuum might also be related to different stages of L2 development; children may move from an integrated single lexicon to a less integrated double lexicon (Taeschner, 1983). One important aspect of this question may indeed be to establish which areas of the L1 are *not* affected by the L2, for example the lexical diversity or productivity studied by Dewaele and Pavlenko (Chapter 7). The concept of the integration continuum is discussed elsewhere in more detail in the context of bilingual concepts in (Cook 2002a, 2002b).

Again there are several alternatives to the integration-continuum way of conceptualising L2 influence on L1. Pavlenko (Chapter 3) describes five forms of 'transfer'; Kecskes and Papp (Chapter 13) describe six variations on the L2→L1 effect. Many of these variations concern whether the second language is the majority or minority language in the community or in the individual (Li Wei, 1994), whether it is taught in a classroom or learnt outside, whether it acts as a lingua franca, and so on.

The integration continuum differs in certain ways from the concept of language modes. Grosjean (2001) puts any language use by an L2 user on a continuum of monolingual and bilingual modes according to the proportions of language A and language B, or indeed language C, that are involved. 'Language mode is the state of activations of the bilingual's languages and language processing mechanisms at a given point in time' (Grosjean, 2001: 3). An L2 user decides the proportions of the two languages to employ at any given moment in the light of multiple factors on a continuum between effectively activating only one language and activating both simultaneously. The language mode continuum is not then about *which* language to use but about *how much* of each. It is like a mixer tap that merges hot and cold water, but neither tap can be completely turned off. The way in which the language mode concept is phrased still implies the existence of *two* (or more) languages, *two* (or more) separate mental entities that strike a balance for each language use rather than integration of the two languages. Grosjean (2001), for instance, questions the methodologies that have produced signs of integration in semantics and word perception by pointing out that they paid insufficient attention to language mode. The partial integration model denies, however, that there are two languages as such and favours a single mental system within which a balance can be struck between elements of a particular aspect of language in a particular situation. This is one of the reasons why this introduction has tried to avoid the word 'transfer' (the other reasons being its confusing multiple definitions and its emotive connotations): it is questionable whether links between elements in the same mind can be considered transfer without in effect 'counting' languages (Cook, 2000).

The Integration Continuum fits with the Dynamic Model of Multi-lingualism (Jessner, Chapter 12) in trying to see the language system of the L2 user as a whole rather than as an interaction between separate language components. It is similar to the Common Underlying Conceptual Base (Kecskes and Papp, Chapter 13) in seeing the effects of the second language as affecting the whole mind. It is also compatible with the integrated neurolinguistic theory of bilingualism (Paradis, 2001) in unifying both L1 and L2 within the same architecture of the mind. The Integration Continuum does not spell out the separate L1 and L2 components of pragmatics, semantics, morphosyntax and phonology that are part of the Paradis model but, without naming the components, implies that the rela-tionship of integration versus separation varies from component to compo-nent. It differs, however, in extending the continuum to concepts, whereas Paradis (2001) has a single unvarying conceptual system. If speakers of different languages do in fact have different concepts, such as relative versus absolute orientation (Levinson, 1996) and form versus substance categorisation of objects (Imai & Gentner, 1997), models of L2 users clearly must accommodate variation in cognition and some relationship between the specifically L1 and specifically L2 concepts (Cook, 2000, 2002b). For example Athanasopoulos (2001) showed that Greeks who knew English had a different perception of the colour 'blue' than Greeks who did not.

## Positive and Negative Effects on the L1?

The integration continuum has been presented here positively as the separation or integration of two languages in the same mind. However these L2→L1 effects could be evaluated in at least three ways: positive effects on the L1, negative effects on the L1, and effects that are essentially neutral.

## The L1 can be enhanced by the use of an L2

It seems obvious that in some sense knowing another language benefits your use of your first language; language teaching classically invoked the concept of 'brain-training' to justify the teaching of Latin for example. Hungarian children who know English use measurably more complex sentences in their first language than those who do not (Kesckes & Papp, 2000). Extensive research into bilingual development shows overall that L2 user children have more precocious metalinguistic skills than their mono-lingual peers (Bialystok, 2001). English children who are taught Italian for an hour a week read English better than those who are not (Yelland *et al.*,

1993). So far as the general use of the first language is concerned, it is an advantage to know a second language, as attested by many celebrated bilingual writers, ranging from Chinua Achebe to John Milton, Samuel Beckett to Rabindranath Tagore. In the present volume the enhancing effects of the second language can be found in the contribution by Murphy and Pine (Chapter 8) on the development of bilingual children in England.

## The L1 can be harmed by the use of an L2

The usual context for discussing possible harmful effects of the L2 on the L1 is language loss or attrition. We will set aside here the effects on the L1 of other factors than the L2, such as aphasia caused by brain damage (Paradis, 2000). As a person gains the ability to use a second language, so he or she may to some extent lose the ability to use the first language. In circumstances where one language becomes less and less used, people do lose their command of it, whether as a group or as individuals. Perhaps this is familiar to everybody whose school-learnt language has effectively vanished from their lives. Research into this has mostly been carried out in the context of the loss of the first language by people who are spending their lives in a situation where it is not used for their major everyday social and professional purposes, whether as immigrants or expatriates. Examples of such research in this volume are Porte's account of expat teachers of English (Chapter 6) and Laufer's account of Russian L1 speakers in Israel (Chapter 2).

## The L1 is different from the L2, without being better or worse

Positive and negative evaluations of differences are to some extent problematic in that they rely on a value judgement about what is good and what is bad. Enhanced metalinguistic ability is valuable only if it is useful in some definable way; losing some aspect of the first language is a disadvantage only if it prevents the L2 user from carrying out some activity successfully.

Many of the effects of the L2 on the L1 simply amount to differences. The L2 user mind is bound to have differences in the first language element because of its more complex linguistic organisation, whether through linking or integration. In phonology the extensive literature on Voiced Onset Times in L2 users, surveyed in Watson (1991), reveals time and again the differences in the first language of L2 users for plosive consonants such as /p/ and /b/ or /k/ and /g/ across pairs of languages such as Spanish/ English (Zampini & Green, 2001), French/English (Flege, 1987), and Hebrew/English (Obler, 1982), which are essentially undetectable in normal language use. In this volume the contribution by Cook *et al.*

(Chapter 10) shows differences in L1 sentence-processing by Japanese L2 users that are hard to regard as either positive or negative; the changes that Jarvis (Chapter 5) finds in the L1 Finnish of a Finn again seem neither good nor bad. L2 users in a sense simply have a different command of the L1, which cannot be either commended or disapproved of. It is a complete system of its own, as the work by Cenoz with Spanish learners of English suggests (Chapter 4).

## Methodology of L2 on L1 Research

We have already seen the breadth of approaches used in looking at the effects of L2 on L1. The basic methodological paradigm is the comparison of monolingual native speakers with speakers of the same language who know a second language. At least two factors are probably more crucial in this type of research than in others.

### Establishing two equivalent groups of speakers of the same language, one with and one without a second language

The need initially is to find two similar groups who differ in whether or not they know a second language. The papers in this volume tackle Russians who do or do not know Hebrew (Laufer, Chapter 2), bilingual and monolingual children in England (Murphy and Pine, Chapter 8), Japanese, Greek and Spanish-speaking adults who do or do not know English (Cook *et al.*, Chapter 10), Canadian Francophones who do or do not know English (Balcom, Chapter 9), Cubans using English in the United States who had been there a short while and those who had been there a long time (Satterfield, Chapter 11), and many other combinations.

Finding two comparable groups with and without an L2 is easier said than done. The consequence of the widespread use of second languages is that monolingual native speakers are hard to come by. Where in the world can one find people who have not at least studied a second language in school? (Actually, given current government proposals to minimise languages in the National Curriculum, this may soon be the case in England.)

If L2 effects on L1 happen only at advanced stages of the L2, it would be safe to count as monolinguals people who had only a smattering of a second language, say as a school subject. Restricting monolingual subjects to those who had never studied a language at school might restrict them to people who had not completed education or who had had a non-standard education, or to those who were too old to have had a compulsory language. Furthermore, as Bialystok (2001) argues, eliminating in advance those with low levels of the L2 would prejudge the issue by assuming that there are no effects at early stages, which is by no means certain. Indeed, if Yelland *et al.* (1993)'s results are correct, one hour of an L2 in the primary school per week can affect the L1, at least in the area of reading.

Or it might be possible to include people who had learnt a second language provided it was a *different* second language. English people who had learnt German might be put in the monolingual group so far as the learning of French was concerned. The danger is that L2 learning in general produces some effects on the L2 user, such as enhanced metalinguistic ability: a grammaticality judgement test might be contaminated if the person had learnt any other language, not just the particular language tested in the experiment. This becomes even more dangerous if the effects of the L2 on people's linguistic judgements cannot be predicted from a conjunction of the first and second languages but are something different from both, as we find in Chapter 10 (Cook *et al.*)

The solution that has often to be resorted to is to abandon the attempt to contrast 'pure' monolinguals with L2 users. One possibility is to try for minimal versus maximal bilinguals, say people who have had the least possible exposure to another language versus those who have studied it at university level, as is done by Cook *et al.* (Chapter 10). Cenoz (Chapter 4) comes to a similar solution by comparing Spanish university students who were 'non-fluent' in English in that they had studied it only at school with those who were 'fluent' by virtue of receiving all their university tuition through English.

Underlying many of these factors is the difficulty in equating the two groups for various social factors. Those who have learnt another language may, compared to the monolingual control, either be in a higher socio-economic group (as with elite bilingualism) or in a lower socio-economic group (as with asylum seekers or migrant workers) or, in the case of university students doing different subjects, may differ in personality profiles and career ambitions.

In addition, the problem is sometimes that the L2 user who is part of a minority in a culture may be socialising with a group of fellow L1 speakers. Over time these isolated L1 communities may evolve their own languages. Gal (1989) described Hungarian speakers living in Austria who invented new Hungarian words as they did not know the actual forms used in Hungary. Many of the EFL students I once taught in West London were members of the expatriate Polish community; one of them, however, was an actress who was in England temporarily to act in the Polish theatre. She told me that members of the audience had complained about her terrible accent in Polish, while in fact she had the educated accent that was then spoken in Warsaw. Languages change. The L1 spoken in the larger L1 community may change, as in this case, so that L2 users who are cut off from it are inevitably out of date in their usage – say at the extreme of Welsh speakers in Patagonia or French speakers in Pondicherry. The L1 used by minority groups may change and adapt to its circumstances, as in Pennsylvania Deitsch in the United States. Cantonese speakers in Newcastle for instance say *tiojau* ('table wine') rather than *jau* ('wine') as used in Hong Kong and *bafong* ('bathroom') rather than *saisanfong* (Li Wei, 1994: 66).

In these complex social situations, it is hard to decide whether there is really an effect of L2 on L1 or there has simply been an evolutionary change in the L1 as spoken by particular groups. The changes in the Finnish woman living in United States described by Jarvis (Chapter 5) are particularly interesting because she does not take part in the Finnish expatriate community. One of the causes of linguistic change overall is indeed the contacts with other cultures; how else could English have absorbed vocabulary such as *bungalow, kangaroo* or *ciabatta* except by eventual effects on the L1s of its speakers?

### Giving both groups the same test of whatever linguistic area is being investigated

The next factor is choosing a testing instrument that can be used with both groups. Among the different possibilities used in this volume are: elicitation of narratives by showing subjects films (Pavlenko, Chapter 3), a standardised discourse completion test (Cenoz, Chapter 4), assignment of the subject of the sentence (Cook *et al.*, Chapter 10), naturalistic observation (Porte, Chapter 6), grammaticality judgements (Balcom, Chapter 9; Laufer, Chapter 2), reaction-time experiments (Murphy and Pine, Chapter 8), and statistical measures of lexical diversity and productivity (Dewaele and Pavlenko, Chapter 7). In their chapters, both Jarvis (Chapter 5) and Kecskes and Papp (Chapter 13) further discuss the issue of research techniques.

The problem that we found with the research reported in Chapter 10 was how the nature of the task varied across languages. A sentence that provides a particular clue to the subject of the sentence (say number agreement) is useless when translated and tested in a language with no agreement; a sentence that in English carries no clue about gender has to specify gender when translated into many other languages, this providing unwelcome additional cues. A task such as grammaticality judgements depends on many cultural attitudes towards correctness and status, which may well be altered in people who know another language – again one of the goals of language teaching is often given as greater tolerance of linguistic variety. Toribio (2001) has pioneered the use of grammaticality judgements with code-switching, a fully appropriate use that recognises the distinctive language of the L2 user.

In particular Grosjean (1998, 2001) has highlighted the effects of the subject's awareness of language mode on experiments. Does the task try to put the L2 users on their mettle as L1 users? Or do they see it as a test of their second language? This links to the observer effect, as emphasised by Li Wei (2000): do they feel the experimenter is a fellow L2 user, or a judgemental monolingual native speaker? How they present themselves is affected by their perception of the testing situation as one in which the first or second language is involved.

The issue of whether the second language affects the first has then provided a rich new question for second language acquisition research to investigate, the first fruits of which are seen in this volume. It has profound implications not only for our conceptualisation of the mind with two languages, but also for our view of all human minds.

## References

Athanasopoulos, P. (2001) L2 acquisition and bilingual conceptual structure. MA thesis, University of Essex.

Bialystok, E. (2001) *Bilingualism in Development*. Cambridge: Cambridge University Press.

Bley-Vroman, R.W., Felix, S. and Ioup, G.L. (1988) The accessibility of Universal Grammar in adult language learning. *Second Language Research* 4 (1), 1–32.

British Council (1999) Frequently asked questions. Online document: http://www.britishcouncil.org/english/engfaqs.htm#hmlearn1.

Caramazza, A. and Brones, I. (1980) Semantic classification by bilinguals. *Canadian Journal of Psychology* 34 (1), 77–81.

Chomsky, N. (2000) *The Architecture of Language*. New Delhi: Oxford University Press.

Cook, V.J. (1991) The poverty-of-the-stimulus argument and multi-competence. *Second Language Research* 7 (2), 103–117.

Cook, V.J. (1997) Monolingual bias in second language acquisition research. *Revista Canaria de Estudios Ingleses* 34, 35–50.

Cook, V.J. (1999) Going beyond the native speaker in language teaching. *TESOL Quarterly* 33 (2), 185–209.

Cook, V.J. (2000) Is transfer the right word? Paper presented at the 7th International Pragmatics Conference, July, 2000. Budapest. On-line at http://privatewww.essex.ac.uk/~vcook/OBS8.htm.

Cook, V.J. (2002a) Background to the L2 user. In V.J. Cook (ed.) *Portraits of the L2 User* (pp. 1–28). Clevedon: Multilingual Matters.

Cook, V.J. (2002b) Bilingual cognition. Paper presented at the EUROSLA Annual Meeting, Basel, September. On-line at http://privatewww.essex.ac.uk/~vcook/OBS33.htm.

Dulay, H.C. and Burt, M.K. (1980) On acquisition orders. In S. Felix (ed.) *Second Language Development: Trends and Issues*. Tübingen: Narr.

Fabbro, F. (2002) The neurolinguistics of L2 users. In V.J. Cook (ed.) *Portraits of the L2 User* (pp. 167–195). Clevedon: Multilingual Matters.

Flege, J.E. (1987) Effects of equivalence classification on the production of foreign language speech sounds. In A. James and J. Leather (eds) *Sound Patterns in Second Language Acquisition* (pp. 9–39). Dordrecht: Foris.

Francis, W. (1999) Cognitive integration of language and memory in bilinguals: Semantic representation. *Psychological Bulletin* 125 (2), 193–222.

Gal, S. (1989) Language and political economy. *Annual Review of Anthropology* 18, 345–67.

Genesee, F. (2002) Portrait of the bilingual child. In V.J. Cook (ed.) *Portraits of the L2 User* (pp. 167–196). Clevedon: Multilingual Matters.

González-Nueno, M. (1997) VOT in the perception of foreign accent. *IRAL* 35/4, 251–267.

Grosjean, F. (1989) Neurolinguists, beware! The bilingual is not two monolinguals in one person. *Brain and Language* 36, 3–15.

Grosjean, F. (1998) Studying bilinguals: Methodological and conceptual issues. *Bilingualism: Language and Cognition* 1 (2), 131–149.

Grosjean, F. (2001) The bilingual's language modes. In J. Nicol (ed.) *One Mind, Two Languages* (pp. 1–22). Oxford: Blackwell.

Hockett, C.F. (1960) The origin of speech. *Scientific American* 203, 88–9.

Imai, M. and Gentner, D. (1997) A cross-linguistic study of early word meaning: Universal ontology and linguistic influence. *Cognition* 62, 169–200.

Kasper, G. and Kellerman, E. (eds) (1997) *Communication Strategies: Psycholinguistic and Sociolinguistic Perspectives*. Harlow: Longman.

Kecskes, I. and Papp, T. (2000) *Foreign Language and Mother Tongue*. Hillsdale, NJ: Lawrence Erlbaum.

Kroll, J.F. and Tokowicz, N. (2001) The development of conceptual representation for words in a second language. In J. Nicol (ed.) *One Mind, Two Languages* (pp. 49–71). Oxford: Blackwell.

Lambert, W.E. (1990) Persistent issues in bilingualism. In B. Harley, P. Allen, J. Cummins and M. Swain (eds) (1990) *The Development of Second Language Proficiency* (pp. 201–220). Cambridge: Cambridge University Press.

Levinson, S.C. (1996) Relativity in spatial conception and description. In J.J. Gumperz and S.C. Levinson (eds) *Rethinking Linguistic Relativity* (pp. 177–202), Cambridge: Cambridge University Press.

Li Wei (1994) *Three Generations, Two Languages, One Family*. Clevedon: Multilingual Matters.

Li Wei (2000) Methodological questions in the study of bilingualism. In Li Wei (ed.) *The Bilingualism Reader* (pp. 475–486). London Routledge.

Long, M. (1990) Maturational constraints on language development. *Studies in Second Language Acquisition* 12, 251–86.

Obler, L. (1982) The parsimonious bilingual. In L. Obler and L. Menn (eds) *Exceptional Language and Linguistics* (pp. 339–345). New York: Academic Press.

Odlin, T. (1989) *Language Transfer: Cross-Linguistic Influence in Language Learning*. Cambridge: Cambridge University Press.

Paradis, J. and Genesee, F. (1996) Syntactic acquisition in bilingual children. *Studies in Second Language Acquisition* 18, 1–25.

Paradis, M. (2000) Bilingual and polyglot aphasia. In R.S. Berndt (ed.) *Handbook of Neuropsychology* (2nd edn). Oxford: Elsevier Science.

Paradis, M. (2001) An integrated neurolinguistic theory of bilingualism 1976–2000. *LACUS Forum*, XXVII.

Taeschner, T. (1983) *The Sun is Feminine*. Berlin: Springer.

Toribio, A.J. (2001) On the emergence of bilingual code-switching competence. *Bilingualism: Language and Cognition* 4 (3), 203–232.

Van Hell, J.G. and Dijkstra, T. (2002) Foreign language knowledge can influence native language performance in exclusively native contexts. *Psychonomic Bulletin and Review.*

Watson, I. (1991) Phonological processing in two languages. In E. Bialystok (ed.) *Language Processes in Bilingual Children* (pp. 25–48). Cambridge: Cambridge University Press.

Weinreich, U. (1953) *Languages in Contact*. The Hague: Mouton.

Weltens, B., De Bot, K. and van Els, T. (1986) *Language Attrition in Progress.* Dordrecht: Foris.

Williams, L. (1977) The perception of consonant voicing by Spanish English bilinguals. *Perception and Psychophysics* 21 (4), 289–297.

Yelland, G.W., Pollard, J. and Mercuri, A. (1993) The metalinguistic benefits of limited contact with a second language. *Applied Psycholinguistics* 14, 423–444.

Zampini, M.L. and Green, K.P. (2001) The voicing contrast in English and Spanish: The relationship between perception and production. In J. Nicol (ed.) *One Mind, Two Languages* (pp. 23-48). Oxford: Blackwell.

# Chapter 2

# The Influence of L2 on L1 Collocational Knowledge and on L1 Lexical Diversity in Free Written Expression

BATIA LAUFER

## Introduction

Most of the work on cross-linguistics influence has focused on the influence that the learners' first languages have on the additional languages they acquire. This was the case of the classical Contrastive Analysis and transfer studies (Lado, 1957; Levenston, 1970; Weinreich, 1953), and also of the later work on interlanguage (e.g. Kellerman, 1978, 1983, 1984; Laufer, 1992; Plag, 1992; Zimmermann, 1992; Zobl, 1982).

Fewer researchers have investigated the acquisition of more than one second language. Some studied the effect that the native and the second language had on the third language (Ringbom, 1978, 1982, 1987; Singleton, 1999, Singh & Carrol, 1979; Sjöholm, 1995). Others tried to answer the question whether it is easier to learn a third than a second language (Cummins, 1978; Ringbom, 1985).

What has hardly been investigated, however, is the influence that foreign languages have on the learner's first language. The reason for this neglect may have been twofold. Firstly, for a long time researchers have been interested in the non-advanced learners of second languages. At the beginning stages of second language learning, the influence is mostly unidirectional, from L1 to L2. Secondly, SLA (Second Language Acquisition) research has been dominated by English as a Second Language. Advanced learners of English who supplied the data for research were immigrants to English-speaking countries, and knowledge of English was vital for their success and integration into the new society. Therefore the development of this knowledge provoked researchers' interest. The state of their native language, on the other hand, was less important and did not raise the same amount of interest. Changes in the first language have been investigated in the framework of language attrition. The increasing dominance of the L2 was presented as one of the factors responsible for the gradual disappearance of the L1 (Berman & Olshtain, 1983; Kaufman & Aronof, 1989; Weltens *et al.*, 1986).

The term 'cross-linguistic influence', which succeeded the traditional notion of language transfer, refers to a wide range of phenomena including transfer, lack of transfer (Kellerman, 1979), avoidance (Hulstijn & Marchena, 1989; Laufer & Elliason, 1993; Schachter, 1974), underproduction (Ringbom, 1987), overall facilitation of learning (Ard & Homburg, 1983), and strategies of communication (Ellis, 1985). There is no reason why these manifestations of cross-linguistic influence could not be explored in the context of second language effects on the first language.

## Background to the Studies

### Lexical knowledge and lexical competence

The purpose of the studies reported in this chapter was to investigate L2 effects on two areas of L1 lexical competence: the knowledge of collocations and lexical diversity in free written expression. The terms 'competence' and 'knowledge' are not synonymous here. I refer to 'knowledge' as the information about a word that is stored in the mental lexicon, e.g. the spoken and written form, grammatical properties, different meanings, paradigmatic and syntagmatic relations with other words. I refer to 'lexical competence' as the way in which lexical knowledge is put to use. Thus lexical competence includes knowledge, but also the willingness to use a word, accessibility to a word (i.e. speed of retrieval of the word), and strategic competence (i.e. strategies compensating for deficiencies in knowledge, such as the use of dictionaries, inferring the meaning from context, and negotiation of meaning).

The studies reported here, therefore, investigate an area of lexical knowledge and an area of lexical use. The first is the ability to judge L1 collocations as correct or incorrect. When an incorrect collocation is judged as correct, the reason is likely to be a change in the way words have become related to other words in the mental lexicon. For example, a native speaker of English living in Israel could judge the collocation *solve dreams* in English as correct. This would indicate that though he or she knows the meaning of the word *dream*, he or she combines it with an incorrect verb *solve*, probably owing to the influence of Hebrew. The second area of investigation is the proportion of infrequent words used in writing. A low percentage of infrequent vocabulary does not necessarily mean that some of the words not used are 'unknown' in the sense of non-existent in the mental lexicon. It means that the subject may not have been able to put this knowledge to use, or had not wanted to. For example, a person may be able to recognise the meaning of *inquire*, but will prefer to use *ask* in writing. One of the reasons may be not remembering how to spell it, another may be forgetting what prepositions follow *inquire*, or simply not accessing it as quickly as the more frequent word *ask*.

### Differential L2 on L1 effect position

Cross-linguistic influence may be noticeable in word 'knowledge' and in the other areas of lexical competence discussed above. But the influence is different in each case. The L1 speaker of English who has used Hebrew as L2 for a long time may say *we don't have any evidences* [here and in later pages, * before a phrase signifies that it is ungrammatical in native speech]. The grammatical feature 'non-count' of *evidence* has apparently been replaced by the 'count' feature of the Hebrew translation equivalent of *evidence*. The L2 influence is obvious to those who know the two languages. The error is easily traceable to L2 since it has resulted in a word that resembles L2 in its features. I refer to this kind of influence as direct, and suggest that direct influence of L2 occurs in the case of L1 lexical *knowledge*.

L2 effects on the other areas of lexical competence are not so obvious. A person whose L2 is becoming dominant may begin to experience some difficulties with retrieving L1 words for use. The speed of retrieval will deviate from the speed of a proficient L1 user, even though the final result will not be a lexical error modelled on another language. When L2 influence results in a deviation from an L1 lexical norm even when there are no obvious L2 features, I refer to such influence as indirect and suggest that it occurs in areas of L1 lexical competence *other than knowledge*. L1 lexical competence that is affected by L2 may exhibit characteristics of direct and indirect influence of L2. The two studies reported in this paper explored the two types of influence.

### Study 1: Collocations

As pointed out earlier, a person who knows a lexical item is familiar with its common collocations, that is to say the other words that it combines with. For example, a person who has collocational knowledge of the word *decision* in English knows that one is supposed to say *make a decision*. Similar knowledge of *decision* in French implies knowledge of the French collocation *prendre une decision* ('take a decision'). The aim of the study was to investigate the influence that a prolonged contact with L2 had on L1 collocational knowledge. Such knowledge was operationalised as the subjects' correctness judgement of sentences, including correct and incorrect collocations.

## Subjects

Two groups participated in the study: a group of immigrants to Israel from the former Soviet Union, and a group of Moscow residents. The immigrant group consisted of thirty subjects. Their L1 was Russian, their L2 was Hebrew. At the time of the experiment, they were all adults with an academic education. They had been living in Israel from 2 to 40 years and all of them could function in Hebrew. There were no subjects whose length of residence was between 7 and 16 years, simply because for some time there was no immigration from the former Soviet Union. The age of arrival was between 11 and 44. One subject arrived at the age of 11, one at 12, one at 13 and two at 15. The rest of the subjects arrived in Israel after the age of 15. The control group consisted of fourteen Moscow residents, i.e. native speakers of Russian who did not move into another language environment. All were adults with an academic education.

## Research questions

The specific research questions were as follows:

(1) How well can immigrants who live and function in an L2 environment recognise and correct non-native-like L1 collocations when compared with people living in an L1 environment?

(2) How is the correctness judgement of collocations affected by the following sociolinguistic variables?

   (a) length of residence in Israel;

   (b) age of arrival in Israel;

   (c) Russian language maintenance;

   (d) frequency of use of Hebrew.

## Methodology

The demographic and sociolinguistic information about the Israeli subjects was collected by means of a questionnaire. Age of arrival in Israel, education and length of residence were stated explicitly by the subjects. Maintenance of Russian and use of Hebrew were determined by answers to five statements:

| | | |
|---|---|---|
| 1 I read magazines and books in | (a) Hebrew | |
| | (b) Russian | |
| | (c) both languages | |
| 2 I watch TV in | (a) Hebrew | |
| | (b) Russian | |
| | (c) both languages | |
| 3 I speak with family and friends in | (a) Hebrew | |
| | (b) Russian | |
| | (c) both languages | |
| 4 In a week, I use Russian | (a) less than 10 hours | |
| | (b) 10–15 hours | |
| | (c) 15–30 hours | |
| | (d) more than 30 hours | |
| 5 In a week, I use Hebrew | (a) less than 10 hours | |
| | (b) 10–15 hours | |
| | (c) 15–30 hours | |
| | (d) more than 30 hours | |

In the first three questions, each language that was used received one point. In the last two questions, each language received 1 to 4 points depending on the answer, (a) to (d), respectively. The results of the five questions were added to calculate the language-use score for each subject, for each language. For example, Subject 6 marked 'Russian' in question 1 and 'both languages' in questions 2 and 3. He also marked (d) in question 4 (used Russian more than 30 hours a week) and (c) in question 5 (used Hebrew 15–30 hours a week). So Subject 6's score for Russian was (1+1+1+4) = 7, and his score for Hebrew was (0+1+1+3) = 5.

Theoretically, the score for each language use could range from 1 to 7. In practice, however, there were no scores of 1 and barely any scores of 2, which indicated that our subjects functioned in both languages.

The test of correctness judgement consisted of 35 sentences: 18 were correct, 17 included wrong collocations that were modelled on Hebrew. An example of such a sentence is *Ja zakryl telvizor*, literally 'I closed the TV'. The correct Russian verb is *vykluchil* 'switched off'. The task was to decide whether or not each sentence was correct and, if it was incorrect, the subjects were expected to correct it. An error that was recognised and corrected counted 2 points; an error recognised but not corrected counted 1 point; an error not corrected counted 0 points; a correct sentence spoiled counted minus 1 point. The immigrants took the test at their homes in Israel, the Russians took the test in their homes in Moscow.

For each subject, a correctness score was calculated as follows: the number of wrong items that were corrected was multiplied by 2, to this figure was added the number of wrong items recognised but not corrected, minus the number of correct items spoiled. For example, Subject 12 recognised and corrected 9 sentences, for which she received (9 x 2) = 18 points. She recognised 2 sentences as incorrect, but could not correct them, for which she received (2 x 1) = 2 points. She failed to recognise 6 sentences as incorrect, and therefore received (0 x 6) = 0 points for these, and she marked one correct sentence as incorrect, for which she received (1 x –1) = –1. Her correctness score was therefore (18+2+0–1) = 19. The maximum score was 34, when 17 items with an error in collocation were recognised and corrected.

## Results

To answer the first research question, regarding the immigrants' ability to perceive and correct incorrect collocations in their L1, mean correctness scores of the two groups (immigrants and Russians) were calculated. The two groups were compared on the number of correct responses by a two-tailed $t$-test. The results are presented in Table 2.1.

**Table 2.1** Scores of collocation correctness judgement (maximum = 34)

|  | $n$ | Mean | Standard deviation | Minimum | Maximum |
|---|---|---|---|---|---|
| **Immigrants in Israel** | 30 | 20.7 | 8.06 | 2 | 32 |
| **Russians in Moscow** | 14 | 28.5 | 2.24 | 23 | 31 |
| **Difference** | | $T$ (d.f. 42) = 7.6   $p = 0.001$ | | | |

The Russian group did not achieve the maximum score, which implies that two of the test sentences may not have been unequivocally wrong. Nevertheless, the difference between the two groups in correct responses was significant. The immigrant group did not spot almost 40% of the wrong collocations (34 –20.7)/34 × 100%. Moreover, the small range and standard deviation of the Russian group show that the members of this group were pretty uniform in their judgement. The immigrants, however, varied considerably and the standard deviation was more than one-third of the mean.

The reasons for this variation were addressed in the second research question, which explored collocational knowledge as a function of age of arrival in Israel, length of residence, and the use of the two languages.

Table 2.2 presents correlations between the above variables and the collocation judgement correctness score.

**Table 2.2**  Collocation judgement correctness and sociolinguistic variables: Correlations

|  | Collocation judgement score | |
|---|---|---|
|  | *R* | *p* |
| Age of arrival | 0.37 | 0.04 |
| Length of residence | -0.65 | 0.0001 |
| Use of Russian | 0.54 | 0.002 |
| Use of Hebrew | -0.28 | ns |

Table 2.2 shows that the amount of Hebrew used by the subjects had no effect on their collocational knowledge. The maintenance of Russian, on the other hand, was moderately but significantly related to the test results. There was a low, but significant, correlation between the age of arrival and the test scores, which means that people who arrived at an older age, and presumably had used Russian for a longer time, were more successful. The strongest effect on the correctness scores was the effect of length of residence. Negative correlation means that, the longer people lived in an L2 environment, the worse their judgement of L1 collocations became.

The importance of the length-of-residence variable led me to perform an additional analysis of the collocation-correctness data. The group of immigrants was divided into two subgroups on the basis of their length of residence in Israel. One group included those who had lived there 2–6 years, the other 17–40 years. As was mentioned earlier, there were no immigrants of 7–16 years' standing. The two new groups of immigrants and the group of Russians were compared by one-way ANOVA (analysis of variance) on their collocational knowledge.

Table 2.3 shows that there was a significant difference between the three groups. Tukey post hoc tests revealed that the group of older immigrants was significantly different from the other two groups. The means in Table 2.3 suggest that most of the attrition in collocational knowledge happened after a long period of residence in a non-L1-speaking environment. The increasing standard deviations mean that, the longer the residence, the less uniform people became in their L1 knowledge. This in turn implies that some other factors (possibly memory, L1 maintenance, identification with L1 group, etc.) may have become more influential.

In sum, the results of the study show that incorrect L1 collocations that were modelled on L2 were not recognised by the immigrants in about 40% of the cases. The decline in collocational knowledge is dependent on the

**Table 2.3** Collocation judgement scores of Russians, recent immigrants and old immigrants (maximum score = 34)

|                   | $n$  | Mean | Standard deviation | Minimum | Maximum |
|-------------------|------|------|--------------------|---------|---------|
| **Russians**      | 14   | 28.5 | 2.24               | 23      | 31      |
| **Recent immigrants** | 22 | 24.7 | 4.04             | 18      | 32      |
| **Old immigrants** | 8   | 9.75 | 6.62               | 2       | 19      |
| **Difference**    | $F(41,2) = 54.2$    $p = 0.0001$ | | | | |

length of residence in the L2 environment. The rate of decline was low at the beginning of contact with the L2, and accelerated later on. The amount of L1 use and the age of arrival also play a moderate but significant role.

## Study 2: Lexical Diversity in Written Expression

Earlier, I made a distinction between word knowledge and word use. A learner of English as an L2 may have the knowledge of *serendipity* reflected in the ability to state what the word means, or may retrieve the word form when given its L1 equivalent. This does not mean that he will use the word at his own will in free expression. He may prefer to use a different term or phrase with a similar meaning, such as *lucky coincidence*. Why is it that some people choose to use sophisticated and varied vocabulary and others opt for frequent everyday words and tend to repeat them? Stylistic considerations aside, people, particularly learners, often avoid the use of some of the words they know for fear of making an error, or using them inappropriately. Furthermore, under the pressure of time, some words may be temporarily inaccessible, even though they are stored in the mental lexicon. Risk avoidance in the use of vocabulary and reduced accessibility to words are characteristic of a transitional competence in a language, whether this competence is developing or suffering attrition.

The aim of the second study was to investigate the influence of prolonged contact with L2 on L1 lexical diversity in written expression. Lexical diversity was defined as the combination of (a) the percentage of infrequent vocabulary (not in the first 2000 most frequent words) in a composition, and (b) the percentage of different words in the total number of words. The first component of lexical diversity is sometimes referred to as the 'lexical sophistication' or 'lexical richness' of the composition. For example, in a 300-word composition, 240 words belong to the 'first 2000 most frequent' vocabulary. The 60 remaining words therefore are infrequent.

The percentage of these words, the lexical richness of the composition, is 20%. The second component of lexical diversity is sometimes termed 'lexical variation'. For example, in a composition of 300 words, the writer uses 150 *different* words. The lexical variation of the composition is 150 / 300×100% = 50%. High lexical variation shows that a person is not repetitive in his choice of words. (For a detailed discussion of lexical measures in free expression and their limitations, see Laufer and Nation, 1995.)

## Subjects

Twenty six immigrants from the former USSR served as subjects in the study. Twenty one were adult educated professionals at the time of the experiment. They had immigrated to Israel between the ages of 20 and 30. They were divided into two groups on the basis of their length of residence in Israel. Eleven subjects had lived 20 years in Israel, 10 subjects had lived 5–10 years. They were all fluent speakers of Hebrew (their L2) and used Russian (their L1) in social domain. A third small group included five young new immigrants, age 20–25. At the time of the experiment they had been living in Israel 1–4 years.

## Research questions

(1)  What is the difference between the three groups of immigrants in the percentage of infrequent words they use in composition?
(2)  What is the difference between the three groups of immigrants in the lexical variation of compositions?

## Methodology

All the subjects were asked to write a composition about the problems facing new immigrants to Israel. The recommended maximum length was 400 words. They wrote the composition on paper and took as much time as they needed. Later, an assistant typed the compositions into a computer. A list of 2000 most frequent words in Russian was typed into the computer as well. In this list, a base word with all its inflections was counted as one word.

A special computer program was written in SAS for mainframe computer, which can also be adapted to SAS for Windows. The program matched the compositions with the list of 2000 words, and calculated the number and the percentage of these 2000 words in each of them. Similarly it calculated the percentage of the words not included in the 2000 words, that is, the less frequent words. In addition, it counted the number of different words that a subject used in a composition and the ratio between the different and the total number of words in a composition, i.e. lexical variation. For calculating the lexical variation (LV), however, the length of compositions was standardised to around 200 words since LV is sensitive to the length of written passages.

## Results

Table 2.4 shows the lexical diversity of the three groups of immigrants, i.e. the mean percentages of frequent and non-frequent words in the compositions, and lexical variation. The table also presents the number of words that each group used in the composition.

**Table 2.4** Lexical diversity and length of residence

|  | *n* | *Most frequent 2000 words* | *Beyond 2000 words* | *Lexical Variation (on text adjusted for length)* | *No. of words in essay* |
|---|---|---|---|---|---|
| **Newcomers** 1–4 years in Israel | 5 | 79% SD 3.57 | 21% SD 3.57 | 68.4% SD 2.88 | 357 SD 87 |
| **5–10 years in Israel** | 10 | 81% SD 5.03 | 19% SD 5.03 | 64.5% SD 2.99 | 354 SD 170 |
| **20 years in Israel** | 11 | 87% SD 4.93 | 13% SD 5.17 | 61.1% SD 5.62 | 199 SD 19.88 |
| **Difference** (one-way ANOVA) | | F=6.48 $p<0.01$ | F=5.82 $p<0.01$ | F=3.16 $p<0.06$ | F=7.65 $p<0.005$ |

Table 2.4 shows that there was a significant difference in lexical richness, i.e. the percentage of frequent and non-frequent words, and also in the number of words that the groups could produce. The percentage of non-frequent words declined as the length of residence increased, as did the number of words in the essays. Lexical variation declined too, but the difference did not reach significance at 0.05 level.

Tukey post hoc tests showed that the significant differences were found only between newcomers and the oldest immigrants. This means that L1 lexical diversity as reflected in lexical use (the use of infrequent and different words) did not decline immediately. It reached a plateau and started decreasing after prolonged contact with L2. Another piece of evidence for this pattern of change was in the number of words that subjects could produce in their compositions. The number did not decline in the second group, but did so in the group of old immigrants.

## Conclusion

The two studies were carried out with immigrants who maintained their first language, Russian, by using it on a daily basis. Most of them were educated adults when they arrived in Israel, which suggests that their L1 competence had fully developed before then. Almost all subjects became fluent in Hebrew, their L2. In spite of good initial L1 knowledge and its continual maintenance, L1 started exhibiting L2 features some time during the contact between the two languages.

Inability to identify wrong collocations implies that the L1 lexical networks in the mental lexicon may have undergone changes. These resulted in some words becoming associated with other wrong words, if we judge them by monolingual standards. For example, *telephone* in Russian became wrongly connected with *close*, since in Hebrew you *close the telephone* when you hang up on someone. In L2 learning, a good collocational knowledge is achieved only at advanced levels of proficiency. (Often a non-native speaker can be identified by the wrong use of collocations in otherwise correct spoken or written language.) It is possible that, once this problem has been overcome and collocations have been mastered in the L2, they start replacing the collocational pattern of the L1. Being able to produce or identify the correct collocations of a word is part of one's word knowledge. Study 1 showed that word knowledge as reflected in identifying wrong collocations was influenced by the L2. This influence is easily traceable since it has resulted in a collocation modelled on the L2. Earlier I referred to this kind of influence as direct.

Study 2 showed that L1 lexical diversity declined as the contact time with L2 increased. The percentage of non-frequent vocabulary and the total number of words produced in free expression significantly decreased as time passed. Lexical variation declined as well, and almost reached a significant level of decrease. Unlike change in lexical knowledge, as it occurs in the case of L2-based L1 collocation, the change in lexical diversity does not result in error, and is therefore not immediately noticeable. It could be detected only by using sophisticated calculations. Even though the changing lexical diversity shows no error, it deviates from the monolingual norm. L2 influence that leads to this kind of change, not readily noticeable, has been referred to as 'indirect' influence.

Both studies demonstrated that a changing L1 lexical competence may at some point start to exhibit characteristics of direct and indirect influence of L2. Direct influence is evident in lexical knowledge, while indirect influence occurs in other areas of lexical competence, such as lexical use. The studies support the position that cross-linguistic influence is not necessarily unidirectional, from L1 to L2, but may take the opposite direction as well (Weinreich, 1953; Cook, 1992). Furthermore, it does not occur only from the dominant language to the less well known one. Subjects' reports revealed that most of them used Russian just as much as, or more than, Hebrew. Yet Russian, the dominant language, did not escape the influence of L2.

In the course of this chapter, the term 'attrition' was avoided intentionally. I am fully aware that the results of the two studies show that the subjects' Russian underwent some changes that are often termed 'attrition'. However, I would prefer to take a more positive and optimistic attitude to the subjects' development of knowledge, by viewing it as the acquisition of multi-competence (Cook, 1991, 1992), which rarely means 100% correctness of L1 + 100% correctness of L2. The subjects in my studies, L1 speakers of Russian, acquired an additional language system. Their L1 declined, deteriorated, or suffered attrition to some degree, if we measure them against people who know one language. Yet, as Cook (1992) points out, most human beings know two or more languages rather than just one. Some L1 attrition, therefore, is a small price to pay for achieving the ordinary state of mankind.

### References

Ard, J. and Homburg, T. (1983) Verification of language transfer. In S. Gass and J. Homburg (eds) *Language Transfer in Language Learning* (pp. 157–176). Rowley, MA: Newbury House.

Berman, R.A. and Olshtain, E. (1983) Features of first language transfer in second language attrition. *Applied Linguistics* 4, 222–234.

Cook, V.J. (1991) The poverty of stimulus argument and multi-competence. *Second Language Research* 7, 103–117.

Cook, V.J. (1992) Evidence for multi-competence. *Language Learning* 42, 557–591.

Cummins, J. (1978) Bilingualism and the development of metalinguistic awareness. *Journal of Cross-cultural Psychology* 9, 131–148.

Ellis, R. (1985) *Understanding Second Language Acquisition*. Oxford: Oxford University Press.

Hulstijn, J. and Marchena, E. (1989) Avoidance: Grammatical or semantic causes? *Studies in Second Language Acquisition* 11, 241–255.

Kaufman, D. and Aronof, M. (1989) Morphological interaction between L1 and L2 in language attrition. In S. Gass, C. Madden, D. Preston and L. Selinker (eds) *Variation in Second Language Acquisition* (pp. 202–215). Clevedon: Multilingual Matters.

Kellerman, E. (1978) Giving learners a break: Native language intuitions as a source of prediction about transferability. *Working Papers in Bilingualism* 15, 59–92.

Kellerman, E. (1979) Transfer and non-transfer: Where are we now? *Studies in Second Language Acquisition* 2, 25–57.

Kellerman, E. (1983) Now you see it, now you don't. In S. Gass and L. Selinker (eds) *Language Transfer in Language Learning* (pp. 112–134). Rowley, MA: Newbury House.

Kellerman, E. (1984) The empirical evidence for the influence of the L1 in interlanguage. In A. Davies, C. Criper and A. Howatt (eds) *Interlanguage* (pp. 98–122). Edinburgh: Edinburgh University Press.

Lado, R. (1957) *Linguistics across Cultures: Applied Linguistics for Language Teachers.* Ann Arbor: University of Michigan Press.

Laufer, B. (1992) Native language effect on confusion of similar lexical forms. In C. Mair and M. Markus (ed.) *New Departures in Contrastive Linguistics* (pp. 199–210). Innsbruck: University of Innsbruck.

Laufer, B. and Elliason, S. (1993) What causes avoidance in L2 learning: L1–L2 difference, L1–L2 similarity, or L2 complexity? *Studies in Second Language Acquisition* 15, 35–48.

Laufer, B. and Nation, P. (1995) Vocabulary size and use: Lexical richness in L2 written production. *Applied Linguistics* 16, 307–322.

Levenston, E.A. (1970) *English for Israelis: A Guide for Teachers.* Jerusalem: Israel Universities Press.

Plag, I. (1992) 'There was a man picking pears'. Participial ing-clauses in native language, interlanguage, and target language. In C. Mair and M. Markus (eds) *New Departures in Contrastive Linguistics* (pp. 223–236). Innsbruck: University of Innsbruck.

Ringbom, H. (1978) The influence of the mother tongue on the translation of lexical items. *Interlanguage Studies Bulletin* 3, 80–101.

Ringbom, H. (1982) The influence of other languages on the vocabulary of foreign language learners. In G. Nickel and D. Nehls (eds) *Error Analysis, Contrastive Analysis and Second Language Learning.* IRAL special issue, pp. 85–96.

Ringbom, H. (1985) *Foreign Language Learning and Bilingualism.* Abo: Research Institute of Abo Akademi.

Ringbom, H. (1987) *The Role of the First Language in Second Language Learning.* Clevedon: Multilingual Matters.

Schachter, J. (1974) An error in error analysis. *Language Learning* 24, 205–214.

Singleton, D. (1999) *Exploring the Second Language Mental Lexicon.* Cambridge: Cambridge University Press.

Singh, R. and Carrol, S. (1979) L1, L2 and L3. *Indian Journal of Applied Linguistics* 5, 51–63.

Sjöholm, K. (1995) *The Influence of Crosslinguistic, Semantic and Input Factors on the Acquisition of English Phrasal Verbs.* Abo: Abo Akademi Press.

Weinreich, U. (1953) *Languages in Contact.* The Hague: Mouton.

Weltens, B., De Bot, K. and van Els, T. (eds) (1986) *Language Attrition in Progress.* Dordrecht: Foris.

Zimmermann, R. (1992) Lexical knowledge: Evidence from L1 and L2 negatives and L1–L2 translations. In C. Mair and M. Markus (eds) *New Departures in Contrastive Linguistics* (pp. 301–311). Innsbruck: University of Innsbruck.

Zobl, H. (1982) A direction for contrastive analysis: The comparative study of developmental sequences. *TESOL Quarterly* 16, 169–183.

# Chapter 3

# *'I Feel Clumsy Speaking Russian':* *L2 Influence on L1 in Narratives* *of Russian L2 Users of English*

ANETA PAVLENKO

## Introduction

The focus of this paper is on second language (L2) influence on first language (L1) in Russian L2 users of English, all of whom learned their English between the ages of 10 and 27 in the target language context. In previous work, I have argued that many seemingly disparate instances of L2 influence on L1 in such diverse areas as morphosyntax, the lexicon or semantics can be brought together within a unitary classificatory framework that ties these instances to conceptual restructuring in bilingual memory (Pavlenko, 1999, 2000). The present paper will use this approach to analyse L2 influence in L1 Russian narratives elicited from Russian L2 users of English. This data set forms part of a larger corpus of narratives, collected by using the same stimuli with monolingual Russians and Americans, Russian foreign language (FL) learners of English, American FL learners of Russian, simultaneous Russian/English bilinguals, and Russian L2 users of English (Pavlenko, 1997). While parts of this corpus have been examined from different perspectives in Pavlenko (1999, 2002a, 2002b), Pavlenko and Jarvis (2002), and Dewaele and Pavlenko (2002, and this volume), the present chapter represents the first attempt to analyse the full set of L2 users' L1 Russian narratives from the perspective of L2 influence on L1. The analysis will be supplemented by evidence from narratives elicited with the use of the same stimuli from simultaneous Russian/ English bilinguals, and from American FL learners of English. Furthermore, to provide a full picture of L2 effects in Russian users of English, I will also refer to in-depth interviews conducted with the study participants.

In my discussion I will follow Kellerman and Sharwood Smith's (1986) suggestions and adopt the term *transfer* to refer to processes that lead to the incorporation of elements from one language into another (e.g. borrowing or restructuring), and the more inclusive term *crosslinguistic influence* to refer to transfer and any other kind of effect that one language may have on the other (e.g. convergence or attrition). I will also argue that L2 influence on L1 in production and perception of individual adult L2 learners and users can be best understood within the multi-competence framework, proposed by Cook (1991, 1992). In accordance with this framework, the participants will be referred to interchangeably as '[late] bilinguals' and 'L2 users' (Cook, 1999), to acknowledge the fact that they are legitimate speakers of both languages.

## Theoretical Framework

A review of the literature on L2 influence on L1 in adult L2 users suggests that a second or additional language may influence the first in all areas of language, whether phonology, morphosyntax, lexis, semantics, pragmatics, rhetoric or conceptual representations (Pavlenko, 2000). In what follows, I will discuss L2 influence on L1 in Russian L2 users of English in several of these areas with the exception of phonology (for an informative discussion of L2 effects on phonology of Russian L2 users of English, see Andrews, 1999). The L2 effects will be further examined within the classificatory framework proposed earlier (Pavlenko, 1999, 2000) and linked to possible changes in L2 users' conceptual representations. The proposed analytical framework theorises instances of L2 influence on L1 as evidence of one or more of the following five phenomena:

(1)  *borrowing transfer*, or addition of L2 elements to the L1: e.g. lexical borrowing, such as the terms *bid* ('bid') or *bebisitter* ('babysitter') in the speech of Russian immigrants in the US, documented in Andrews (1999);

(2)  *convergence*, or creation of a unitary system, distinct from both L1 and L2: e.g. the use of the same phonetic realisation rules for French and English /t/, which results in a moderately aspirated stop, different from both L1 and L2 values, documented by Flege (1987) in the speech of late French/English bilinguals;

(3)  *shift*, or a move away from L1 structures or values to approximate L2 structures or values: e.g. semantic extension of the meaning of the verb *correr* ('to run') documented by Otheguy and Garcia (1988) in the speech of Cuban immigrants in the US, where, under the influence of English, the verb has acquired the metaphoric meaning of running for office (e.g. *correr para gobernador* 'to run for governor');

(4)  *restructuring transfer*, or incorporation of L2 elements into L1 resulting in some changes, substitutions or simplifications: e.g. the loss of

possessive clitics in the L1 Finnish of Finnish L2 users of Swedish, attributed by Boyd and Andersson (1991) to Swedish influence;

(5) *L1 attrition*, i.e. loss of (or inability to produce) some L1 elements due to L2 influence: e.g. acceptance of syntactically deviant L1 sentences under the influence of L2 constraints, documented by Altenberg (1991) in a case study of two German users of English.

In what follows, I will demonstrate how this framework could be successfully applied to an analysis of L2 effects in the L1 narratives.

## Research Design and Methodology

### Objective

The purpose of the present study is to examine L2 influence on L1 in Russian narratives elicited from Russian L2 users of English. Transfer patterns identified in these narratives will be compared with those identified in Russian narratives elicited from simultaneous Russian/English bilinguals and from American FL learners of Russian.

### Subjects

Thirty Russian L2 users of English (14 males, 16 females), aged between 18 and 31, participated in the study. All were middle-class urban adults, students at Cornell University, Ithaca, New York. Twenty were undergraduates (mean age = 19.5, SD = 0.5, range 18–21) and ten were graduate students (mean age = 27, SD = 1.4, range 24–31). All participants are seen as 'late' bilinguals, as they had learned their English between the ages of 10 and 27 (mean = 16, SD = 2.7), upon arrival in the US, through ESL classes, public or private school attendance, and naturalistic exposure. By the time of the study 23 subjects had spent between 3 and 8 years in the US (mean = 6, SD = 0.95). Among the seven outliers, four subjects had spent 1.5 years in the US, and three had spent between 10 and 14. Despite the differences in the length of exposure, I will consider these participants as members of the same group, since a previous study (Pavlenko & Jarvis, 2002) demonstrated that in this corpus of L2 users' narratives, differences in the length of exposure do not significantly affect either directionality or amount of language transfer. Because Cornell has a sizeable Russian student population, all the participants interacted both in Russian and English on a daily basis. According to the background questionnaires, the participants used Russian with their families, relatives and Russian-speaking friends, and English with English-speaking friends, as well as for educational and interactional purposes.

Two additional groups of participants provided narratives for comparative purposes: (a) four simultaneous Russian/English bilinguals who had arrived in the US between the ages of 1 and 3 and had grown up in Russian-speaking families, and (b) twelve American FL learners of Russian enrolled in advanced Russian classes. All these participants were undergraduate students at Cornell University, closely matched with the main group in age and socio-economic background.

### Stimuli

Four 3-minute long films, with a sound track but no dialogue, were used to elicit the narratives. Narratives, rather than grammaticality judgements or spontaneous conversations, were used in the present study for several reasons. To begin with, narratives present researchers with samples of language use in context and, for this reason, have been used in previous studies of both bilinguals' and L2 learners' L2 competence (e.g. Berman, 1999; Rintell, 1990; Wenzell, 1989) and L1 attrition (Schmid, 2000). At the same time, it has been noted that personal and spontaneous narratives exhibit a significant amount of variation across participants and contexts. For this reason, the present study used video retelling, a task that has a number of advantages. Doughty and Long (2000) argue that a narrative orientation to displaced time and space allows for a greater complexity of output. Pavlenko and Jarvis (2002) suggest that presenting uniform non-verbal prompts allows researchers to keep the data more or less homogeneous by holding the semantic referents constant. At the same time, using films rather than pictures permits researchers to make the storytelling task less artificial and more similar to spontaneous narratives (Tannen, 1980, 1993). Consequently, video retelling has been successfully used for narrative elicitation purposes in several studies in the field of Second Language Acquisition (SLA) (Bardovi-Harlig & Bergström, 1996; Becker & Carroll, 1997; Hyltenstam, 1988; Jarvis, 1998; Klein & Perdue, 1992; Perdue, 1993).

The four films used as stimuli in the present study were specifically made to allow the researcher to manipulate content and context as variables in examination of language use by Russian/English bilinguals. Prior studies, using the same stimuli with Russian and American English monolinguals (Pavlenko, 1997, 2002a), have shown differences in the participants' interpretation of the content of the four films and have linked them to differences between the two speech communities in the conceptualisation of emotions and privacy. Two films, *The Ithaca Story* and *Kiev Story*, portrayed a situation interpreted by monolingual American participants as an invasion of personal space: a stranger sitting down too close to someone. Monolingual Russians, in contrast, perceived the situation as an attempt at a pick-up. The other two films, *The Letter* and *Pis'mo* (The Letter), portrayed a roommate reading someone else's letter without that person's permission. This situation was perceived by monolingual Americans as a violation of informational privacy and by monolingual Russians as an attempt to invade someone's emotional and spiritual world. The first film of each pair was made in the US, and the second in Kiev, Ukraine, to see whether the context in which the interaction takes place has any influence on the linguistic means chosen by bilingual storytellers. Ukraine, rather than Russia, was chosen for reasons of production cost. As expected, although the film was actually made in Kiev, the participants inferred that the action was taking place in Russia, or 'somewhere in the former Soviet Union'.

During the course of the study, eleven participants (6 males, 5 females), saw *The Ithaca Story,* nine (4 males, 5 females) saw *The Letter,* four (1 male, 3 females) saw *Kiev Story,* and six (3 males, 3 females) saw *Pis'mo.* The impact of context and content variables on L2 influence on L1 will not, however, be a subject of discussion, as previous research (Pavlenko & Jarvis, 2002) has determined that differences in content of the narratives and the context in which the action took place did not significantly affect directionality or amount of transfer in this narrative corpus.

## Method

To induce a Russian language mode (Grosjean, 1998) or at least to activate Russian, all participants were greeted and interacted with in Russian by the bilingual researcher. Each participant was shown one film, then given a portable tape recorder and the following instructions: *Pozhaluista, rasskazhite chto vy videli v fil'me* ('Please, tell what you just saw in the film'). Subsequently, all narratives were transcribed and analysed in Russian. All instances of language use that appeared to be errors (or deviations from the range of language variation exhibited by monolingual native speakers of Russian) were compared with patterns of language use in the monolingual narratives elicited previously by the same films (Pavlenko, 1997, 2002a).

Even though no explicit directions were given with regard to code-switching, the amount of code-switching in the data was negligible, possibly because of negative attitudes towards code-switching in the Russian community in the US (Andrews, 1999). At the same time, since the study took place in a US context, it cannot be claimed that the participants told their stories in an exclusively Russian mode. Most likely, they remained in a somewhat bilingual mode, common for their interactions with other Russian speakers in the US. In fact, from the multi-competence perspective, it is possible that they no longer have access to a purely monolingual Russian mode. Consequently, it is Russian produced in a bilingual mode in an American setting that is the focus of this paper.

## Results and Discussion

### Narratives

Thirty narratives were collected from the main group of participants, one from each subject, with a mean length of around 35 clauses. In terms of word length the narratives were about 158 words in total (*Ithaca Story* mean = 155; *Kiev Story* mean = 153; *The Letter* mean = 183; *Pis'mo* mean = 142) – for more details see Dewaele and Pavlenko's chapter in this volume.

In what follows, to give the reader an idea of what these tape-recorded oral narratives looked like, I will provide two stories, elicited by two different films, and then discuss the results of the analysis of the corpus. To demonstrate that the L2 effects in my corpus are not limited to participants who had spent several years in an English-speaking context, I have on purpose selected narratives told by participants with a relatively limited period of exposure to English: 1.5 years in the first case and 3 years in the second.

The first narrative is elicited by *The Ithaca Story* and is told by a 24-year-old male who arrived in the US at the age of 23 (all instances considered to be L2 influence on L1 are underlined):

(1) Центр города... скорее всего/мне сперва показалось, весна, но потом к концу уже фильма, я подумал, что это уже где-то конец лета... итак, центр города... жизнь кипит там... много прохожих, музыканты... жонглёры, и в это время... прогуливается де/девушка... мм, просто, наверное, какая-то очередная обычная прогулка... проходит мимо... мимо кафе... по-моему, Декаданс, на... Коммонсе... на Коммонсе... потом... на случ/наталкивается на знакомых людей, на/на пару, на знакомую пару... там, здоровается с ними там, привет-привет, и дальше идет... это, <u>показалось, что она хочет быть... одной, но в то же время бу/будучи не одинокой, то есть, она хочет быть внутри с/ внутри одной но/но чтобы ее окружали какие-то люди, чтобы она не была одинокой</u>... ну, потом она там проходит, садится... около деревья какого-то... и там достает чего-то там, пытается писать, потом, нет, и в это время подходит/думает о чем-то там, я не знаю там, медитирует, в это время подходит какой-то парень, садится рядом с ней, ну, она так, чуть-чуть в сторону отодвигается, потом... о... ну, я подумал, что, ну все нормально, но потом опять парень, опять как-то/ей хочется быть одной, а он все время, он как-то сделал какое-то движение, ну, убрал/ поднял ноги, положил, ну, на это... на какой-то, ну на... на... на

бетон, где они сидели... ну, это мне так показалось, что... м... э... как-то она почувствовала, что он... мм... <u>вторгается в ее одиночество</u>... отодвинулась в сторону, потом, в конце концов, встала и ушла. Всё.

'Downtown... most likely/at first it seemed to me it was spring, but then, by the end of the movie I thought it was the end of summer... so, downtown... life is busy there... many passersby, musicians... jugglers, and at that time... a gi/girl is walking around... mm... simply, possibly on a regular common walk... she passes by... by a café... I think, 'Decadance', on the... on the Commons... on the Commons... then... sudden/ she bumps into some acquaintances, a/a couple, a couple she knows... well, says hi to them, hello-hello, and keeps going... <u>it seemed that she wants to be... alone at the same time not be/ being lonely, in other words, she wants to be alone in/inside, but/but to be surrounded by some people so that she wouldn't be lonely</u>... well, then, she walks by, sits down... next to some tree... and then gets something out, tries to write, then, no, and at that point comes over/thinking about something, I don't know, meditating, at that point some guy comes over, sits down next to her, so, she moves away a little, then... well, I thought, well, everything is OK, but then again, the guy again somehow/she wants to be alone, and he keeps, he made some movement, well, moved away/put up his legs, put them on that... on some... well, on... on... on the cement where they were sitting... well, so it seemed to me that... m... eh... somehow she felt that he... mm... <u>was invading her solitude</u>... [she] moved away, then finally she got up and left. That's it.'

The second narrative is elicited by *The Letter* and is told by an 18-year-old male who arrived in the US at the age of 15 (all instances considered to be L2 influence on L1 are underlined):

(2)   Я только что посмотрел кино... какое-то... женщина шла по улице, потом она зашла в свой дом, когда она <u>заходила через дверь</u> у неё в руке были письма, её почта... она зашла, она по... прошла в комнату, и <u>села в кресле</u>, к нам... спиною, она положила почти что все/всю почту на стол и открыла одно письмо... она его читала, где-то в середине письма <u>она стала... мм... она выглядела как будто бы она была зла на кого-то и в то же время ей было или страшно или она была очень расстроена</u>, она вначале бросила письмо, потом она его опять подобрала и начала его читать опять, и <u>она стала ещё более расстроенная, но она не выглядела как будто бы она была зла</u>, она, потом она его опять положила, и она/она не плакала, но <u>она</u>

<u>выглядела как будто бы ей было очень не грустно, но</u>, но, не зн/ непонятно что с ней было, потому что её волосы закрывали её лицо, поэтому мы не могли видеть её лицо, потом зашла другая женщина, она подошла к окну вначале, потом она увидела женщину которой было грустно, и она подошла к ней, э, она у нее что-то спросила и та, наверное, сказала про письмо, потому что женщина подобрала письмо и начала его читать, но женщина которой письмо это было адресовано, его забрала у той и бросила его опять на стол, и что-то ей сказала, другая женщина не поняла почему первая так <u>действовала</u>, и она села в кресло, перед этим первая женщина вышла из комнаты.

'I have just seen a film... some [film]... a woman was walking down the street, then she entered her house, when she <u>was entering through the door</u> she had some letters in her hand, her mail... she entered, she ca... came into the room, and sat down in <u>an armchair</u>, with her... back to us, she put almost all/all mail on the table, and opened one letter... she was reading it, somewhere in the middle of that letter <u>she became... uhm... she looked as if she were angry at someone and at the same time she was either scared or very upset</u>, she first threw the letter down, then picked it up and started reading it again, and <u>she became even more upset, but she didn't look as if she were angry</u>, she, then she put it down again, and she/she wasn't crying but <u>she looked as if she were not sad, but</u>, but I don't/it is not clear what was happening to her, because her hair covered her face, and so we couldn't see her face, then another woman came in, she first came to the window, then she saw the woman who was sad and came over to her, uhm, asked her something, and the other one probably said something about the letter, because the woman picked up the letter and started reading it, but the woman to whom the letter was addressed, took it away, and threw it back on the table, and said something to her, the other woman did not understand why the first one was <u>acting</u> this way and she sat down in an armchair, before this the first woman left the room.'

## Data analysis

As already mentioned, the first step in the data analysis involved identifying instances of deviation from standard Russian. In all cases where particular uses were questionable, comparisons were made with the 80 narratives elicited by the same films from monolingual Russian speakers (Pavlenko, 1997, 2002a), in order to see whether particular instances fall within the range of acceptable language variation. These comparisons were made possible by the fact that these elicited narratives required storytellers to refer to a common – and limited – set of visual representations. Thus, resulting narratives were relatively short, employed a limited range of morphosyntactic and semantic means, and allowed for meaningful comparisons across various groups. These comparisons allowed me to eliminate instances that represent deviation from standard Russian, but are nevertheless part of colloquial Russian speech. Then, I have analysed remaining instances and excluded obvious performance errors and errors whose origin could not be traced to English (and which might also be performance errors). The remaining instances were compared with those identified in narratives elicited from simultaneous Russian/English bilinguals and from American FL learners of Russian to ensure that the patterns identified indeed reflect the cross-linguistic influence of English on Russian. The patterns were also compared with those identified by other researchers in the speech of Russian L2 users of English (Andrews, 1993, 1999; Schmitt, 2000). Altogether, I have found 56 instances of L2 influence on L1 in the narratives of 21 Russian L2 users. Below, I will describe the L2 effects in three broadly defined areas of language use:

(1) lexicon and semantics
(2) morphosyntax, and
(3) linguistic framing.

### L2 influence on L1 in the lexicon and semantics

Lexical and semantic influence of L2 on L1 are extremely well documented in the literature on language contact, and in particular on immigrant bilingualism, where the need to name new phenomena in the new reality and the desire to keep the referential meaning constant may prompt lexical borrowing and semantic extension (Romaine, 1995). Many scholars suggest that the lexicon is the first and the main area where L2 influence on L1 is visible. Four main types of L2 effects on L1 lexis have been documented in the literature: lexical borrowing (Andrews, 1993, 1999; Boyd, 1993; Haugen, 1953; Li, 2001; Otheguy & Garcia, 1988, 1993), loan translation (Jaspaert & Kroon, 1992; Latomaa, 1998), semantic extension (Otheguy & Garcia, 1988), and difficulties in lexical retrieval (Latomaa, 1998; Olshtain & Barzilay, 1991). In the present corpus, all four types of L2 influence on L1 were observed in the lexicon and semantics of the study participants, who produced 29 L2-influenced lexical and semantic errors.

Six instances of _lexical borrowing_ (i.e. L2 items adopted phonologically and, in the first case, morphologically) were identified in the narratives of four participants: _intruzivnost'_ 'intrusiveness', _dauntaun_ 'downtown', _lendlord_ 'landlord', _apointment_ 'appointment', and _boifrend_ 'boyfriend' (the last item was used by two different participants). The latter two items were also documented by Andrews (1999: 90–91, 96) as common items in the speech of immigrant Russians, designating concepts that have no exact counterparts in Russian.

Three instances of *loan translation*, or literal translations of compound words, idioms, and lexical collocations from the source language, were found in three different narratives:

(3) он... мм... <u>вторгается в её одиночество</u>
   'he... uhm... <u>invades her solitude</u>'

   он <u>вторгается в её эмоции, чувства</u>
   'he <u>invades her emotions, feelings</u>'

   предлагает ей какую-то <u>эмоциональную помощь</u>
   'offers her some <u>emotional help</u>'

The first two instances are prompted by the fact that Russian lacks the notion of privacy, and thus, in order to describe what they see as an invasion of privacy, the participants have to appeal to its translation equivalents in Russian, such as *odinochestvo* 'solitude'. The third instance was a literal translation of a collocation 'emotional help' where an appropriate Russian expression would have been *podderzhka* '[moral, emotional] support'.

L2 influence was also observed in the area of *semantic extension*, that is to say, extension in the use of L1 words and expressions to include the meaning of a perceived L2 translation equivalent (a phenomenon also known as loan shift). Twenty instances of semantic extension were found in the narratives of 13 participants; they can be further subdivided into four subcategories. The first subcategory, extension per se, involves attribution of a meaning of a polysemous English word to the Russian word that shares some but not all of the meanings of its 'translation equivalent', as in the examples below:

(4) поменять как бы... сцену
   'to change <u>the scene</u> somehow' – an appropriate lexical choice would be обстановку 'surroundings'

   она явно становится... становится как-то <u>неудобно</u> и неуютно
   'she clearly becomes... becomes somehow <u>uncomfortable</u> and ill at ease' – an appropriate lexical choice would be некомфортно 'uncomfortable [psychologically]'

The first instance illustrates semantic extension of the Russian word *stsena* 'scene, stage.' While in Russian *stsena* could also mean an embarrassing display of anger or bad manners, like its English counterpart, its primary or core meaning is that of a theatre stage. It does not refer to areas or spheres of activity (e.g. the fashion scene) or places where events or actions occurred (e.g. the scene of the accident). The utterance does not constitute a loan translation, however, because there is a Russian expression *pomeniat' obstanovku* 'to change one's surroundings', which would have been appropriate. In a similar vein, two participants extended the meaning of the English 'uncomfortable' to the Russian adverb *neudobno* 'uncomfortable', which is typically used in apologies (*mne tak neudobno* 'I am so sorry') or when discussing physical discomfort. The speakers, however, used the adverb to refer to the psychological discomfort of being close to a stranger. This type of semantic extension was also encountered in the narratives of American FL learners of Russian and that of simultaneous Russian/English bilinguals, in particular with regard to the use of *neudobno*. In contrast, Russian monolinguals and some Russian L2 users of English used *nekomfortno* 'uncomfortable' or *diskomfort* 'discomfort' in the same context.

The second subcategory involves instances that may be interpreted as a loss of semantic and conceptual distinctions, and, in the first example, as semantic narrowing. These instances contain references to human emotions:

(5)  но ещё была очень как бы... <u>зла</u> на кого-то
     'and also [she] was very somehow... <u>angry</u> at someone' – an appropriate lexical choice would be сердита 'cross, angry at the moment'

     она видит, что её дочь не очень такая... <u>счастливая</u>
     'she sees that her daughter is not that... <u>happy</u>' – an appropriate lexical choice would be недовольная 'dissatisfied' or грустная 'sad'

With regard to the first instance, Russian has three translation equivalents of angry – *serdityi* 'cross', 'angry at the moment', *zloi* 'malicious', 'very angry', 'mean' (typically used as a personality characteristic), and *gnevnyi* 'irate', 'in wrath' – each adjective more intense than the preceding one. Russian monolinguals favoured the first term, *serditaia* 'cross/Fem', in their narratives. In contrast, some Russian L2 users of English appear to have collapsed the distinctions, using instead the short adjective *zla* 'malicious', 'angry/Fem' in describing the main protagonist. In the second case, the participant similarly misused the adjective *schastlivaia* 'happy/Fem' which in Russian refers to a lasting state of happiness. In contrast, the English 'happy' has a much wider range of usage and may be used to mean 'pleased' or 'satisfied' (for an argument that the English 'happy' is weaker than its Russian counterpart, see Wierzbicka, 1999: 53).

The third subcategory of semantic extension involves the use of references in the inappropriate register:

(6) девочка ходила по улице

    'a [little] girl was walking down the street' – an appropriate lexical choice would be девушка 'young woman'

Here, two of the participants in the study referred to the main character in the movies as *devochka* 'little girl' and *devchonka* (pejorative term for a young girl), confounded by the overlap in the core meanings of the English 'girl' and the Russian *devochka, devchonka* 'girl'. The English word, however, has a much broader range of meanings and, depending on the context, may refer to women of all ages. In Russian, however, *devochka* can only mean a little girl up to the age of 10 to 13, at which point she transforms into *devushka* 'a young woman', which would have been an appropriate term to use in this context.

The last subcategory involves the attribution of a particular meaning to the word, based on superficial word-structure similarities, for example:

(7) просматривала письма, которые она выбрала из почтового ящика

    '[she] was looking through the letters which she chose from the mailbox' – an appropriate lexical choice would be вынула 'took out'

In the example above, the participant used the verb *vybrat'* 'to choose, to pick out' in the meaning of 'taking out' [the mail]. In doing so, he reinterpreted the meaning of the Russian verb, based on the literal meaning of its constituents *vy/*'out'+*brat'*/'take.' Similarly, another participant used the word *sozhitel'nitsa* (literally: 'co-habitant'/Fem) to mean 'roommate', whereas in Russian the word is used exclusively as a derogatory or ironic reference to a female who cohabitates with a male without being married to him.

Finally, ten narratives and five subsequent interviews also provided evidence of lexical access and retrieval difficulties (see also the discussion section). In some cases, the participants hesitated specifically at points where they were having problems with lexical choice or were about to violate either syntactic or semantic constraints of Russian – see narratives in (1) and (2), as well as examples (4) and (5). Others explicitly admitted difficulties in expressing their thoughts in Russian where particular concepts, such as privacy, were involved:

(8) мне пришло в голову понятие, но я не нашел слов в русском языке, чтобы это описать... в общем, пришлось бы достаточно долго и неточно как-то описывать

'A notion came to me, but I didn't find Russian words to describe it... I would have had to describe it for a long time and inexactly'

когда парень убирает, ставит ноги, я уже не/не знаю как по-русски это обьяснять... она уже, я так подумал, что это уже, для неё это уже было, что он пересек, то есть, что она уже не может быть одна 'when the guy moves away, puts his legs on, I already don't/I don't know how to describe this in Russian... she already, I thought, that this already, that for her it was, that he crossed, in other words, that she can no longer be alone'

Together, the narratives and the interviews provide convincing evidence that English influences both the Russian lexicon and the semantics of these Russian L2 users of English, and may also prompt temporary difficulties in access to Russian lexical items.

## L2 influence on L1 in morphosyntax

Previous research on L2 influence on L1 in late bilinguals suggests that the lexicon is not the only area that is vulnerable to L2 influence, and that L1 morphosyntactic performance (and at times even competence) could also be subject to L2 influence and L1 attrition in adulthood (Pavlenko, 2000). L2-induced changes are particularly visible in L1 speakers who had spent a substantial amount of time in their L2 environment, generally between ten and twenty years (De Bot *et al.*, 1991; Py, 1986; Waas, 1996), and at times even forty years or longer (Altenberg, 1991; Schmid, 2000). De Bot and Clyne (1994) argue that L1 attrition may be visible much earlier, and that immigrants who managed to maintain their language in the first years of their stay in the L2 context are likely to remain fluent L1 speakers. Most pronounced changes and attrition are found in those who have few if any contacts with the speakers of L1 (De Bot *et al.*, 1991; Waas, 1996) and in those who have negative attitudes toward the L1 (Schmid, 2000). Considering the fact that L1 attrition is a complex phenomenon that cannot be reduced to L2 influence (for an up-to-date treatment, see Schmid, 2000), the focus of the present chapter will be exclusively on the L2 effects on L1. To date, the L2 influence on L1 morphosyntax of adult L2 users has been documented in the areas of case-, gender- and number-marking (Håkansson, 1995; Schmid, 2000), preposition choice (Py, 1986; Schmid, 2000), and word-order rules and subcategorisation (Boyd & Andersson, 1991; Py, 1986; Schmid, 2000; Seliger & Vago, 1991; Waas, 1996), where some L2 users not only extend L2 rules to their L1 but also accept sentences syntactically deviant in the L1 but permissible in the L2 (Altenberg, 1991).

In the present study, seventeen L2-influenced errors were identified in the L2 users' narratives in four areas: tense and aspect, subcategorisation, case marking and prepositional choice. It is not surprising that the participants' morphosyntax is less affected than their lexicon. Most of them had spent less than ten years in the L2 environment, and only three participants had been in the US for ten years or longer (interestingly, they are not the ones who exhibited traces of L2 influence on L1 morphosyntax, which confirms De Bot and Clyne's (1994) observations). In addition, all participants indicated that they interacted both in English and in Russian on a daily basis, and were very committed to maintaining their native language (even though, as will be discussed later, several informants found L1 maintenance to be a daunting task). As a result, this section will examine trends and possible areas of influence rather than make sweeping claims about the present population. In what follows, I will discuss each area in turn, with the understanding that future work may uncover L2 English effects on other areas of Russian morphosyntax.

The first area where difficulties may arise and changes occur in Russian/ English contact is that of tense and aspect (see Wenzell, 1989, for a discussion of L1 transfer in the use of tense/aspect by Russian learners of English). English verbs have an inherent lexical aspect (activity, state, accomplishment, achievement) and a grammatical one (simple, perfective, progressive). In turn, each Russian verb is either perfective or imperfective, and most of them have an aspectual pair. Thus, an English verb would typically have two corresponding Russian verbs (e.g. 'to do' corresponds to *delat'* 'to be doing something' and *sdelat'* 'to have done something'). The Russian verbs that make an aspectual pair generally have the same lexical meaning, but refer to the action from different perspectives (Vasilenko *et al.*, 1982). The imperfective form, which is the unmarked member of the pair, names the action without referring to its temporal limits, manner, direction, etc. The perfective form refers to a completed action; it is usually derived from the imperfective by the addition of a prefix or a suffix (in some cases, however, it is a verb with a different stem). Both types of verbs are marked for tense (past, present, perfect) and could be translated into English in a variety of ways (e.g. *ushel* 'left', 'has left', 'had left' vs. *ukhodil* 'was leaving', 'left several times', 'used to leave'). Just as Russian learners of English find the English tense system challenging (Wenzell, 1989), American FL learners of Russian have considerable difficulties in learning Russian aspectual distinctions, because they do not fully correspond to the perfective/ progressive aspect in English. The difficulties are compounded by the fact that at times both members of an aspectual pair may be grammatically acceptable in a sentence, and lexical choice is ultimately determined by context. Consequently, learners are often under a false impression that imperfective is the unmarked option and can be used in a wider variety of contexts than is acceptable in Russian. Additional difficulties are created by the fact that Russian verbs of motion have several imperfective forms, subcategorised into determinate and indeterminate (e.g. *idti/khodit'* 'to walk'). Determinate verbs describe motion generally proceeding in a forward direction, usually at a given point in time (*idti po ulitse* 'to be walking down the street), while indeterminate verbs describe aimless and/ or multidirectional motion, and habitual or repeated motion (*khodit' tuda siuda* 'to walk back and forth'; *khodit' v shkolu* 'to go to school every day') (Muravyova, 1986). As a result of this seeming prevalence of the imperfective and the fact that it refers to action in general, American FL learners of Russian often opt for the imperfective when referring to accomplished past tense actions, as seen in the FL learners' narratives in the present study. Influenced by the lack of distinction between indeterminate and determinate verbs in English, at times they also appeal to indeterminate verbs when referring to specific movement proceeding forward:

(9) она <u>ходится</u> по улице
'she <u>is walking [herself]</u> down the street' – an appropriate lexical choice would be идет по улице, as the woman is moving forward in a specific direction; the narrator also erroneously used the verb as a reflexive and chose an inappropriate preposition, на/'on', which refers to location, rather than по/'on', which refers to direction

когда она <u>входила</u> в комнату, она постала спокойную классическую музыку
'when she <u>was entering</u> the room, she turned on some quiet classical music' –an appropriate lexical choice would be вошла 'entered', as the two actions are sequential, not simultaneous, the first was completed before the second

та же самая женщина пришла домой, видимо, домой... э, бабушка <u>шла</u>, не знаю, мимо
'the same woman came home, it seems, home... mm, a grandmother <u>was walking</u>, I don't know, by' – an appropriate lexical choice would be прошла 'walked by', as the action was singular and completed, with no simultaneous actions described

я только что <u>смотрел</u> фильм, который происходил в каком-то русском городе
'I <u>was</u> just <u>watching</u> a movie that took place in some Russian city' – an appropriate lexical choice would be посмотрел 'saw', as the reference

is to a completed action, with no simultaneous actions described, and the intended meaning is 'I have just seen/watched a movie'

и парень <u>сидел</u> на эту скамейку
'and a guy <u>was sitting</u> on that bench' – in the context of this story, which describes a series of completed actions, the intended meaning is 'sat down' and an appropriate lexical choice would be сел 'sat down'; the case markings on the determiner and the noun confirm that this was the meaning intended by the speaker

Similar problems occur in the speech of simultaneous Russian/English bilinguals dominant in English:

(10) она пришла, хотела <u>сесть</u>, сама быть
'she arrived, wanted <u>to sit down</u> (meaning: to sit for a while), to be alone' –since the reference in this context is to a progressive action limited in time, an appropriate lexical choice would be the perfective verb посидеть 'to sit for a while'

женщина <u>ходит</u> по улице
'a woman <u>is walking</u> down the street' – in this context, an appropriate lexical choice is идёт since the woman is moving forward in a specific direction, and not walking back and forth

The L2 users' narratives indicate that the perfective/imperfective and determinate/indeterminate distinctions in Russian may also be getting somewhat blurred for some Russian L2 users of English, who, just like FL learners, may be perceiving imperfective verbs and indeterminate verbs of motion as unmarked options. In the present corpus, seven instances of tense and aspect errors were identified in the narratives of five participants. All instances involved the use of imperfective aspect where perfective was required (and used by Russian monolinguals); some instances involved the use of verbs of motion and the additional use of indeterminate rather than determinate verbs. What makes it impossible to discard these instances as performance errors is that they mirror the patterns of L1 transfer in narratives told by American FL learners of English and simultaneous Russian/English bilinguals:

(11) пришел... мм... какой-то парень и <u>сидел</u> рядом с ней
'some guy arrived and <u>was sitting</u> down next to her' – an appropriate lexical choice would be сел 'sat down'

она шла через мост, в Итаке, скорее всего в центре внизу в Итаке...
мм... мимо неё <u>проезжала</u> машина
'she was walking across the bridge, in Ithaca, most likely in downtown
Ithaca ... uhm... a car <u>was passing</u> by her' – since проезжать refers to
repeated or multiple actions, appropriate lexical choices here would
be проехала 'passed by' if one car was involved, and проезжали 'were
passing by' if multiple cars were involved

девочка <u>ходила</u> по улице
'a young girl <u>was walking</u> down the street' – in this context, an appropriate lexical choice is шла 'was walking', since the woman was
walking forward in a specific direction; the verb ходить generally
implies repeated or habitual action, or multiple directions

я <u>смотрела</u> фильм
'I <u>was watching</u> a movie' – in the context of the story, an appropriate
lexical choice would be посмотрела 'I just watched, I have watched, I
have just seen', since the reference is to a completed action with no
mention of events taking place simultaneously

она <u>смотрела</u> на свою почту
'she <u>was looking</u> at her mail' – in the context of the story, an appropriate lexical choice would be посмотрела 'looked', as the woman
glanced at the mail briefly

The second area where L2 influence was observed is that of subcategorisation. In the present study, five violations of subcategorisation
constraints were found in the narratives of five participants, involving
instances such as the following two:

(12) она чувствовала <u>грустная</u>
     'she felt <u>sad</u>'

     она явно становится... становится <u>как-то неудобно и неуютно</u>
     'she clearly becomes... becomes <u>somehow uncomfortable and ill at
     ease</u>'

In the first instance, the participant violated subcategorisation constraints
which specify that, as a reflexive verb, *chuvstvovat'* 'to feel' subcategorises
either for a limited range of adverbs, or for nouns and adjectives in Instrumental case and, as a non-reflexive verb, for nouns in Accusative case.
Instead, the reflexive particle required in this context is omitted, and the
verb is followed by the adjective in Nominative case, as it would have been
in English. In the second case, another participant violated the constraints

for the verb *stanovit'sia* 'to become' which in Russian subcategorises only for nouns and adjectives in Instrumental case. However, there are no adjectives in Russian that correspond to the English 'uncomfortable', and to complete the thought the speaker violated the constraints and used two adverbs that correspond in meaning to 'uncomfortable' (see also the discussion in the previous section on the problems with the lexical choice in this example). To use these adverbs, the sentence should have been constructed in the passive voice, with the subject pronoun 'she' in the Dative case (*ei*) and not in the Nominative (*ona*) – see also further discussion of this example in the section on linguistic framing.

The discussion above demonstrates that not only Russian subcategorisation constraints but also Russian case marking is subject to L2 influence. Two more study participants produced the utterances below where a noun and a subject pronoun were marked incorrectly:

(13) она села в <u>кресле</u>
'she sat down in an <u>armchair</u>'/Prep – should have been <u>кресло</u>/Acc

он <u>её</u> не только начинает не нравится, но очень даже раздражает
'he not only displeases <u>her</u>/Acc, but really starts irritating her' – should have been <u>ей</u>/Dat

Both errors can be explained by the fact that Russian has a six-case system with obligatory morphological case marking, while English has three cases with case marking most visible in pronouns (e.g. *he/him*). Thus, under the influence of English, the distinction between the cases in question may have become subject to intralinguistic simplification. It is also possible that in the second example we are witnessing a performance error where the pronoun is in agreement with the verb *razdrazhat'* 'to irritate' which introduces the new topic, rather than with the one immediately following it. Schmitt (2000) observed similar instances of subcategorisation violations and of case marking errors in the speech of Russian immigrant children living in the US. In the present study, case-marking errors, all in prepositional phrases, have also been observed in the narratives of FL learners (the first three instances) and simultaneous Russian/English bilinguals (the last two):

(14) сначала фотоаппарат следовал... <u>какую-то девушку</u>
'first the camera followed... <u>some girl</u>/Acc – an appropriate wording would be за какой-то девушкой/Instr

она... мм... пошла на мосте
'she... uhm... walked over the bridge'/Prep – an appropriate wording
would be по мосту/Dat or через мост/Acc

похоже на Москве
'similar to Moscow'/Prep – an appropriate choice would be Москву/
Acc

она... вх... вых... выходит из комната
'she l... le... leaves the room'/Nom – an appropriate choice would be
комнаты/Gen

кто-то пришел, сел к неё
'someone came, sat down next to her'/Acc – an appropriate choice
would be к ней/Dat

The examples above illustrate not only patterns of case-marking errors
but also the difficulties that FL learners and simultaneous bilinguals have
in selecting appropriate prepositions in Russian. This area may also be of
interest in future investigations of L2 influence on L1 in Russian L2 users of
English. In the present study, two Russian L2 users produced three L2-
influenced errors in selecting a preposition (the second instance was
repeated twice):

(15) когда она заходила через дверь, у неё в руке были письма
   'when she was entering through the door, there were letters in her
   hand' – an appropriate prepositional choice is в дверь 'in the door',
   moreover, in this context, the mention of the door is simply redundant

   села на кресле
   'sat on the chair' – an appropriate prepositional choice is в кресло 'in
   the chair'

In sum, the present study identified four specific areas of Russian
morphosyntax (tense and aspect, subcategorisation, case marking, and
prepositional choice) that are likely to be subject to L2 influence in Russian–
English contact and may also be the first areas to exhibit such influence.
Clearly, to make substantial claims about L2 influence on L1 competence,
rather than performance, a significantly larger database will need to be
assembled, in particular from speakers who have been exposed to and
interacting in English for decades.

### L2 influence on L1 linguistic framing

Another important area where L2 influence on L1 of the study participants was evident is that of *linguistic framing*, or the choice of a structural

category or grammatical class to express a mental representation (Slobin, 1996). To give an example, in satellite-framed languages, such as English, information about the motion path is provided in a satellite of the verb (prefixes or particles), while in verb-framed languages, such as French, the path is indicated through the main verb. To this researcher's knowledge, to date this category has not yet been examined in the study of L2 influence on L1 (see, however, Pavlenko, 2002b; Pavlenko & Jarvis, 2002). In the present study, ten instances of L2 influence on L1 framing were identified in seven narratives, all involving references to emotions. This is not surprising, as the two speech communities in question differ in the framing of emotions, and two of the four films aimed to elicit such differences. In what follows, then, I will first discuss differences in linguistic framing of emotions between Russian and English, and then proceed to discuss the L2 effects.

Previous research on Russian discourses of emotions suggests that experiences comparable to 'joy', 'sadness,' or 'anger' are often conceptualised in Russian as inner activities in which one engages more or less voluntarily (Wierzbicka, 1992). As a result, these activities involve duration and are often designated by verbs, rather than by adjectives (e.g. *radovat'sia* 'to rejoice', 'to be actively happy, joyful'; *serdit'sia* 'to be angry', 'to rage'; *stydit'sia* 'to be ashamed', 'to be experiencing shame'). While it is possible in Russian to use perception copulas and change-of-state verbs when discussing emotions, such references would be typically made in passive voice (e.g. *ei bylo/stalo grustno*; literally 'it was/became sad for her'). In contrast, in English emotions are conceptualised as passive states caused by external and/or past causes; as a result, they are more commonly expressed by means of adjectives and pseudo-participles, such as 'worried', 'sad' or 'disgusted'. Moreover, as Wierzbicka (1992: 401) points out, English has only a very limited number of intransitive emotion verbs, such as 'to rejoice', 'to grieve', 'to worry,' or 'to pine' – and the whole category may be losing ground in modern English.

Pavlenko's (2002a) study of emotion narratives of monolingual speakers of Russian and English provides empirical support for these claims, demonstrating that American narrators favour an adjectival pattern in their emotion narratives, while Russian narrators favour a verbal one. Moreover, not only did Russian speakers use more verbs than adjectives in their narratives, they also used predominantly imperfective and reflexive emotion verbs that stressed the processual aspect of the experience. Of particular importance in the Russian corpus was the verb *perezhivat'* 'to suffer things through', which, together with the noun *perezhivania* 'feelings', 'emotions', 'suffering' accounted for 9% of all emotion word tokens in the monolingual Russian corpus. *Perezhivat'* has no translation equivalent in

English. The meaning of the verb's perfective counterpart *perezhit'* is 'to live through' (e.g. difficult times), while the meaning of the imperfective lemma (literally referring to 'suffering through') is more immediate and refers to the act of experiencing, processing and dealing with particular emotions caused by unfortunate experiences. It is difficult to render the verb precisely in English, as its closest counterparts 'experiencing' and 'processing' lack the emotional overtone of being nervous, anxious, suffering and engaged in observable actions, crucial for understanding of *perezhivat'*.

In the present study, under the influence of the L2, some Russian L2 users of English attempted to substitute verbs for adjectives and, consequently, incorporated perception copulas and change-of-state verbs in their texts. The first L2-influenced tendency, found in the narratives of five different participants (see also narrative in (2) above), is to use the verb *stat'* (perfective)/*stanovit'sia* (imperfective) 'to become' with emotion adjectives, in contexts where monolingual participants use action verbs such as *rasserdit'sia* 'to get angry' or *rasstroit'sia* 'to get upset'. This framing transfer also involves subcategorisation violations, as in Russian the verb subcategorises for adjectives in Instrumental (and not in Nominative) case:

(16) она явно <u>становится</u>... <u>становится</u> как-то неудобно и неуютно
'she clearly <u>becomes</u>... <u>becomes</u> somehow uncomfortable and ill at ease' – an appropriate linguistic framing here, as discussed earlier, would be ей стало как-то некомфортно

она <u>стала</u> ещё более расстроенная
'she <u>became</u> even more upset'/Nom – an appropriate linguistic framing here is она ещё более расстроилась 'she got even more upset'

она <u>была, стала</u>... сердиться
'she <u>was, became</u> (meaning: started) ... getting angry' – an appropriate linguistic framing here is она рассердилась 'she got angry'

она <u>становится</u> очень какая-то такая... трудно, я даже не знаю как это сказать... ну, как-то меланхолическое у неё состояние
'she <u>becomes</u> so very... it's hard, I don't even know how to say that... well, she is in a melancholic state' – an appropriate linguistic framing here is passive voice ей становится 'it becomes for her'

Another L2-influenced framing pattern involved the use of perception verb *vygliadet'* 'to look as if':

(17) она <u>выглядит как</u>, может быть, она будет плакать
'she <u>looks as if</u>, maybe, she will be crying' – here the subject missed an obligatory particle будто 'if' which should have followed как 'as'

она <u>выглядела как будто бы</u> она была зла на кого-то
'she <u>looked as if</u> she were angry at someone'

она <u>не выглядела как будто бы она</u> была зла... она <u>выглядела как будто бы ей</u> было очень не грустно, но не зн/непонятно что с ней было
'she <u>didn't look as if</u> she were angry... she <u>looked as if</u> she were not sad, but I don't kn/it's not clear what was going on with her'

The uses of this verb exemplified above are inauthentic for a number of reasons. To begin with, the use of *vygliadet'* is a rhetorical strategy, not encountered in the narratives produced by monolingual Russians, who favour either action verbs, such as *rasstroit'sia* 'to get upset' or direct descriptions of states such as *ona rasstroena* 'she [is] upset'. In contrast, monolingual speakers of English in the previous study (Pavlenko, 2002a) preferred to phrase their opinions in a qualified way, stating that the woman 'seemed upset' or 'looked as if she was upset.' Secondly, the use of *vygliadet'* is inappropriate in this context for pragmatic reasons, as in Russian it is used in a limited range of contexts to tell people that they either look well (*khorosho vygliadet'*) or do not (*plokho vygliadet'* 'to look badly', i.e. tired). Finally, the use of *vygliadet'* also creates morphosyntactic problems for the participants. To begin with, the Russian verb is most frequently used with a limited range of adverbs, such as the ones above; in rare cases when it is used with adjectives, it subcategorises for adjectives in Instrumental case. In contrast, in English the verb may subcategorise for multiple adjectives and pseudo-participles (e.g. 'to look dapper, elegant, confused'). Thus, the participants often pause, hesitate, and then resort to the construction *kak budto* 'as if', which allows them to avoid subcategorisation errors (in particular, if they are no longer comfortable with case marking) by producing a subordinate clause. Not surprisingly, similar uses of *vygliadet'* are documented in the narratives by simultaneous Russian bilinguals and by FL learners of Russian, for example:

(18) и <u>выглядела</u> как она была очень тронутая
'and <u>looked as</u> she were very moved' – note that the actual Russian adjective used тронутая, while literally meaning 'moved', in reality means 'crazy'; also the particle будто 'if' is missing

L2 effects were also seen in the inappropriate use of the verb *chuvstvovat'* 'to feel', already illustrated in example (12). Similar to *vygliadet'* 'to look as if', this verb is frequently used with a limited range of adverbs such as *khorosho* 'well' (as in *chuvstvovat' sebia khorosho* 'to feel well') or *plokho* 'badly' (*chuvstvovat' sebia plokho* 'to feel badly', i.e. to be ill). With adjectives the verb subcategorises for Instrumental (and not for Nominative) case. In addition, it is obligatory to use the reflexive form of the verb that includes the particle *sebia* 'self' (e.g. *ona chuvstvovala sebia neschastnoi* 'she felt [herself] unhappy'/Inst).

In sum, it appears that L2 influence on L1 prompted some study participants to frame emotions linguistically as states, rather than as active processes, violating both semantic and syntactic constraints of Russian. In many cases, the speakers realised that they were not using the appropriate frames and, as seen in the narrative in (2) and in some of the examples above, started pausing, stumbling, stuttering, self-correcting and offering a metalinguistic commentary.

## Discussion

The analysis above shows that L2 effects were identified in narratives elicited from 21 Russian L2 users of English, some of whom have been in the target language context for less than 10 years (and in some cases only 1.5 years). It is possible that, if more extensive data were collected, the L2 effects would have been visible in the speech of the other participants as well. In the present study, the L2 influence on L1 was found in the areas of the lexicon, semantics and morphosyntax, and in linguistic framing that involves both semantics and grammar. From the point of view of the theoretical framework presented earlier, the results of the study are interpreted as evidence for four out of five processes taking place in the bilingual mental lexicon: borrowing, shift, restructuring and L1 attrition (but not convergence).

The first and most important process evident in the present data is *borrowing* or internalisation of new concepts, which are either differentially encoded in English and in Russian (e.g. emotion concepts) or encoded in English but not in Russian (e.g. 'privacy'). The fact that Russian L2 users of English are internalising new concepts is evident in instances of lexical borrowing, all of which refer to concepts non-existent in Russian culture (see also Andrews, 1993, 1999), instances of loan translation and hesitation whereby participants declare the inability to express a notion or a concept, and in the few instances of code-switching. As seen in the excerpt below, the study participants are aware of these conceptual differences between their two speech communities, which may lead to difficulties in lexical choice:

(19) Или, например, privacy?... какая privacy?... по-русски этого нету, я не могу сказать по-русски, знаешь, ну я могу сказать 'Я хочу побыть одна', но это звучит слишком драматично, да?.. когда ты говоришь

по-английски 'I need my privacy' это более как ежедневная вещь и никто, никого это не волнует...

'Or take, for instance, *privacy*... what *privacy*?... in Russian this doesn't exist, I cannot say in Russian, you know, well, I can say "I want to be alone", but this sounds too dramatic, yes?.. when you say in English "I need my privacy" this is more like an everyday thing and no one, it doesn't bother anyone...'

Another process evident in the data is *shift*, whereby some conceptualisations shift towards L2 conceptual domains. This shift is particularly evident in the domain of emotions, where the participants appeal to English means of encoding emotions and, in the process, violate syntactic (in particular, subcategorisation) and semantic constraints of Russian. Once again, some are aware that English is becoming their preferred mode of self-expression. In the interview below, a 25 year old female study participant who arrived in the US five years earlier complains that her Russian is no longer adequate to describe her feelings and newly-acquired concepts (note that she also code-switches when describing how she feels, using first the English word 'clumsy', and only then the Russian approximation *nelovko*):

(20) Что я хочу сказать? Что я чувствую себ/все более и более clumsy, неловко, когда я говорю по-русски, мне трудно подбирать слова, и очень часто мне кажется, что мне легче выразить это по-английски, даже не потому что я не знаю слов по-русски, а потому что выражение, которое я хочу употребить в данной ситуации, оно настолько английское, и оно настолько... например...что-то очень трудно сделать, да?.. и я не знаю получится у меня или нет, я говорю себе сама по-английски 'I can make it'... почему – потому что по-русски это не звучит, это не то же самое, и нету такой... уверенности, что ты, да, ты сможешь это сделать, нет такой бравады, нет такого спокойствия, ещё чего-то такого, нет вот этого, нету...

'What do I want to say? That I feel more and more *clumsy*, uncomfortable, when I speak Russian, it is difficult for me to choose words, and very often it seems to me that it is easier for me to express something in English, not even because I do not know Russian words, but because the expression I want to use in a particular situation, it is so English, and it is so... for example... something is very difficult to accomplish, yes? ... and I do not know if I will be able to succeed or not, and I say to myself in English "I can make it"... why – because in Russian it doesn't sound right, it is not the same, and there is no such... confidence, that you, yes, you will be able to do this, there is no such bravado, no such calm, and something else, it is not there, no...

A further process we have witnessed is *restructuring,* in which the violation of syntactic and semantic constraints suggests that the Russian of some of the study participants may be incorporating some L2 elements and undergoing some intralinguistic simplification in the domains of tense and aspect and case marking, as well as with regard to particular lexical items, such as *zloi* 'angry' or *schastlivyi* 'happy.' These data also point in an interesting direction for future research in the area of tense and aspect. Slobin (1996, 2000) has repeatedly argued that speakers of different languages vary in the ways in which they perceive and encode motion. Some languages (such as French) are verb-framed and indicate 'path' through the main verb, and others (such as English) are satellite-framed and thus indicate 'path' by a satellite to the verb while focusing on 'manner of motion'. What is interesting about Russian is that, even though it is considered to be a satellite-framed language, Russian motion verbs encode both 'path' and 'manner of motion', with 'path' often being doubly encoded through both prefixes and prepositions. Moreover, as discussed earlier, Russian also distinguishes between determinate and indeterminate motion. If L2 influence did indeed begin to impact on ways in which tense and aspect, and in particular motion, are encoded by Russian L2 users of English, in the future it would be interesting to investigate whether some aspects of motion (such as determinacy or even path) that are emphasised by Russian but not by English are becoming less salient for Russian L2 users.

Finally, self-corrections, hesitations, pauses, metalinguistic comments and explicit statements indicate that the participants are aware of lexical retrieval difficulties that may be interpreted as a sign of – at least temporary – L1 *attrition* (limited perhaps to on-line performance). One 18-year-old male participant, who arrived in the US four years earlier, mentioned that during his annual summer visits to Moscow people tease him about his Russian:

(21) they say that I have an accent in Russian (laughs)... no, I don't make mistakes, but... I have a bit of an accent, but sometimes I forget words...

On the conceptual level, attrition is evident in the fact that, not only do American conceptualisations of emotions surface in the narratives, but also only one of all the study participants referred to the specifically Russian notion of *perezhivat'* 'to suffer through', which dominated the narratives of Russian monolinguals (see also Pavlenko, 2002b).

At the same time, despite the signs of perhaps inevitable L2 influence, for many, if not all, of the study participants, Russian remains an important means of self-expression. They are fully invested in maintaining their Russian competence – even though they cannot help but witness the interaction between their two linguistic systems, described as follows in one of the interviews:

(22) if I am with my Russian friends, I think it's very important that I do speak Russian to them, but there is always that mixing of two languages, which personally I don't appreciate, especially when people try to conjugate Russian or American verbs or like different words in Russian way, so... I mean, you can mix it but to a certain point, and that's what I do...

The awareness of the dynamic nature of linguistic competence prevents us ultimately from seeing the instances discussed in this study as language loss, a phenomenon which, according to Schmid (2000: 191) may not even exist. Rather, they may constitute a case of temporary inhibition or deactivation of particular linguistic items and morphosyntactic constraints.

## Conclusion

The data discussed above provide evidence that L2 influence on L1 takes place in the lexicon, semantics and morphosyntax of Russian L2 users of English who learned their L2 in late childhood or adulthood. In the area of morphosyntax, the L2 influence was exhibited in violations of tense and aspect, case-marking rules, subcategorisation constraints, and prepositional choice. In the area of lexicon and semantics, the influence was visible in the instances of lexical borrowing, loan translation and semantic extension, as well as in lexical retrieval difficulties. L2 influence was also found in the area of linguistic framing, where both semantic and syntactic constraints were violated by the narrators.

Clearly, the present investigation is limited in a number of ways. To begin with, the data collected here consist of relatively short oral narratives, elicited by specific visual stimuli. While these data allow us to conduct very useful across-group comparisons, in future studies of L2 influence on L1 it would also be important to collect longer samples consisting of both oral and written performance, both elicited and spontaneous. In future studies with Russian participants, it would be interesting to examine L2 influence on L1 in participants who emigrated to the US at various socio-historic points, as language and assimilation attitudes of various groups of immigrants may differ and have important implications for L1 maintenance and L2 influence on L1 (Schmid, 2000; for discussion of three Russian emigration waves, see Andrews, 1999). To encourage cross-linguistic inquiry, it is also important to move beyond numerous comparisons of language X and English, and in particular to examine interaction between languages rich in inflectional morphology. It is equally important to examine cross-linguistic influence as a multidirectional phenomenon that may involve simultaneous L1 influence on L2 and L2 influence on L1 (Pavlenko & Jarvis, 2002) and the interaction between three or more languages (Cenoz *et al.*, 2001).

In sum, I argue that the complex phenomenon of L2 influence on L1 is best understood from a multi-competence perspective, advanced by Cook (1991, 1992), which sees multilinguals' linguistic repertoires as a 'unified, complex, coherent, interconnected, interdependent ecosystem, not unlike a tropical forest' (Sridhar, 1994: 803). This dynamic perspective accommodates the framework proposed here, and allows us to examine further which L2-influence processes take place in which language areas, and what prompts particular changes. Most importantly, it allows us to see L2 influence as a potentially positive and enriching phenomenon, beautifully described by the Polish/English writer Eva Hoffman:

> When I speak Polish now, it is infiltrated, permeated, and inflected by the English in my head. Each language modifies the other, crossbreeds with it, fertilises it. Each language makes the other relative.
> (Hoffman, 1989: 273)

## Acknowledgements

An early draft of this chapter was presented at the International Workshop on Effects of the Second Language on the First Language, organised by Vivian Cook at Wivenhoe House, Colchester, UK, in April 2001; I am very thankful to the workshop audience for their comments and suggestions. I am also deeply grateful to Vivian Cook, Istvan Kecskes, Monika Schmid and Masha Shardakova for their insightful and constructive comments on the earlier versions of this chapter. Finally, I would like to acknowledge the fact that many of the ideas discussed in the chapter were born in discussions of the data with two outstanding and generous colleagues, Jean-Marc Dewaele and Scott Jarvis. All errors and inaccuracies remain my own.

## References

Altenberg, E. (1991) Assessing first language vulnerability to attrition. In H. Seliger and R. Vago (eds) *First Language Attrition* (pp. 189–206). Cambridge: Cambridge University Press.

Andrews, D. (1993) American-immigrant Russian: Socio-cultural perspectives on borrowings from English in the language of the third wave. *Language Quarterly* 31 (3–4), 153–176.

Andrews, D. (1999) *Sociocultural Perspectives on Language Change in Diaspora: Soviet Immigrants in the United States*. Amsterdam/Philadelphia: John Benjamins.

Bardovi-Harlig, K. and Bergström, A. (1996) Acquisition of tense and aspect in second language and foreign language learning: Learner narratives in ESL and FFL. *The Canadian Modern Language Review* 52 (2), 308–330.

Becker, A. and Carroll, M. (1997) *The Acquisition of Spatial Relations in a Second Language*. Amsterdam/Philadelphia: John Benjamins.

Berman, R. (1999) Bilingual proficiency/proficient bilingualism: Insights from narrative texts. In G. Extra and L. Verhoeven (eds) *Bilingualism and Migration* (pp. 187–208). Berlin: Mouton De Gruyter.

Boyd, S. (1993) Attrition or expansion? Changes in the lexicon of Finnish and American adult bilinguals in Sweden. In K. Hyltenstam and A. Viberg (eds) *Progression and Regression in Language: Sociocultural, Neuropsychological and Linguistic Perspectives* (pp. 386–411). Cambridge: Cambridge University Press.

Boyd, S. and Andersson, P. (1991) Linguistic change among bilingual speakers of Finnish and American English in Sweden: Background and some tentative findings. *International Journal of the Sociology of Language* 90, 13–35.

Cenoz, J., Hufeisen, B. and Jessner, U. (eds) (2001) *Cross-linguistic Influence in Third Language Acquisition: Psycholinguistic Perspectives*. Clevedon: Multilingual Matters.

Cook, V. (1991) The poverty of the stimulus argument and multi-competence. *Second Language Research* 7, 103–117.

Cook, V. (1992) Evidence for multi-competence. *Language Learning* 42, 557–591.

Cook, V. (1999) Going beyond the native speaker in language teaching. *TESOL Quarterly* 33, 185–209.

De Bot, K. and Clyne, M. (1994) A 16 year longitudinal study of language attrition in Dutch immigrants in Australia. *Journal of Multilingual and Multicultural Development* 15 (1), 17–28.

De Bot, K., Gommans, P. and Rossing, C. (1991) L1 loss in an L2 environment: Dutch immigrants in France. In H. Seliger and R. Vago (eds) *First Language Attrition* (pp. 87–98). Cambridge: Cambridge University Press.

Dewaele, J-M. and Pavlenko, A. (2002) Emotion vocabulary in interlanguage. *Language Learning* 52 (2), 265–329..

Doughty, C. and Long, M. (2000) Eliciting second language speech data. In L. Menn and N. Ratner (eds) *Methods for Studying Language Production* (pp. 149–177). Mahwah, NJ: Lawrence Erlbaum.

Flege, J. (1987) The production of 'new' and 'similar' phones in a foreign language: evidence for the effect of equivalence classification. *Journal of Phonetics* 15, 47–65.

Grosjean, F. (1998) Transfer and language mode. *Bilingualism: Language and Cognition* 1 (3), 175–176.

Håkansson, G. (1995) Syntax and morphology in language attrition: A study of five bilingual expatriate Swedes. *International Journal of Applied Linguistics* 5 (2), 153–171.

Haugen, E. (1953) *The Norwegian Language in America: A Study in Bilingual Behavior*. Philadelphia, PA: University of Pennsylvania Press.

Hoffman, E. (1989) *Lost in Translation: A Life in a New Language*. New York: Penguin Books.

Hyltenstam, K. (1988) Non-native features of near-native speakers. On the ultimate attainment of childhood L2 learners. In R. Harris (ed.) *Cognitive Processing in Bilinguals* (pp. 351–368). Amsterdam: Elsevier Science Publishers.

Jarvis, S. (1998) *Conceptual Transfer in the Interlingual Lexicon*. Bloomington, IN: Indiana University Linguistics Club Publications.

Jaspaert, K. and Kroon, S. (1992) From the typewriter of A.L.: A case study in language loss. In W. Fase, K. Jaspaert, and S. Kroon (eds) *Maintenance and Loss of Minority Languages* (pp. 137–147). Amsterdam/Philadelphia: John Benjamins.

Kellerman, E. and Sharwood Smith, M. (eds) (1986) *Crosslinguistic Influence on Second Language Acquisition*. Oxford: Pergamon Press.

Klein, W. and Perdue, C. (1992) *Utterance Structure. Developing Grammars Again*. Amsterdam/ Philadelphia: John Benjamins.

Latomaa, S. (1998) English in contact with 'the most difficult language in the world': The linguistic situation of Americans living in Finland. *International Journal of the Sociology of Language* 133, 51–71.

Li, D. (2001) L2 lexis in L1: Reluctance to translate out of concern for referential meaning. *Multilingua* 20 (1), 1–26.

Muravyova, L. (1986) *Verbs of Motion in Russian*. Moscow: Russky Yazyk Publishers.

Olshtain, E. and Barzilay, M. (1991) Lexical retrieval difficulties in adult language attrition. In H. Seliger and R. Vago (eds) *First Language Attrition* (pp. 139–150). Cambridge: Cambridge University Press.

Otheguy, R. and Garcia, O. (1988) Diffusion of lexical innovations in the Spanish of Cuban Americans. In J.L Ornstein-Galicia, G.K. Green and D. Bixler-Marquez (eds) *Research Issues and Problems in US Spanish: Latin American and Southwestern Varieties* (pp. 203–242). Brownsville: University of Texas.

Otheguy, R. and Garcia, O. (1993) Convergent conceptualisations as predictors of degree of contact in US Spanish. In A. Roca and J. Lipski (eds) *Spanish in the US: Linguistic Contact and Diversity* (pp. 135–154). Berlin: Mouton de Gruyter.

Pavlenko, A. (1997) *Bilingualism and Cognition*. PhD thesis, Cornell University.

Pavlenko, A. (1999) New approaches to concepts in bilingual memory. *Bilingualism: Language and Cognition* 2 (3), 209–230.

Pavlenko, A. (2000) L2 influence on L1 in late bilingualism. *Issues in Applied Linguistics* 11 (2), 175–205.

Pavlenko, A. (2002a) Emotions and the body in English and Russian. *Pragmatics and Cognition* 10 (1/2), 201–236.

Pavlenko, A. (2002b) Bilingualism and emotions. *Multilingua* 21 (1), 45–78.

Pavlenko, A. and Jarvis, S. (2002) Bidirectional transfer. *Applied Linguistics* 23 (2), 190–214.

Perdue, C. (ed.) (1993) *Adult Language Acquisition: Crosslinguistic Perspectives*. Cambridge: Cambridge University Press.

Py, B. (1986) Competence and attrition in the native language of immigrants. In E. Kellerman and M. Sharwood Smith (eds) *Crosslinguistic Influence in Second Language Acquisition* (pp. 163–172). Oxford: Pergamon Press.

Rintell, E. (1990) That's incredible: Stories of emotion told by second language learners and native speakers. In R. Scarcella, E. Andersen and S. Krashen (eds) *Developing Communicative Competence in a Second Language* (pp. 75–94). Boston, MA: Heinle and Heinle Publishers.

Romaine, S. (1995) *Bilingualism* (2nd edn). Oxford: Basil Blackwell.

Schmid, M. (2000) First language attrition, use, and maintenance: The case of German Jews in Anglophone countries. PhD thesis, Heinrich-Heine-Universität Düsseldorf, Germany.

Schmitt, E. (2000) Overt and covert codeswitching in immigrant children from Russia. *International Journal of Bilingualism* 4 (1), 9–28.

Seliger, H. and Vago, R. (1991) The study of first language attrition: An overview. In H. Seliger and R. Vago (eds) *First Language Attrition* (pp. 3–15). Cambridge: Cambridge University Press.

Slobin, D. (1996) From 'thought and language' to 'thinking for speaking.' In J. Gumperz and S. Levinson (eds) *Rethinking Linguistic Relativity* (pp. 70–96). Cambridge: Cambridge University Press.

Slobin, D. (2000) Verbalised events: A dynamic approach to linguistic relativity and determinism. In S. Niemeier and R. Dirven (eds) *Evidence for Linguistic Relativity* (pp. 107–138). Amsterdam/Philadelphia: John Benjamins.

Sridhar, S. (1994) A reality check for SLA theories. *TESOL Quarterly* 28, 800–805.

Tannen, D. (1980) A comparative analysis of oral narrative strategies: Athenian Greek and American English. In W. Chafe (ed.) *The Pear Stories: Cognitive, Cultural, and Linguistic Aspects of Narrative Production* (pp. 51–87). Norwood, NJ: Ablex.

Tannen, D. (1993) What's in a frame? Surface evidence for underlying expectations. In D. Tannen (ed.) *Framing in Discourse* (pp. 14–56). New York: Oxford University Press.

Vasilenko, E., Yegorova, A. and Lamm, E. (1982) *Russian Verb Aspects*. Moscow: Russian Language Publishers.

Waas, M. (1996) *Language Attrition Downunder: German Speakers in Australia.* Frankfurt: Peter Lang.

Wenzell, V. (1989) Transfer of aspect in the English oral narratives of native Russian speakers. In H. Dechert and M. Raupach (eds) *Transfer in Language Production* (pp. 71–97). Norwood, NJ: Ablex.

Wierzbicka, A. (1992) *Semantics, Culture, and Cognition: Universal Human Concepts in Culture-specific Configurations.* New York/Oxford: Oxford University Press.

Wierzbicka, A. (1999) *Emotions across Languages and Cultures: Diversity and Universals.* Cambridge: Cambridge University Press.

## Chapter 4

# The Intercultural Style Hypothesis: L1 and L2 Interaction in Requesting Behaviour

JASONE CENOZ

## Interlanguage Pragmatics

The study of speech acts from a linguistic perspective, comparing either the linguistic realisation of speech acts in different languages (contrastive pragmatics), or the speech acts produced by native speakers and second language learners (interlanguage pragmatics) has experienced an important development in the last few years (Cohen 1996; Kasper & Dahl, 1991; Kasper & Blum-Kulka, 1993a; Kasper & Schmidt, 1996; Kasper & Rose, 1999; Gass & Neu, 1995). Research in contrastive pragmatics points in the direction of a universal and a language-specific component in the realisation of speech acts. Universal pragmatic knowledge is shared across languages and explains how, for example, the same basic strategies (direct, conventionally indirect and non-conventionally indirect or hints) are used in the realisation of requests in different languages (Blum-Kulka & Olshtain, 1984). At the same time, there are different interactional styles and important cross-linguistic differences in the selection, distribution and realisation of speech acts. According to some studies, German speakers are more direct than British English speakers when making requests (House & Kasper, 1981), and Hebrew speakers are more direct than American English speakers (Blum-Kulka, 1982). For example, German speakers produce a higher percentage of requests such as *Du solltest das Fenster zumachen* ('You should close the window') and English speakers use more indirect utterances such as *Can you close the window?* (House & Kasper, 1981). Nevertheless, the universality vs. culture-specificity issue is still controversial (Fraser, 1985; Wierzbicka, 1991), particularly when non-Western languages and cultures are considered (Kachru, 1994).

Research in *interlanguage pragmatics* has focused on 'the study of non-native speakers' use and acquisition of linguistic action patterns in a second language' (Kasper & Blum-Kulka, 1993b: 3). This approach has followed the general trend in second language acquisition (SLA) by considering deviations from native speaker forms as examples of pragmatic failure. For example, a learner of English may say *Pass me the water, please* when having dinner with an English-speaking family instead of using more appropriate expressions such as *Could you...?* or *Would you mind...?* Pragmatic failure differs from other types of failure in that it is not easily recognisable by interlocutors who may judge the speaker as being impolite or uncooperative or attribute the pragmatic errors to the speaker's personality. Moreover, pragmatic failure is common not only among students with low proficiency in the target language but also among advanced language learners with a good command of grammatical and lexical elements (Bardovi-Harlig & Hartford, 1990). The most common explanation for pragmatic failure is pragmatic negative transfer (Thomas, 1983), defined as 'the influence of L1 pragmatic competence on IL pragmatic knowledge that differs from the L2 target' (Kasper & Blum-Kulka, 1993b: 10). Pragmatic negative transfer can take place at the pragmalinguistic and sociopragmatic levels (Blum-Kulka, 1991; Thomas, 1983). In the case of pragmalinguistic failure, the learner uses linguistic elements that do not correspond to native forms and can produce breakdowns in communication or socially inappropriate utterances. At the sociopragmatic and cultural level, the learner produces an inappropriate utterance because he/she is not aware of the social and cultural rules affecting speech act realisation in a particular language. These rules can involve a different perception of social psychological elements, such as social distance, relative power and status or legitimisation of a specific behaviour.

Most research in interlanguage pragmatics presents two characteristics which are common in other areas of second language development:

(1) The exalted ideal monolingual native speaker is held up as the model of pragmatic competence for second language users and deviations from the native speaker norm are considered examples of pragmatic failure. Grosjean (1989, 1992) and Cook (1992, 1993, 1995) have criticised this 'monolingual prejudice' or 'the monolingual view of bilingualism', and propose a more holistic view. According to Grosjean (1992) the language competence of bilinguals should not be regarded as simply the sum of two monolingual competencies, but rather should be judged in conjunction with the user's total linguistic repertoire. Cook (1992) has proposed the notion of 'multi-competence' to designate a unique form of language competence that is not necessarily comparable with that of monolinguals.

(2)   The direction of influence is from the L1 to the L2; most studies in
      interlanguage pragmatics do not consider a bi-directional relationship
      between the two languages. As Kecskes and Papp (2000) point out,
      there is evidence to prove that the L2 can also exert an important
      influence on different areas of the L1. According to these researchers,
      the Common Underlying Conceptual Base (CUCB) 'is a container of
      mental representations that comprise knowledge and concepts that
      are either language and culture neutral or language and culture
      specific' (Kecskes & Papp, 2000: 41). CUCB develops as the result of
      language acquisition and it can explain the specific characteristics of
      multi-competence and the interaction between the different lang-
      uages at different levels, including the pragmatic level.

The interaction between the L1 and the L2 at the pragmatic level has
been reported by Blum-Kulka (1990) and Blum-Kulka and Sheffer (1993),
who found that requests issued in English (L1) and Hebrew (L2) by
American immigrants to Israel who were fully competent in the two
languages differed significantly from both the Israeli and the American
patterns. These requests presented a level of directness that can be situated
in between American and Israeli requests. Blum-Kulka (1991) proposes the
'Intercultural Style Hypothesis' to define the development of an intercultural pattern that reflects bi-directional interaction between the languages.
Research with immigrant populations in other countries is also compatible
with this hypothesis; Kecskes and Papp (2000) claim that the hypothesis is
supported in foreign language acquisition contexts when exposure to the
foreign language is intensive. As Kasper and Blum-Kulka (1993b) point
out, there is also considerable anecdotal support for this hypothesis, but
more research is needed in the field of interlanguage pragmatics.

The chapter aims to investigate the similarities and differences in the
requesting behaviour presented by Spanish speakers in English and
Spanish in order to test the 'Intercultural Style Hypothesis' (Blum-Kulka,
1991; Kasper & Blum-Kulka, 1993b). Requests are pre-event acts that have
been considered *face-threatening* (Brown & Levinson, 1978) as they impose
the speaker's interests on the hearer. Requests can be regarded as a
constraint on the hearer's freedom of action and, for this reason, requests in
different languages present a rich variety of strategies and modifiers
necessary to mitigate their impositive effect.

The cross-linguistic comparison of requests has focused on the comparison of requests uttered by native and non-native speakers. Non-native
speakers have been reported to use a more restrictive and less complex
requesting repertoire than native speakers (Blum-Kulka, 1982, 1991; House

& Kasper, 1987; Faerch & Kasper, 1989; Niki & Tajika, 1994). When the requesting strategies of native speakers and learners have been compared, learners have been found to be more direct than native speakers in some studies (House & Kasper, 1987; Tanaka, 1988; Koike, 1989; Fukushima, 1990), but not in others (Blum-Kulka 1982, 1991). Learners' requests have been reported to differ from those of native speakers in that learners modify their requests externally by adding more mitigating supportives than do native speakers (Blum-Kulka & Olshtain, 1986; House & Kasper, 1987; Faerch & Kasper, 1989). However, the use of mitigating supportives has also been related to English proficiency (Cenoz & Valencia, 1996).

As the specific aim of this research study is to test the 'Interactional Style Hypothesis', we take into account the fact that similarities in the production of speech acts in the L1 and the L2 can be explained in terms both of uni-directional influence from the L1 to the L2 and of bi-directional interaction between the two languages. Anecdotal evidence seems to support this interaction; it is common for students who receive intense exposure to English to report that people tell them that their formulation of requests has changed (see also Kasper & Blum-Kulka, 1993b: 4). For example, some Spanish advanced learners of English are said to use *por favor* ('please') and the conditional *podría* ('could you?') more often than other Spanish speakers do. The influence of English requesting behaviour on Spanish can also be observed at a wider sociolinguistic level. For example, the expression translated from English *¿Puedo ayudarle?* ('Can I help you?') is used very commonly by shop assistants nowadays and has the same function as the more traditional Spanish questions *¿Qué desea?* ('What do you wish?') or *¿Le atienden?* ('Are you being served?'). Nevertheless, it is necessary to go beyond anecdotal evidence and to analyse requests in different languages in order to confirm the 'Intercultural Style Hypothesis'. The specific research questions of this study are the following:

(1) Do learners of English present differences when formulating requests in the L 1 and L2 or do they develop an intercultural style for the two languages?
(2) Are there differences between the requests formulated in the L1 by speakers who differ in the level of proficiency in a foreign language?

## Method

### Participants

The participants were 69 university students (14.7% male, 85.3% female) with a mean age of 20.68 years. They were all students at the University of the Basque Country, and they were all native speakers of Spanish who had studied Basque as a second language and English as a third language. The subjects were divided into two groups according to their proficiency in English. The 'fluent in English' group was composed of 49 subjects who were specialising in English Studies and the rest of the subjects ($n = 20$) were psychology students with a very low command of English (the 'non-fluent in English' group). All the subjects had studied English as a compulsory subject at school, but members of the 'fluent in English' group received all their instruction in English at the University and were required to pass a test of English equivalent to the Cambridge Proficiency test as part of their English language course requirements. The 'non-fluent in English' group had studied English only at school up to three years before this study was conducted, and had not had further contact with English.

### Instruments and procedure

The data were obtained via a general background questionnaire and a discourse completion test (DCT), based on the Cross-Cultural Speech Act Realisation Project, CCSARP (Blum-Kulka *et al.*, 1989). The 'fluent in English' group ($n = 49$) completed the DCT in both English and Spanish on different days, and the 'non-fluent in English' group ($n = 20$) completed the tests only in Spanish. The DCT used in this research contained the following request situations:

(1)   A teacher asks a student to get a book from the library.
(2)   A student asks a fellow student for handouts given in a previous class.
(3)   You ask a colleague to make a long-distance phone call from his/her apartment.
(4)   A traffic warden asks a driver to move his/her car.

The DCTs were codified according to the CCSARP coding manual (Blum-Kulka *et al.*, 1989). The five elements considered in this paper are the following: alerters, request strategies, syntactic downgraders, lexical downgraders and mitigating supportives.

*Alerters* are used to draw the hearer's attention, and include titles/roles, surnames, first names, nicknames, endearment terms, offensive terms, pronouns, attention getters or combinations of these elements: *John, eh, you*, etc.

*Request strategies* refer to the linguistic elements used to convey the head act of the request. The most common strategies are the conventionally indirect ones that include *want* statements (*I'd like to*), suggestory formula (*How about?*) and preparatories (*Can I, Could I*).

*Syntactic downgraders* mitigate the request by using interrogatives (*Can I?*), the past tense (*I wanted to*), conditional clauses, etc. *Lexical and phrasal downgraders* are also used to mitigate the impositive force of the request and include expressions such as *please, I'm afraid, you know* and *will you*. *Mitigating supportives* include justifications, promises of reward and preparators (*I'd like to ask you...*)

## Results

The first research question concerned the differences between the requests produced in English and in Spanish by the same group of speakers, that is to say the 'fluent in English' group who were tested in both languages. The mean number of alerters, preparatory strategies, syntactic downgraders, lexical downgraders and mitigating supportives in their English and Spanish requests was compared. T-tests (paired samples) were carried out. Then the specific means for each of the requests were compared to see if there were differences related to the situations.

The results of the *t*-tests (paired samples) comparing the mean number of elements produced by the same learners in English and Spanish in the four requests are presented in Table 4.1 (min = 0, max = 4).

**Table 4.1** Requests in English and Spanish by the 'fluent in English' group (*n* = 49)

|  | English | | Spanish | | *t* | *s* |
|---|---|---|---|---|---|---|
|  | Mean | SD | Mean | SD | | |
| alerters | 2.58 | 1.45 | 2.52 | 1.55 | 0.43 | 0.66 |
| preparatory strategy | 3.39 | 0.81 | 3.37 | 0.84 | 0.15 | 0.88 |
| syntactic downgraders | 3.81 | 0.49 | 3.79 | 0.50 | 0.33 | 0.74 |
| lexical downgraders | 1.93 | 0.99 | 1.85 | 0.98 | 0.47 | 0.64 |
| mitigating supportives | 2.50 | 0.96 | 2.33 | 0.95 | 1.21 | 0.23 |

The results indicate that, for the 'fluent in English' group, there are no significant differences between the means for the two languages corresponding to the total number of alerters, preparatory strategies, syntactic downgraders, lexical downgraders and mitigating supportives in English and Spanish.

Tables 4.2–4.6 include the mean number of elements used in the formulation of each of the requests in English and Spanish by the same 'fluent in English' group (min = 0, max = 1). These means correspond to the percentages of subjects using each of the linguistic elements.

**Table 4.2** Mean number of alerters in English and Spanish in each request

| Request | English | | Spanish | | t | s |
|---|---|---|---|---|---|---|
| | Mean | SD | Mean | SD | | |
| (1) teacher/student | 0.67 | 0.47 | 0.67 | 0.47 | 0.00 | 1.00 |
| (2) student/student | 0.71 | 0.46 | 0.65 | 0.48 | 1.00 | 0.32 |
| (3) colleague/colleague | 0.69 | 0.47 | 0.63 | 0.49 | 1.13 | 0.26 |
| (4) warden/driver | 0.51 | 0.46 | 0.59 | 0.50 | -1.10 | 0.29 |

**Table 4.3** Mean number of preparatory strategies in English and Spanish in each request

| Request | English | | Spanish | | t | s |
|---|---|---|---|---|---|---|
| | Mean | SD | Mean | SD | | |
| (1) teacher/student | 0.85 | 0.35 | 92 | 0.28 | -1.35 | 0.18 |
| (2) student/student | 0.85 | 0.35 | 80 | 0.41 | 0.82 | 0.41 |
| (3) colleague/colleague | 0.83 | 0.38 | 81 | 0.39 | 0.37 | 0.71 |
| (4) warden/driver | 0.81 | 0.39 | 84 | 0.37 | 0.37 | 0.71 |

**Table 4.4** Mean number of syntactic downgraders in English and Spanish in each request

| Request | English | | Spanish | | t | s |
|---|---|---|---|---|---|---|
| | Mean | SD | Mean | SD | | |
| (1) teacher/student | 0.93 | 0.24 | 98 | 0.14 | 1.43 | 0.15 |
| (2) student/student | 1.00 | 0.00 | 96 | 0.19 | -1.42 | 0.16 |
| (3) colleague/colleague | 0.95 | 0.20 | 92 | 0.27 | -1.00 | 0.32 |
| (4) warden/driver | 0.87 | 0.33 | 96 | 0.19 | 2.06 | 0.04* |

*significant at the 0.05 level

**Table 4.5** Mean number of lexical downgraders in English and Spanish in each request

| Request | English | | Spanish | | t | s |
|---|---|---|---|---|---|---|
| | Mean | SD | Mean | SD | | |
| (1) teacher/student | 0.53 | 0.50 | 51 | 0.26 | 0.24 | 0.81 |
| (2) student/student | 0.38 | 0.49 | 26 | 0.44 | 1.63 | 0.11 |
| (3) colleague/colleague | 0.22 | 0.42 | 25 | 0.43 | -0.29 | 0.76 |
| (4) warden/driver | 0.77 | 0.42 | 81 | 0.39 | 0.53 | 0.59 |

**Table 4.6** Mean number of mitigating supportives in English and Spanish in each request

| Request | English | | Spanish | | t | s |
|---|---|---|---|---|---|---|
| | Mean | SD | Mean | SD | | |
| (1) teacher/student | 0.34 | 0.48 | 24 | 0.43 | 1.21 | 0.23 |
| (2) student/student | 0.59 | 0.49 | 65 | 0.48 | -0.90 | 0.37 |
| (3) colleague/colleague | 0.81 | 0.39 | 73 | 0.44 | 1.15 | 0.25 |
| (4) warden/driver | 0.77 | 0.42 | 73 | 0.44 | 0.49 | 0.62 |

The results indicate that, in general terms, the differences between requests uttered in the two languages are not significant, the only exception being the use of more syntactic downgraders in the fourth request in Spanish than in English. The first research question is then answered negatively: people with a high level of fluency in the L2 make requests in their L1 and L2 in essentially the same way.

The second research question concerned differences in the L1 according to proficiency in the L2. Several *t*-tests (independent samples) were carried out to analyse the differences between the requests produced in Spanish by the two different groups of learners – the 'fluent in English' and the 'non-fluent in English'.

The results of the general comparison between the requests formulated by the two groups of learners are given in Table 4.7 (min = 0, max = 4).

**Table 4.7** Requests in Spanish by the two groups of fluent and non-fluent

| Request | Fluent in English | | Fluent in Spanish | | *t* | *s* |
|---|---|---|---|---|---|---|
| | *Mean* | *SD* | *Mean* | *SD* | | |
| alerters | 2.52 | 1.55 | 2.95 | 1.39 | -1.06 | 0.29 |
| preparatory strategy | 3.37 | 0.84 | 3.25 | 0.96 | 0.53 | 0.59 |
| syntactic downgraders | 3.76 | 0.50 | 3.45 | 0.88 | 1.72 | 0.09[#] |
| lexical downgraders | 1.85 | 0.98 | 1.70 | 0.86 | 0.60 | 0.54 |
| mitigating supportives | 2.33 | 0.95 | 2.15 | 1.18 | 0.67 | 0.50 |

[#]marginally significant

The results indicate that there are no significant differences between the requests produced by the two groups in terms of the total number of elements, although in the case of syntactic downgraders the differences are marginally significant.

Tables 4.8–4.12 present the results of the *t*-tests (independent samples) corresponding to each of the requests.

**Table 4.8** Mean number of alerters in English and Spanish in each request

| Request | Fluent in English | | Fluent in Spanish | | *t* | *s* |
|---|---|---|---|---|---|---|
| | *Mean* | *SD* | *Mean* | *SD* | | |
| (1) teacher/student | 0.67 | 0.47 | 0.80 | 0.41 | -1.11 | 0.27 |
| (2) student/student | 0.65 | 0.48 | 0.75 | 0.44 | -0.77 | 0.44 |
| (3) colleague/colleague | 0.63 | 0.49 | 0.60 | 0.50 | 0.19 | 0.85 |
| (4) warden/driver | 0.59 | 0.50 | 0.80 | 0.41 | -1.79 | 0.08[#] |

[#]marginally significant

**Table 4.9** Mean number of preparatory strategies in English and Spanish in each request

| Request | Fluent in English | | Fluent in Spanish | | t | s |
|---|---|---|---|---|---|---|
| | Mean | SD | Mean | SD | | |
| (1) teacher/student | 0.92 | 0.28 | 1.00 | 0.00 | -2.06 | 0.04* |
| (2) student/student | 0.80 | 0.41 | 0.70 | 0.47 | 0.84 | 0.39 |
| (3) colleague/colleague | 0.81 | 0.39 | 0.85 | 0.37 | -0.36 | 0.71 |
| (4) warden/driver | 0.84 | 0.37 | 0.70 | 0.47 | 1.16 | 0.25 |

* significant at the 0.05 level

**Table 4.10** Mean number of syntactic downgraders in English and Spanish in each request

| Request | Fluent in English | | Fluent in Spanish | | t | s |
|---|---|---|---|---|---|---|
| | Mean | SD | Mean | SD | | |
| (1) teacher/student | 0.97 | 0.14 | 1.00 | 0.00 | -0.63 | 0.52 |
| (2) student/student | 0.95 | 0.19 | 0.95 | 0.22 | 0.16 | 0.86 |
| (3) colleague/colleague | 0.91 | 0.27 | 0.85 | 0.36 | 0.81 | 0.41 |
| (4) warden/driver | 0.95 | 0.19 | 0.65 | 0.48 | 3.75 | 0.01** |

** significant at the 0.01 level

**Table 4.11** Mean number of lexical downgraders in English and Spanish in each request

| Request | Fluent in English | | Fluent in Spanish | | t | s |
|---|---|---|---|---|---|---|
| | Mean | SD | Mean | SD | | |
| (1) teacher/student | 0.51 | 0.50 | 0.80 | 0.41 | -2.48 | 0.01** |
| (2) student/student | 0.26 | 0.44 | 0.25 | 0.44 | 0.12 | 0.89 |
| (3) colleague/colleague | 0.25 | 0.43 | 0.25 | 0.44 | 0.00 | 1.00 |
| (4) warden/driver | 0.81 | 0.39 | 0.40 | 0.50 | 3.31 | 0.00** |

** Significant at the 0.01 level

**Table 4.12** Mean number of mitigating supportives in English and Spanish in each request

| Request | Fluent in English | | Fluent in Spanish | | t | s |
|---|---|---|---|---|---|---|
| | Mean | SD | Mean | SD | | |
| (1) teacher/student | 0.24 | 0.43 | 0.15 | 0.36 | 0.92 | 0.36 |
| (2) student/student | 0.65 | 0.48 | 0.55 | 0.51 | 0.79 | 0.43 |
| (3) colleague/colleague | 0.72 | 0.44 | 0.65 | 0.48 | 0.64 | 0.52 |
| (4) warden/driver | 0.73 | 0.44 | 0.80 | 0.41 | -0.56 | 0.57 |

The results of the *t*-tests indicate that there are significant differences between the two groups in some of the measures corresponding to requests 1 and 4: preparatory strategies, syntactic downgraders and lexical downgraders. The results of the *t*-tests also indicate that the differences between the two groups are marginally significant for alerters.

## Analysis of the Results

When the direction of the differences in those cases in which the differences are significant (or marginally significant) is analysed, it can be observed that the 'non-fluent in English' group uses more alerters (request 4), more preparatory strategies (request 1), fewer syntactic downgraders (request 1), more lexical downgraders (request 1) and fewer lexical downgraders (request 4).

Though a quantitative analysis is useful in providing a general perspective on the use of different elements in the formulation of requests, qualitative analysis can provide more information on the type of elements produced. The qualitative analysis was carried out with the five elements considered in this study: alerters, request strategies, syntactic downgraders, lexical downgraders and mitigating supportives.

## Alerters

The main difference between the two groups is that students in the 'fluent in English' group tended to use their interlocutors' first name more frequently than did those in the 'non-fluent in English' group. It was also observed that there were no differences between the utterances produced in English and Spanish by the same subjects in the fluent group.

*Examples in English*

(1)  Sandra, I'd like to phone my parents and I know it's a bit expensive. So, I'll phone and give you the money. ('fluent in English' group)

(2)  Hey, Mike, would you lend me your lecture notes? ('fluent in English' group)

*Examples in Spanish*

(3)  Jon, por favor, ¿me podrías traer este libro de la biblioteca? ('fluent in English' group)
('Jon, please, could you bring me this book from the library?')

(4)  Oye, Mikel, ¿podrías pasarme los apuntes de ayer? ('fluent in English' group)
('Listen Mikel, could you lend me the class notes you got yesterday?')

(5)  ¿Me puedes traer un libro de la biblioteca, por favor? ('non-fluent in English' group)
('Can you bring me a book from the library, please?')

(6)  ¿Podría hacer una llamada al extranjero? ('non-fluent in English' group)
('Could I make a phone call abroad?')

**Request strategies**

Though the preparatory strategy is the preferred strategy for both groups, there are some interesting differences when other strategies are used. The 'non-fluent in English' group tends to use more direct strategies than the 'fluent in English' group, particularly in requests 2 and 4 – see examples (11) and (12). No differences were observed when the strategies used in English and Spanish by the same subjects were compared.

*Examples in English*

(7)  Would you please get me this book from the library? ('fluent in English' group)

(8)  Excuse me, could you move your car? ('fluent in English' group)

*Examples in Spanish*

(9)  Ayer no pude venir a clase, ¿podría darme las fotocopias? ('fluent in English' group)
('I couldn't come to class yesterday, could you give me the handouts?')

(10) ¿Le importaría moverse, señora? Está prohibido dejar el coche aparcado aquí ('fluent in English' group)
('Would you mind moving on, madam? Parking is not allowed here.')

(11) Mueva el coche señora, aquí está prohibido aparcar. ('non-fluent in English' group)
('Move your car, madam. Parking is not allowed here.')

(12) Por favor, Ana, déjame los apuntes de ayer, no vine ya que fui al médico y necesito los apuntes. ('non-fluent in English' group)
('Please, Ana, lend me your class notes from yesterday, I didn't come because I went to the doctor and I need the class notes.')

## Syntactic downgraders

The main difference is that, while students in the 'fluent in English' group use a wide range of syntactic downgraders (aspect, tense, conditional clause, interrogatives), the 'non-fluent in English' group tends to use a single type of syntactic downgrader, the interrogative.

*Examples in English*

(13) I wonder if I could make a long distance phone call from here. I'll pay for it as soon as the bill gets here. ('fluent in English' group)

(14) I need a great favour from you. I must make a long distance phone call. Would you mind if I used your telephone? ('fluent in English' group)

*Examples in Spanish*

(15) ¿Le importaría si hago una llamada a larga distancia? Le pagaré el importe. ('fluent in English' group)
('Would you mind if I make a long distance phone call? I'll pay for it.')

(16) Mikel, ¿te importaría ir a la biblioteca y coger el libro de historia? ('fluent in English' group)
('Mikel, would you mind going to the library and getting me the history book?')

(17) ¿Me puede dar una de las fotocopias que repartió ayer? ('non-fluent in English' group)
('Could you give me the handout you gave yesterday?')

(18) Proceda, por favor, a mover el coche. ('non-fluent in English' group)
('Please be so kind as to move the car.')

## Lexical downgraders

The 'fluent in English' group uses a wider range of lexical downgraders (understater, politeness markers), and the 'non-fluent in English' group tends to use a single type of lexical downgrader, namely politeness markers.

*Examples in English*

(19) Sandra, I really need to make a call to Spain if you don't mind. I'll try not to be long. ('fluent in English' group)

(20) Please, madam, would you be able to move your car a little? It is interrupting the entrance. Thank you. ('fluent in English' group)

*Examples in Spanish*

(21) John, ¿te importaría si llamo de tu casa al extranjero? Será poco rato ('fluent in English' group)
('John, would you mind if I phone abroad from your house? It will be for a short time.')

(22) ¿Le importaría mucho mover el coche un poco hacia adelante? ('fluent in English' group)
('Would you mind moving your car a little bit forward?')

(23) Por favor Miren, ¿podrías ir a la biblioteca y traerme este libro? ('non-fluent in English' group)
Please Miren, could you go to the library and bring me this book?')

(24) Por favor, ¿te importaría dejarme llamar por teléfono al extranjero? ('non-fluent in English' group)
('Please, would you mind allowing me to phone abroad?')

## Mitigating supportives

The 'fluent in English' group uses a wider range of mitigating supportives (preparator, reward, grounder) and the 'non-fluent in English' group tends to use a single type of mitigating supportive, grounders.

*Examples in English*

(25) Could I make a long distance phone call, John? I promise you I'll pay it, okay? ('fluent in English' group)

(26) Sandra, I have to make a phone call to Spain and I know it is expensive but could I call? I'll pay you the call. ('fluent in English' group)

*Examples in Spanish*

(27) John, ¿te importa que haga una llamada al extranjero? Es importante.
('fluent in English' group)
('John, do you mind if I make a phone call abroad? It is important.')

(28) Sandra, tengo que llamar a mis padres y se que es bastante caro. Si te parece llamo y luego te doy el dinero que cueste la llamada aproximadamente. ('fluent in English' group)
('Sandra, I have to phone my parents and I know it is quite expensive. If you agree, I'll phone and then I'll give you the money for the approximate cost of the phone call.')

(29) Tengo un problema ¿podría hacer una llamada al extranjero? ('non-fluent in English' group)
('I have a problem, could I make a phone call abroad?')

(30) Ayer no pude venir a clase ¿me podría dar las fotocopias que repartió? ('non-fluent in English' group)
('I couldn't come to class yesterday, could you give me the handouts you used?')

## Discussion

The results presented in this chapter indicate that subjects whose first language is Spanish and who are fluent in English do not exhibit differences when they formulate requests in English and Spanish. They tend to use a similar number of alerters, preparatory strategies, syntactic downgraders, lexical downgraders and mitigating supportives. Furthermore, the qualitative analysis indicates that they also tend to use the same type of elements when formulating requests in English and Spanish. The use of similar pragmalinguistic elements to formulate requests in the two languages could be due to transfer from the first language (Spanish) into English. Pragmatic transfer is well documented in second language acquisition research and it is related to several factors, including proficiency in the target language or length of residence in the target community (see Kasper, 1992; Kasper & Rose, 1999). The existence of pragmatic transfer from the first into the second language does not exclude the possibility of a more complex bi-directional interaction between the two languages. According to the 'Intercultural Style Hypothesis', English could also influence the production of speech acts in Spanish. In this case, the 'fluent in English' group, who are exposed to English in their everyday life because they are specialising in English Studies, could be using similar pragmalinguistic elements in the two languages because there is interaction between the two systems and their influence on each other. This interpretation is supported by the fact that the requests produced in English by Spanish subjects and other non-native speakers of English also differ from requests produced in English by native speakers (Cenoz & Valencia, 1996).

Comparing the requests formulated in the first language (Spanish) by the two groups provides more evidence to support the 'Intercultural Style Hypothesis'. In fact, these results reveal some quantitative and qualitative differences when requests are formulated in Spanish by the 'fluent in English' and the 'non-fluent in English' groups. Speakers who are fluent in English use their interlocutor's first name more often, use more indirect strategies and have a wider range of syntactic downgraders, lexical downgraders and mitigating supportives. These findings support the existence of the 'Intercultural Style Hypothesis' proposed by Blum-Kulka (1991) because they show that learners who present a high level of proficiency in English seem to have developed an intercultural pattern that is reflected both in the similarity between the requests uttered in Spanish and English and in the differences between these requests and those formulated by other native speakers of Spanish.

It is interesting to observe that there are more differences between the two groups of students in requests 1 and 4, which correspond to interlocutors with a different status (teacher–student; traffic warden–driver), than when the interlocutors share the same status. These results could be related to the differences between English and Spanish requests and orders. According to Haverkate (1994) the use of specific linguistic elements can distinguish requests and orders in Spanish, but this distinction is not conveyed linguistically in English because it is based on the social relationship between the interlocutors.

The findings reported in this chapter clearly indicate that there is interaction between the languages spoken by the multilingual speaker, so that not only can we refer to cross-linguistic influence from Spanish into English but we also have to consider a bidirectional relationship between the two languages. This interaction is compatible with the 'Common Underlying Conceptual Base' proposed by Kecskes and Papp (2000) and the dynamic model of multilingualism proposed by Herdina and Jessner (2000, 2001). Moreover, this interaction has important implications for the study of multilingual competence. If the first language is affected by the process of acquiring a second or a third language, bilingual and multilingual speakers certainly present specific characteristics that distinguish them from monolingual speakers. Moreover it cannot be assumed that multilingual competence is the sum of several monolingual competences (see also Cook 1992,

1993, 1995 and Grosjean, 1989, 1992). The fact that multilinguals are exposed to different dimensions of communicative competence in several languages and, in the case of pragmatic competence, to different ways of achieving pragmalinguistic and sociopragmatic competence in the different languages, could enhance the use of simplification strategies. In this way, multilinguals could use the same common underlying conceptual base and develop an intercultural style that explains the similarities of their requests in different languages. Monolinguals do not need to use these simplification strategies and their requests correspond to their experience in a single language. Another explanation that is also compatible with the 'Intercultural Style Hypothesis' could be related to the important influence on Spanish of English reflected mainly in the mass media. Students who are fluent in English will find the pragmalinguistic elements borrowed from English more familiar than will students who are not fluent in English. As a result, they are able to use these elements in their production both in English and in Spanish.

The limitations of this study are that it deals with only a single speech act, and the data have been collected by means of a Discourse Completion Test, which presents some advantages and disadvantages (Hartford & Bardovi-Harlig, 1992; Bardovi-Harlig & Hartford, 1993; Rose & Ono, 1995). DCTs necessarily produce more stereotyped responses but, as Beebe and Cummings (1995) indicate, they are highly effective as a means of 'ascertaining the canonical shape of speech acts in the minds of the speakers' (Beebe & Cummings, 1995: 80). Moreover, they permit comparisons among different groups because the contexts in which speech acts are produced are controlled. The results of this study clearly indicate the existence of interaction between the languages at the pragmatic level, and the need to analyse different aspects of the L2/L3 effect on L1. This analysis will certainly yield useful insights for the definition of the characteristics of multilingual competence.

## References

Bardovi-Harlig, K. and Hartford, B.S. (1990) Congruence in native and nonnative conversations: Status balance in the academic advising session. *Language Learning* 40, 467–501.
Bardovi-Harlig, K. and Hartford, B.S. (1993) Refining the DCT: Comparing open questionnaires and dialogue completion tasks. *Pragmatics and Language Learning* 4, 143–165.
Beebe, L. and Cummings, M.C. (1995) Natural speech act data versus written questionnaire data: How data collection method affects speech act performance. In S. Gass and J. Neu (eds) *Speech Acts Across Cultures*. Berlin: Mouton de Gruyter.

Blum-Kulka, S. (1982) Learning how to say what you mean in a second language: A study of the speech act performance of learners of Hebrew as a second language. *Applied Linguistics* 3, 29–59.

Blum-Kulka, S. (1990) You don't touch lettuce with your fingers: Parental politeness in family discourse. *Journal of Pragmatics* 14, 259–89.

Blum-Kulka, S. (1991) Interlanguage pragmatics: The case of requests. In R. Phillipson, E. Kellerman, L. Selinker, M. Sharwood Smith and M. Swain (eds) *Foreign/Second Language Pedagogy Research* (pp. 255–272). Clevedon: Multilingual Matters.

Blum-Kulka, S., House, J. and Kasper, G. (1989) *Cross-Cultural Pragmatics: Requests and Apologies*. Norwood, NJ: Ablex.

Blum-Kulka, S. and Olshtain, E. (1984) Requests and apologies: A cross-cultural study of speech act realisation patterns. *Applied Linguistics* 5, 196–213.

Blum-Kulka, S. and Olshtain, E. (1986) Too many words: Length of utterance and pragmatic failure. *Studies in Second Language Acquisition* 8, 47–61.

Blum-Kulka, S. and Sheffer, H. (1993) The metapragmatic discourse of American-Israeli families at dinner. In G. Kasper and S. Blum-Kulka (eds) *Interlanguage Pragmatics* (pp. 196–223). Oxford: Oxford University Press.

Brown, P. and Levinson, S.D. (1978) *Politeness*. Cambridge: Cambridge University Press.

Cenoz, J. and Valencia, J.F. (1996) Cross-cultural communication and interlanguage pragmatics: American vs. European requests. *Pragmatics and Language Learning* 7, 41–54.

Cohen, A. (1996) Developing the ability to perform speech acts. *Studies in Second Language Acquisition* 18, 253–267.

Cook, V. (1992) Evidence for multi-competence. *Language Learning* 42, 557–591.

Cook, V. (1993) *Linguistics and Second Language Acquisition*. Basingstoke: Macmillan.

Cook, V. (1995) Multi-competence and the learning of many languages. *Language, Culture and Curriculum* 8, 93–98.

Faerch, C. and Kasper, G. (1989) Internal and external modification in interlanguage request realisation. In S. Blum-Kulka, J. House and G. Kasper (eds) *Cross-Cultural Pragmatics: Requests and Apologies* (pp. 221–47). Norwood, NJ: Ablex.

Fraser, B. (1985) On the universality of speech act strategies. In S. George (ed.) *From the Linguistic to the Social Context* (pp. 43–69). Bologna: CLUEB.

Fukushima, S. (1990) Offers and requests: Performance by Japanese learners of English. *World Englishes* 9, 317–25.

Gass, S. and Neu, J. (1995) *Speech Acts Across Cultures*. Berlin: Mouton de Gruyter.

Grosjean, F. (1989) Neurolinguists, beware! The bilingual is not two monolinguals in one person. *Brain and Language* 36, 3–15.

Grosjean, F. (1992) Another view of bilingualism. In R.J. Harris (ed.) *Cognitive Processing in Bilinguals* (pp. 51–62). Amsterdam: North Holland.

Hartford, B.S. and Bardovi-Harlig, K. (1992) Experimental and observational data in the study of interlanguage pragmatics. *Pragmatics and Language Learning* 3, 33–52.

Haverkate, H. (1994) *La Cortesía Verbal*. Madrid: Gredos.

Herdina, P. and Jessner, U. (2000) The dynamics of third language acquisition. In J. Cenoz and U. Jessner (eds) *English in Europe: The Acquisition of a Third Language* (pp. 84–98). Clevedon: Multilingual Matters.

Herdina, P. and Jessner, U. (2001) *A Dynamic Model of Multilingualism*. Clevedon: Multilingual Matters.

House, J. and Kasper, G. (1981) Politeness markers in English and German. In F. Coulmas (ed.) *Conversational Routine* (pp. 157–85). The Hague: Mouton.

House, J. and Kasper, G. (1987) Interlanguage pragmatics: Requesting in a foreign language. In W. Lörscher and R. Schulze (eds) *Perspectives on Language in Performance* (pp. 1250–88). Tübingen: Narr.

Kachru, Y. (1994) Cross-cultural speech act research and the classroom. *Pragmatics and Language Learning Monograph Series* 5, 39–51.

Kasper, G. (1992) Pragmatic transfer. *Second Language Research* 8, 203–231.

Kasper, G. and Blum-Kulka, S. (eds) (1993a) *Interlanguage Pragmatics*. Oxford: Oxford University Press.

Kasper, G. and Blum-Kulka, S. (1993b) Interlanguage pragmatics: An introduction. In G. Kasper and S. Blum-Kulka (eds) *Interlanguage Pragmatics* (pp. 3–17). Oxford: Oxford University Press.

Kasper, G. and M. Dahl (1991) Research methods in interlanguage pragmatics. *Studies in Second Language Acquisition* 13, 215–47.

Kasper, G. and Rose, K. (1999) Pragmatics and SLA. *Annual Review of Applied Linguistics* 19, 81–104.

Kasper, G. and R. Schmidt (1996) Developmental issues in interlanguage pragmatics. *Studies in Second Language Acquisition* 18, 149–169.

Kecskes, I. and Papp, T. (2000) *Foreign Language and Mother Tongue*. Mahwah, NJ: Erlbaum.

Koike, D.A. (1989) Pragmatic competence and adult L2 acquisition: Speech acts in interlanguage. *Modern Language Journal* 73, 79–89.

Niki, H. and Tajika, H. (1994) Asking for permission vs. making requests. *Pragmatics and Language Learning Monograph Series* 5, 110–24.

Rose, K.R. and Ono, R. (1995) Eliciting speech act data in Japanese: The effect of questionnaire type. *Language Learning* 45, 191–223.

Tanaka, S. (1988) Politeness: Some problems for Japanese speakers of English. *JALT Journal* 9, 81–102.

Thomas, J. (1983) Cross cultural pragmatic failure. *Applied Linguistics* 4, 91–112.

Wierzbicka, A. (1991) *Cross-cultural Pragmatics: The Semantics of Human Interaction*. Berlin: Mouton de Gruyter.

# Chapter 5

## Probing the Effects of the L2 on the L1: A Case Study

SCOTT JARVIS

The study described in this chapter evolved from a conference paper (Jarvis & Pavlenko, 2000) presented at the Second Language Research Forum in 2000 as part of a colloquium on the end state of second language acquisition (SLA). One of the purposes of that paper was to argue that tenable claims about a learner's end state cannot be made until the learner has been shown to have reached a permanent halt in the restructuring of his or her knowledge of both the L2(s) and the L1. To develop this argument, we first examined naturalistic longitudinal L2 spoken data produced by an advanced adult Finnish-speaking learner of English named Aino. On the surface, Aino's data seemed to suggest that her English interlanguage had reached a final steady state that contained several apparently fossilised grammatical and semantic errors, most of which were clear instances of L1 influence (Selinker, 1992; Selinker & Lakshamanan, 1992). We then examined corresponding L1 data that indicated that Aino's L1 knowledge had conversely not remained in a steady state, but rather had begun to take on some of the characteristics of the L2 (Pavlenko, 1997; Pavlenko & Jarvis, 2002; Sharwood Smith, 1989). We interpreted the data as suggesting that Aino (like perhaps most advanced L2 learners) was engaged in a perpetual pursuit of equilibrium in her language competence(s) by restructuring and resolving perceived incompatibilities within and between her L1 and L2. During the period of data collection, Aino's restructuring appeared to be concentrated mainly on her knowledge of the L1. However, we have no reason to assume that the restructuring pendulum would not eventually swing back to the L2 interlanguage, especially after she returned to a more intensive L1 environment, i.e. Finland. Based on the available evidence, we concluded that the end state of second language acquisition, if there is one, is probably best characterised as a dynamic and partially integrated multicompetence of all of the languages that a learner knows, rather than as separate, rigid, steady-state grammars for the L1 and L2(s) (e.g. Cook, 1991, 1992, 1999; Jarvis, 1998; Pavlenko, 1999).

The present chapter probes deeper into the nature of L2 effects in Aino's use of her L1 through an examination of a greater variety of L1 data than were considered in the earlier study. In addition to observed naturalistic data, the present study also examines elicited oral narrative data, meta-lingual judgements and self-report data. The purpose of the present study is to explore the following questions:

(1)   In which areas of L1 use do L2 effects occur?
(2)   Are the same L2 effects detectable in different types of language tasks?
(3)   Are L2 effects really the result of restructured L1 competence, or are they merely a performance-level phenomenon (Nakuma, 1998)?

Such questions cannot, of course, be sufficiently answered by a case study of a single learner. But it is hoped that the detail and depth of analysis in the present study will nevertheless produce some insights into these questions that might otherwise be overlooked in a larger-scale cross-sectional study (Gass & Selinker, 2001: 30–37).

## L2 Effects: L1 Attrition and L1 Maintenance

Most of the past work on L2 effects in the L1 has been approached from the perspective of language loss, or attrition. The lion's share of such studies has looked at language loss as a societal, sociocultural phenomenon, focusing on language shift or language death affecting entire speech communities. Fewer studies have looked at language loss as an individual, psycholinguistic phenomenon, focusing on processes of L1 attrition in individuals (for a discussion of this distinction, see Andersen, 1982; Pavlenko, 2000; Sharwood Smith, 1983). The present study follows the latter approach by looking at L2 effects in an individual's use of her L1. Most of the studies in this tradition have looked at L2 effects in cases where individuals clearly are losing their ability to function in the L1 (Jaspaert & Kroon, 1992; Kaufman & Aronoff, 1991; Kouritzin, 1999; see Pavlenko, 2000 for a review of such studies). By contrast, the present study considers a case where L2 influence seems to have led to an expanded L1 repertoire – i.e. where L1 rules and structures appear to have remained intact, having been augmented rather than replaced by L2 rules, structures and meanings. Cases such as this have been alluded to in the literature, but researchers tend to classify these, too, as instances of attrition because they represent changes in L1 competence that result in deviations from L1 monolingual norms (Sharwood Smith, 1989: 188–189). In the present study, I will follow

Pavlenko (2000; see also her chapter in this volume) and Pavlenko and Jarvis (2001) in distinguishing cases of L2 influence that result in an inability to access, comprehend or produce L1 structures (i.e. L1 attrition) from cases of L2 influence where the person retains a full ability to perform language functions and express desired intentions in the L1 (i.e. L1 maintenance). It is important to point out that investigations of L2 effects in situations of L1 maintenance are severely lacking in the field, though it is encouraging to see the emergence of some recent work on the expanding and enriching effects of the L2 (Kecskes & Papp, 2000; Pavlenko, 1997; and the chapters in this volume).

I now turn to a brief mention of past studies that have investigated L2 English effects on L1 Finnish. As far as I can tell, nearly all such studies fall into one or both of the following categories:

(1)  studies that focus on the role of English in the shift and death of Finnish in Finnish immigrant communities in English-speaking countries (Hirvonen, 1998; Karttunen, 1977);
(2)  studies that investigate intrasentential code-switching and lexical borrowing in the bilingual utterances of first-generation Finnish immigrants in English-speaking countries (Halmari, 1998; Poplack *et al.*, 1989; Watson, 2001).

One of the general findings from these studies is that first-generation Finnish immigrants tend to be highly successful in maintaining their Finnish proficiency. They also tend to be quite proficient in English and often incorporate their knowledge of English into their use of Finnish, especially through code-switching, lexical borrowing and lexicosemantic transfer from English. By the second generation, the L1 and L2 status of Finnish immigrants is unclear given that they often grow up with both languages (Karttunen, 1977). The lexical and semantic influence of English on the Finnish of the second generation is stronger than it is on the first generation, and English influence also becomes quite noticeable in the second generation's Finnish phonology and morphology. Third-generation Finnish immigrants in English-speaking countries, in turn, tend to be essentially monolingual English speakers with only a limited knowledge of Finnish (Hirvonen, 1998). The present study deals with a first-generation Finnish immigrant living in the US who – consistent with past research on first-generation Finnish immigrants – has maintained a high level of Finnish proficiency.

## The Present Study

This investigation nevertheless differs from past studies on first-generation Finnish immigrants in a few important ways. First, Aino – the subject to be examined in the present study – has never lived in a community with a recognisable Finnish immigrant population. This is noteworthy because immigrant communities often develop their own L2-influenced varieties of Finnish that differ from the Finnish spoken in Finland (Karttunen, 1977). Second, the present study is not concerned with L2 influence at the level of the speech community, as many of the related past studies have been, but instead looks at L2 influence as an individual, psycholinguistic phenomenon. Third, the present study will not be concerned with code-switching or lexical borrowing. I acknowledge that these are important phenomena that must be taken into account as part of the complete picture of L2 effects on the L1, but they also provide ambiguous evidence concerning whether L2 effects are to be found in L1 competence or merely in performance (for instance through switching back and forth between languages). In the present study, I will therefore focus on utterances produced by Aino entirely in Finnish and void of English loan words and nonce borrowings (Poplack *et al.*, 1989).

Unlike subjects in several past studies on L2 effects and L1 attrition (Kaufman & Aronoff, 1991; Kouritzin, 1999), Aino grew up a fully proficient monolingual speaker of the L1. She was born and raised in the metropolitan area of Helsinki, the capital of Finland. Both her parents are monolingual Finnish speakers, and all her interactions with friends and family during her formative years were in Finnish. Like most Finns, she began studying English in the third grade (age 8), and continued taking English classes for ten years (i.e. grades 3–12). She also studied Swedish for six years, beginning in the seventh grade (i.e. grades 7–12). Until the age of 15, Aino was essentially a monolingual Finnish speaker, whose knowledge of L2 English and Swedish was limited primarily to what she had learned in her foreign-language classes at school. (Note, though, that Finns are exposed to a great deal of English through television, radio and other media sources.) At the age of 15, however, she went to the United States for one year as an exchange student, during which time she acquired near-native English proficiency vis-à-vis common conversational topics. She returned to Finland at the age of 16, and attempted to maintain her English proficiency by corresponding with American friends through letters, speaking with English speakers living in Finland whenever she could, and attending English-language conversation classes for about an hour a week. In most domains, she continued functioning almost exclusively in Finnish, but was nevertheless able to maintain a high level of English proficiency through her limited but regular use of English.

Aino got married at the age of 23, and that same year she and her husband moved from Finland to the US. Aino is now 34 years old, and has been living in the US with her immediate family for the past 11 years. During that time, approximately half of her communicative language use has been in English with native English-speaking friends, neighbours and other contacts, and roughly the remaining half of her communicative language use has been in Finnish. She has continued to use Finnish on a daily basis with family and friends through face-to-face interactions, e-mail and telephone conversations, and by reading magazines, books and internet sources written in Finnish. Her spoken interactions in Finnish involve her immediate family, two or three native Finnish-speaking friends living temporarily in the same small community in Ohio (for example a Finnish-speaking neighbour with whom she has shared a daily baby-sitting arrangement for the past several months), and Finnish friends with whom she frequently converses over the telephone. Aino also occasionally hosts visitors from Finland, and has herself returned to Finland three times during the past 11 years, in 1991, 1995 and 2000. The duration of each trip ranged from 2 weeks to 7 months (total: 11 months).

Two points about Aino should be emphasised. First, she is a highly advanced, near-native speaker of English who is detectable as a foreigner by many, but not all, of the native English speakers with whom she inter-acts. She displays occasional errors in her use of English articles, preposi-tions, tense/aspect, word choice, idiom and pronunciation (e.g. *dump truck* vs. *tump druck*), but these are sufficiently infrequent and non-distracting that they often go unnoticed by her interlocutors (Jarvis & Pavlenko, 2000). The second point of emphasis is that Aino does not fit the normal profile of an L2 learner who is likely to undergo L1 attrition. Past research documents losses in individuals' ability to function in the L1 primarily only in cases of immigration where the person in question has become emotionally and physically isolated from the L1 speech community, or does not use the L1 regularly with native speakers tied to the homeland (Jaspaert & Kroon, 1992; Kaufman & Aronoff, 1991; Kouritzin, 1999). This is not the case with Aino. Even though Aino technically fits the definition of an immigrant, she does not view herself in this way. She has retained her Finnish citizenship and considers herself to be a typical Finn who is living temporarily (for an unspecified amount of time) in the US. Perhaps more importantly, she communicates regularly and frequently in the L1 with Finns who either live in Finland or have maintained close ties with the homeland. Thus, Aino's physical, emotional, social and other demographic conditions seem more than adequate for her to maintain her L1 (Baker, 1996: 44–45; Kokko, 1998: 164–170) and, as I will attempt to show in the following sections, the L2 effects that do emerge in her use of the L1 probably should not be classified as symptoms of L1 attrition.

This does not, however, mean that her Finnish still sounds fully native-like. Her L1 utterances often include inflectional forms, word usages, and phrasal expressions that other Finns sometimes point out as being *huonoa suomea* ('bad Finnish'), and most of these deviant structures have their origins in L2 English. Despite her use of such structures, Aino's L1 speech is not marked by frequent pauses, hesitations or code-switches, which would be symptomatic of deteriorating or eroding L1 abilities (Jaspaert & Kroon, 1992; Kouritzin, 1999). Instead, she appears to have remained a fluent, fully-functioning native speaker of Finnish whose idiolect sometimes violates the norms of conventional Finnish, but which is nevertheless fully comprehensible to, and conversationally successful with, other native Finnish speakers. Additionally, as I will explain in the following section, Aino's use of deviant structures alternates with her use of corresponding conventional structures, which suggests that through L2 influence she has gained rather than lost linguistic resources pertaining to her knowledge of the L1 (Sharwood Smith, 1983: 226).

In the present study I will examine four of the following five general types of data that are characteristic of language acquisition studies (Ellis, 1994: 670):

(1)  natural use data (i.e. observations of unsolicited language use);
(2)  clinical elicitation data (i.e. elicited but unguided language use, such as film recalls);
(3)  experimental elicitation data (i.e. guided language use, such as cloze tests);
(4)  metalingual judgements (i.e. grammaticality or appropriateness judgement tasks);
(5)  self-report data (i.e. introspection, retrospection, or think-aloud tasks).

Each of these types of data has its own unique strengths and weaknesses. Consequently, some of the most useful studies are those that consider the consistency of language patterns across different types of data, and which give some indication of the source(s) of any variability encountered (Ellis, 1994: 670–676). This is the goal of the present study, which examines data of types 1, 2, 4 and 5, as described in the following section.

## Results and Discussion

### Natural-use data

With Aino's permission, I conducted approximately 50 separate observations of her natural use of spoken Finnish during the period from January 2000 until April 2001. Although the observer's paradox is difficult to avoid (Labov, 1972: 209), in this case I was already part of Aino's social network before I began the study, so my observations of her informal oral interactions in Finnish involved conditions similar to those of prior social events that Aino and I had participated in simultaneously. Although I am not a native speaker of Finnish, I am relatively proficient in the language, so it was not unusual for Aino to speak Finnish in my presence, or even to me personally. Most of the natural-use data come from my observations of Aino's speech directed at native speakers of Finnish, but some of the data also involve utterances directed specifically towards me. In no case did her speech to me exhibit patterns that were not also found in her speech to native Finnish speakers. Most of the natural-use data were collected in the US, but a good deal was also collected during Aino's three-month trip to Finland during the summer of 2000. These latter data were collected by two members of Aino's family living in Finland, who agreed to help with the study.

Aino's natural-use data contain several instances of erroneous or otherwise unconventional uses of Finnish. Because Finnish is not my L1, I asked native speakers of Finnish living in Finland to confirm whether the patterns I identified were indeed unconventional. The monolingual and bilingual Finnish speakers I consulted disagreed somewhat (I will return to this point later), but the monolinguals unanimously identified as unconventional the patterns I discuss below. Leaving aside performance errors such as slips of the tongue or mistakes, I will focus only on the 15 unconventional patterns that occur repeatedly in the data. Examples of these patterns are listed in the left-most column of Table 5.1, along with corresponding conventional forms and English glosses. The second column indicates the country or countries where each pattern was observed, and the final column shows the relative frequency with which each pattern occurred in relevant contexts. The raw frequencies in parentheses indicate the number of times the underlined deviant pattern was observed, divided by the total number of relevant contexts where it could have occurred. For example, the first deviant form *pihassa* ('in the yard', British equivalent 'in the garden') occurred 6 times in the 25 recorded instances of Aino's locational use of *piha* ('yard'); she used the conventional form *pihalla* (literally, 'on the yard') in the remaining 19 instances. (Note: Because of certain inconsistencies in the recording of the data, the frequencies listed in Table 5.1 are approximate estimations, although I am confident that the relative frequencies are reasonably accurate.)

**Table 5.1** Deviant patterns found in Aino's natural-use data

| | Observed pattern | Where observed | Frequency |
|---|---|---|---|
| **Grammar** | | | |
| (1) | *Ne on pihassa<br>(conventional: pihalla)<br>('They are in the yard') | US, Finland | 24% (6/25) |
| (2) | *Mä tarvitsen mennä Lancasteriin<br>(conventional: Mun tarvitsee)<br>('I need to go to Lancaster') | US | 71% (5/7) |
| (3) | *Se on se joka tapaa niitten kanssa<br>(conventional: niitä)<br>('She is the one who meets with them') | US | 50% (3/6) |
| **Lexicosemantics** | | | |
| (4) | *Meinasin pudota<br>(conventional: kaatua)<br>('I almost fell down') | US, Finland | 25% (3/12) |
| (5) | *Mä voisin kattoo Katieä muutaman päivän viikossa<br>(conventional: vahtia)<br>('I could watch/baby-sit Katie a few days a week') | US, Finland | 58% (11/19) |
| (6) | *Se haluu jakaa sen sun kanssa<br>(conventional: antaa sulle vähän siitä)<br>('He wants to share it with you') | US, Finland | 57% (8/14) |
| (7) | *Toivon, että hänelle jää hyvä muisti siitä tapahtumasta<br>(conventional: muisto)<br>('I hope that he'll have a good memory of that occasion | US | 40% (2/5) |
| (8) | *Mihin se on nyt mennyt?<br>(conventional: kadonnut/hävinnyt)<br>('Where has it gone/disappeared to now?') | US, Finland | 79% (15/19) |

| Idiom | | | |
|---|---|---|---|
| (9) | *Toivon, että me pääsemme pian yli flunssistamme<br>(conventional: toivumme)<br>('I hope that we get over the flu soon') | US | 31% (5/16) |
| (10) | *Yks kerta se tuli ja sanoi, että...<br>(conventional: kerran)<br>('One time she came and said that...') | US, Finland | 36% (4/11) |
| (11) | *Mun pitää ottaa suihku<br>(conventional: mennä suihkuun or käydä suihkussa)<br>('I need to take a shower') | US | 22% (2/9) |
| (12) | *Lapset ottavat koulussa paljon kokeita<br>(conventional: Lapsilla on kokeita)<br>('The kids take a lot of tests at school') | US, Finland | 50% (4/8) |
| (13) | *Me voidaan ottaa bussi<br>(conventional: mennä bussilla)<br>('We can take the bus') | US, Finland | 25% (5/20) |
| (14) | *Mihin tämä menee?<br>(conventional: laitan/panen tämän)<br>('Where does this go – i.e. where should I put this?') | US, Finland | 67% (10/15) |
| (15) | *M-U-M-M-I-L-T-A. Mitä se kirjottaa?<br>(conventional: siinä lukee)<br>('M-U-M-M-I-L-T-A. What does that spell?') | US, Finland | 20% (2/10) |

In Table 5.1, I have categorised each of Aino's deviant Finnish patterns into one of three general areas of language knowledge: grammar (functional morphology and subcategorisation frames), lexicosemantics and idiom. It is noteworthy that every one of the 15 deviant patterns across categories reflects influence from L2 English. In the interests of space, I will illustrate this point by describing only the 10 deviant patterns observed in both the US and Finland. To begin, in example (1) *Ne on pihassa ('they are in the yard') the deviant pattern involves the use of the inessive case suffix -ssa (roughly corresponding in meaning to the English preposition in) on the word piha ('yard'). This gives the word pihassa the meaning of 'in the yard', which is a conventional way of referring to yards in English, but is unconventional in Finnish. The conventional form in Finnish would be pihalla (roughly equivalent to 'on the yard'). Next, in example (4), the clause *Meinasin pudota* ('I almost fell'), involves the use of the Finnish verb *pudota* ('fall'), which prototypically carries the meaning of falling through the air from a higher to a lower level. However, Aino was observed using this verb on three occasions to describe instances where she had almost tripped (almost falling from a vertical to a horizontal position) which is conventionally referred to in Finnish with the verb *kaatua* ('fall, fall down, fall over'). Thus, on the three occasions in question Aino appears to have extended the meaning of *pudota* on the model of the English verb *fall*.

Example (5) *Mä voisin kattoo Katieä muutaman päivän viikossa* ('I could watch/babysit Katie a few days a week') involves the use of the verb *katsoa* ('look, watch') to refer to watching children or babysitting. Several monolingual Finnish speakers whom I surveyed about this verb agreed that it is sometimes used in Finnish to refer to watching a child temporarily for a short amount of time, but not on a regular basis, as was meant in example (5). The appropriate verbs in Finnish would have been *vahtia* ('guard, watch') or *hoitaa* ('care for'). Thus, Aino's use of *katsoa* to refer to a regular babysitting arrangement seems to reflect the influence of one of the meanings of the English verb *watch*. Example (6) *Se haluu jakaa sen sun kanssa* ('He wants to share it with you') is similar. The Finnish verb *jakaa* means 'divide', 'distribute' or 'split (evenly)', yet Aino often uses this verb to carry the meaning of the English verb *share*. The actual sentence shown in example (6) was uttered by Aino in Finland when she was telling her son that a friend of theirs wanted to share a chocolate bar with him. The friend heard her say this, and responded by saying that he did not want to *jakaa* the chocolate bar with her son; he only wanted to give him a small piece of it. Next, example *8 *Mihin se on nyt mennyt?* ('Where has it gone/disappeared to now?') involves the use of the verb *mennä* ('go') to refer to getting lost, in the sentence *Mihin se on nyt mennyt?* ('Where has it now gone?'). It is, of course, quite common in English to refer to disappearances with the verb *go* as in *Where did it go?* but, in Finnish, inanimate objects that do not have wheels or motors generally cannot 'go.' Instead, the appropriate verb in Finnish would have been *kadota* ('get lost') or *hävitä* ('disappear').

The remaining examples do not involve the choice of individual suffixes or isolated words, but instead relate to the way that verbal messages are phrased through linguistic frames (Pavlenko & Jarvis, 2002). Example (10) *Yks kerta se tuli ja sanoi, että...* ('One time she came and said that...') involves the use of the phrase *yks kerta* ('one time') where Finns would normally use the single adverb *kerran* ('once'). The choice of *yks kerta* is ostensibly motivated by the English phrase *one time*. The latter appears to be more common than *once* in the American English that Aino has been exposed to, especially in personal narratives beginning with phrases such as *I remember* <u>*one time*</u> *when we...* or more simply <u>*One time*</u> *we.* I should point out, however, that the *yks kerta* structure is becoming more and more common in informal Finnish – especially among Finns who are proficient in English – so it is unclear whether this should really be categorised as a deviant pattern. However, this and the other examples listed in Table 5.1 do clearly diverge from the norms of spoken Finnish used by monolinguals (according to the monolingual Finnish speakers I consulted), and Aino has even been corrected by native Finnish speakers on her use of many of these. This was the case with examples (12) to (15), which I will describe next.

Examples (12) and (13) both involve the use of the verb *ottaa* ('take') in English-influenced ways that are unconventional in Finnish, such as in phrases corresponding to 'take tests' and 'take a bus.' After uttering the sentence listed as (13), for example, Aino was told by a native Finnish speaker that this was inappropriate because it had the implicit meaning of stealing a bus. Finns do not 'take buses' that do not belong to them, but rather 'go somewhere by bus' (*mennä jonnekin bussilla*). Next, example (14) *\*Mihin* <u>*tämä menee?*</u> ('Where does <u>this go?</u>' i.e. 'Where should I put this?') is a question that Aino addressed to her mother concerning where to put a dish that she had just taken out of the dishwasher. She asked *Mihin tämä menee?* ('Where does this go?'), which is essentially how an English speaker would phrase the question. This is not true of Finnish speakers, however. Aino's mother responded by saying that the dish did not have legs and would not go anywhere on its own. She also informed Aino that she should say *Mihin minä laitan tämän?* ('Where should I put this?') or *Mihin tämä laitetaan?* ('Where is this put?') in this context. Finally, the deviant pattern found in (15) *\*M-U-M-M-I-L-T-A. Mitä* <u>*se kirjottaa*</u> ('M-U-M-M-I-L-T-A. What does <u>that spell</u>?') involves the use of the Finnish verb *kirjottaa* ('write') to carry the meaning of the English verb *spell*. The conventional way of expressing this meaning in Finnish is through the verb *lukea* ('read'), in constructions such as *Mitä siinä lukee?* (literally: 'What in it [one] reads?'). Not only is Aino's word choice English-like in this case, but so is the way she phrases the expression; she uses a Wh-word DIRECT OBJECT + SUBJECT + VERB construction (i.e. *Mitä se kirjottaa*; literally: 'What it writes?') instead of the more conventional Wh-word DIRECT OBJECT + LOCATIVE EXPRESSION + VERB construction represented in *Mitä siinä lukee.*

There are three important points that I would like to make about the deviant patterns in Aino's natural-use data. First, in these data, whole systems of grammar do not seem to be affected by the L2. Instead, most of the regularly-occurring deviant patterns that I have identified are word-specific, involving mainly word–concept associations and metaphorical extensions (Lakoff, 1987). This is interesting because word–concept associations and metaphorical extensions are areas of language knowledge that change and develop throughout a language user's lifetime, and this is true for both monolinguals and bi-/multilinguals (Jarvis, 1998: 8). Consequently, Aino's data may suggest that the processes underlying L2 influence in her use of the L1 may not be so very different from the normal changes that take place in all language users' vocabulary knowledge and idiolect throughout their lifetimes. The fact that Aino's deviant patterns tend to be item-specific instead of system-level may also suggest that her L2 effects are limited to areas where a steady-state L1 competence should not be expected in the first place.

A second important point is that Aino's L2-influenced deviant patterns do not seem to have replaced her previously acquired conventional L1-based patterns. One can see in the 'Frequency' column of Table 5.1 that Aino's deviant patterns never occur 100% of the time in relevant contexts. Instead, her use of deviant forms such as *pihassa* ('in the yard') alternate with corresponding conventional forms such as *pihalla* ('on the yard'), and in many cases the deviant forms represent only a minor proportion of the relevant instances. To me, this suggests that L2 influence in Aino's natural-use data is best characterised as the addition of new concepts and linguistic options to her already-existing L1 linguistic and conceptual repertoire, rather than as the loss, deterioration or replacement of existing L1 knowledge.

Finally, it is pertinent to point out that some of the native Finnish speakers whom I consulted concerning Aino's data failed to confirm the unnaturalness of all 15 patterns. I found that older, monolingual speakers of Finnish did consider all 15 patterns to be unacceptable, but younger Finns with high levels of English proficiency (especially those who had had extensive conversational interaction with native English speakers) often considered examples (3), (5), (6), (9), (10) and (11) to be perfectly acceptable. This finding has several important implications concerning language-contact-induced changes that may currently be underway in Finnish, and it also has implications concerning the interpretations that can be made on the basis of the present data. One issue is whether the controversial patterns really do represent deviant uses of Finnish. A related issue concerns whether Aino's so-called deviant patterns really did originate in her own speech, or whether they simply reflect conventions of her social network of Finnish/English bilinguals (note the earlier-mentioned distinction between L2 effects as an individual, psycholinguistic phenomenon vs. a societal, sociocultural phenomenon). It is impossible to answer these questions definitively in the present study, but my observations of Aino's interactions with other members of her social network of Finnish/English bilinguals do suggest that several of her L2-induced deviant patterns are uniquely her own. Even so, in studies of this type it is crucial for the researcher to remain vigilant of the distinction between L2 effects that originate as a psycholinguistic phenomenon in the mind of an individual L1 speaker and L2 effects that are passed on from one L1 speaker to another as a sociolinguistic phenomenon.

## Clinical elicitation data

The clinical elicitation data were collected in April 2001, after I had finished collecting the natural-use data. I used the 15 deviant patterns from the natural-use data as the basis for the clinical elicitation, which involved oral narrative descriptions of several short film segments. The purpose of the film-elicitation task was to determine whether Aino would produce the same deviant patterns as before, this time under more controlled conditions. To do this, I created a number of short film segments that portrayed children playing in a yard, someone tripping, a group of children sharing some sweets, and so forth, all of which were related to the deviant structures just described. There were three structures (items (2), (3) and (7) in Table 5.1 and Table 5.2) that I did not attempt to elicit because of the difficulty of devising film scenes that would elicit the relevant structures, and there was also one additional structure – item (8) – that I was unable to elicit even with a relevant film scene.

To collect the data, I showed Aino the film segments one at a time, and asked her to describe in Finnish each film segment as a story while speaking into a tape recorder. She was unaware of the specific purpose of the task, but her speech was clearly more formal and deliberate during this task than it was during the natural-use observations. The structures that were targeted through this task, as well as the structures that were actually produced by Aino, are shown in Table 5.2.

The most conspicuous result from the film elicitation data is that in this task Aino did not produce a single one of the deviant forms that she had produced in her natural, informal speech. The only two elicited structures that are in any way questionable in the elicited data are items (10) and (12). The elicited structure in (10) *yhden kerran* ('one time') was produced in response to a film segment that showed a boy swinging on a rope in his yard, and then his father came outside and told him to come in the house. The boy motioned with his finger that he wanted to swing just one more time, to which his father replied with a stern look and a finger emphasising just once more. In this case, Aino's use of the word *yhden* ('one' accusative

**Table 5.2** Film elicitation results

| Targeted structure | Elicited structure |
|---|---|
| (1) *pihassa ('in the yard') | pihalla ('on the yard') |
| (2) *Mä tarvitsen mennä ('I need to go') | (elicitation not attempted) |
| (3) *tavata niitten kanssa ('meet with them') | (elicitation not attempted) |
| (4) *pudota ('fall') | kaatua ('fall down') |
| (5) *katsoa ('look at, watch') | vahtia ('watch, baby-sit') |
| (6) *jakaa ('divide, distribute, split') | antaa ('give') |
| (7) *muisti ('memory') | (elicitation not attempted) |
| (8) *Mihin se meni? ('Where did it go?') | (unable to elicit relevant structure) |
| (9) *päästä yli flunssasta ('get over the flu') | olla taas terveenä ('be well again') |
| (10) *yks kerta ('one time') | yhden kerran ('once, one time') |
| (11) *ottaa suihku ('take a shower') | mennä suihkuun ('go to the shower') |
| (12) *ottaa koe ('take a test') | ?tehdä koe ('do a test') |
| (13) *ottaa bussi ('take a bus') | mennä bussilla ('go by bus') |
| (14) *Mihin tämä menee? ('Where does this go?') | Mihin se laittaa sen? (Where should he put it?) |
| (15) *Mitä se kirjottaa? (What does it write?') | Mitä siinä lukee? ('What does it read?') |

case) is probably quite appropriate with *kerran* ('time, once' accusative) because of the scene's high emphasis on the meaning of 'one.' The elicited structure in (12) *tehdä koe* ('do a test'), on the other hand, may be less appropriate. This item was elicited with a film scene that showed a boy finishing a written test. While describing this scene Aino said *Se teki kokeen* ('He did a test'). The use of the verb *teki* ('did') is awkward in this case, and is also ambiguous (i.e. it could mean that he created a test). My understanding, based on interviews with Finns living in Finland, is that the conventional way of expressing the notion of taking a test in Finnish would be to say *suoritti kokeen* ('performed a test') or *kirjotti kokeen* ('wrote a test'). Still, it is interesting that L2 English influence seems to play little or no role in Aino's choice of *teki* or of any other structures that she produced in the film elicitation task. This underscores the idea that her L1 knowledge is still intact, regardless of the L2 influence that she often demonstrates in her more casual language use. Alternatively, it may suggest that her explicit knowledge of Finnish (which she ostensibly relied on more in this task than in her natural conversations) allows her to avoid deviant forms by consciously controlling her L1 production, even though her implicit knowledge of Finnish may have begun to take on some of the characteristics of L2 English. I address this question further in the following section.

## Metalingual judgements

Like the clinical elicitation task, the metalingual judgement task was also based on the 15 deviant structures that I identified in Aino's natural-use data with the help of monolingual speakers of Finnish. The purpose of the metalingual judgement task was to determine whether Aino would recognise her own regularly-occurring deviant patterns as being non-standard in Finnish. To do this, and in order to conceal the specific purpose of the task from Aino, I created sentences that contained each of the targeted 15 structures, and placed them on a written metalingual judgement test along with 20 additional sentences selected from an online Finnish newspaper, *Iltalehti*. (In the interests of space, I have not included the metalingual judgement test in this chapter, but interested readers can obtain it from me personally.) When I gave the test to Aino, I asked her if she would look over the sentences carefully and correct anything that she considered to be incorrect or inappropriate in Finnish. She did so willingly, and seemed to think that I had written all the sentences myself and needed help from a native Finnish speaker in order to make sure that they were correct. She ended up suggesting corrections to 20 of the 35 sentences, including 8 of the 20 sentences taken from the online Finnish newspaper (which were written by native Finnish-speaking journalists for a native Finnish-speaking audience). Her suggestions dealt mainly with word choice and phrasing, but she also offered some suggestions concerning word order, grammatical inflections, pronunciation, and a couple of spelling errors.

**Table 5.3** Metalingual judgement results

| Targeted structure | Judgement | Corrected? |
|---|---|---|
| (1) *pihassa ('in the yard') | Accepted | |
| (2) *hän tarvitsi mennä ('he needed to go') | Rejected | Yes |
| (3) *tapaisi heidän kanssaan ('would meet with them') | Accepted | |
| (4) *putosi suoraan kasvoillensa ('fell flat on her face') | Rejected | Yes |
| (5) *katsomaan...tyttärensä poikaa ('to watch...her grandson') | Accepted | |
| (6) *jakoi...työtovereidensa kanssa ('divided...with his colleagues') | Accepted | |
| (7) *hyvä muisti tilaisuudesta ('a good memory of the event') | Accepted | |
| (8) *ei tiedä mihin se on mennyt ('doesn't know where it has gone') | Accepted | |
| (9) *ei ollut päässyt yli nuhastansa ('hadn't gotten over his cold') | Accepted | |
| (10) *yks kerta ('one time') | Rejected | Yes |
| (11) *otettuansa pitkän suihkun ('after taking a long shower') | Rejected | No |
| (12) *joutuisi ottamaan lisää kokeita ('would have to take more tests') | Rejected | No |
| (13) *päättivät ottaa bussin ('decided to take the bus') | Accepted | |
| (14) *mihin...asiakirja menee ('where...the document goes') | Rejected | Yes |
| (15) *mitä D-A-N-G-E-R kirjottaa ('what D-A-N-G-E-R writes') | Accepted | |

The results of Aino's responses to the sentences with deviant structures are shown in Table 5.3. For purposes of presentational consistency, the targeted structures listed in the left column are shown in the same order as they were in Tables 5.1 and 5.2, even though their numbering on the actual metalingual judgement test was different. The second column of Table 5.3 indicates whether Aino suggested corrections to the targeted structures in question. 'Accepted' means that she did not suggest any corrections to the structure, and 'Rejected' means that she indicated that the structure was wrong. In most cases of rejection, she also offered a more appropriate alternative, as indicated in the final column of Table 5.3.

Contrary to the film elicitation results presented earlier, which suggest that Aino knows what is appropriate and conventional in Finnish, the metalingual judgement results suggest that Aino nevertheless does not always know what is inappropriate and unconventional in Finnish. Table 5.3 shows that Aino accepted 9 out of the 15 deviant structures. Some of the targeted structures listed in Table 5.3 are superficially well-formed, but the full sentences used on the metalingual judgement test create contexts that make them inappropriate in conventional Finnish. For example, the part of item (5) shown in Table 5.3 – *katsomaan ... tyttärensä poikaa* ('to watch her grandson') – is superficially well-formed, but the full sentence on the test was *Kyseessä oli hänen tyttärensä poika, jota hän oli tarjoutunut katsomaan aina tyttärensä ollessa töissä* ('At issue was her grandson, whom she had offered to watch whenever her daughter was at work'). This refers to a long-term babysitting arrangement, making the use of the verb *katsomaan* ('look at, watch') inappropriate. Similarly, the part of item (6) shown in Table 5.3 is superficially well-formed, but the full sentence on the test makes it clear that the person who shared with his colleagues kept most of the winnings for himself, making the use of the verb *jakoi* ('divided, distributed, split [evenly]') inappropriate. With respect to the six deviant structures that Aino rejected, in the cases where she offered a more appropriate alternative, she always offered a structure that is conventional in Finnish. The two cases where she did not offer any alternative at all involve the use of the verb *ottaa* ('take'), and in both cases she marked the structures as wrong by underlining them and drawing a smiling face. In previous conversations, she and I had discussed inappropriate uses of the verb *ottaa*, so she probably assumed that I knew how to correct these myself. On the other hand, in the case of item (12) I have reason to believe that, although she recognises *ottaa kokeita* ('take tests') as unacceptable in Finnish, she might not know an acceptable alternative. Evidence for this comes from the film elicitation data discussed earlier, as well as from the self-report data described below.

## Self-report data

The self-report data was the last set of data I collected from Aino. It involved sitting down with Aino after she had finished the metalingual judgement task and interviewing her concerning her impressions of the 15 targeted structures. Regardless of whether she had indicated any problems with these structures on the metalingual judgement task, I asked her three questions about each targeted structure: (a) whether she thought it was acceptable to Finns living in Finland, (b) whether it sounded okay to her despite what Finns in Finland might think, and (c) whether she would ever use that structure herself. She had, of course, used all of the targeted structures in her own informal speech, but I wanted to determine whether she was aware of this fact. The results of my interview with her are as follows.

Regarding item (1) *pihassa* ('in the yard'), when I asked her about this structure, she said that it sounded fine. But when I asked her to compare it with *pihalla* ('on the yard'), she suddenly realised that *pihassa* is unacceptable in conventional Finnish. She then said that it does not sound good to her when she thinks about it, and said that she would never use it. (I heard her using it again later that same day.) Regarding item (2) *hän tarvitsi mennä* ('he needed to go'), she said that she does not think that this is acceptable in conventional Finnish, and it also does not sound good to her. She said that she would not use it. In contrast, she considered item (3) *tapaisi heidän kanssaan* ('would meet with them') to be perfectly acceptable both to her and to Finns living in Finland.

With respect to item (4) *putosi* ('fell'), Aino said that this verb cannot be used to refer to tripping, and that it also does not sound right to her. She said that she would not use it in that way. Regarding (5) *katsomaan* ('to watch'), Aino said that her understanding is that this verb cannot be used to refer to regular child-care arrangements, but said that it nevertheless sounds fine to her in this context. Item (6) *jakoi* ('divided, split [evenly]'), she said has exactly the same meaning as *shared*, and said that this is true for her and for Finns living in Finland. With respect to item (7) *muisti* ('memory, ability to memorise'), Aino initially said that this noun can be used when referring to mental pictures and impressions (i.e. memories) but, when I asked her to compare it with the word *muisto* ('memory, mental impression'), she changed her mind. Concerning item (8) *mihin se on mennyt* ('where it has gone'), she said that it is perfectly acceptable in Finnish to refer to disappearances with the verb *mennä* ('go').

Aino's self-reported impressions of Items (9) to (15) can be summarised in the following way. First, only one item – (10) *yks kerta* ('one time') – did not sound good to Aino. All the rest she recognised as being unacceptable in conventional Finnish, but said they sounded perfectly natural to her. With respect to item (14) *mihin ... asiakirja menee* ('where ... the document goes'), she said that that is the way that she would say it, and with respect to items (12) and (15), she said that she does not know a better way to express these notions in Finnish. Of course, her performance on the film description task, which was discussed earlier, indicates that she does indeed know a better way of expressing the notion represented in (15), but it is interesting that she was unable to access this knowledge while reflecting on the metalingual judgement task. Finally, when explaining why items (11) to (15) are unacceptable in conventional Finnish, she frequently referred to what her mother and sister had told her on her last trip to Finland concerning the unacceptability of these structures.

One of the most interesting findings from the self-report data is that Aino's implicit and explicit knowledge of Finnish are often at odds. She recognises 12 out of the 15 deviant structures as being unacceptable in conventional Finnish, but in 7 of these cases her own language intuitions tell her that these structures are perfectly sensible.

## Conclusion

To conclude this chapter I will return to the research questions I raised in the introduction. The first question was: in which areas of L1 use do L2 effects occur? As discussed above, the results of the present study have shown L2 effects in certain limited areas of grammar, and more broadly in areas of lexicosemantics and general idiom. Crucially, all the L2-influenced deviant structures produced by Aino seem to be item-specific (i.e. occurring with only a few specific morphemes, words and phrases), and do not appear to affect whole systems of grammar (e.g. tense, aspect, agreement, case marking). The only evidence I have seen in the data that suggests a possible system-level L2 effect is something that was not discussed above. It is the fact that, on the metalingual judgement task, Aino changed the word order of some of the sentences to a canonical SVO order. Finnish has a relatively flexible word order, and the word orders Aino corrected were all produced by native Finnish speakers living in Finland, so Aino's behaviour in this regard may suggest that she has imposed some of the rigidity of English word order on her knowledge of Finnish. Needless to say, this is only speculative at this point, but it seems like a promising avenue for future research. A final comment related to the first research question is that the present results relate to a single-language user, and should not be generalised to all cases of L2 influence unless or until they are confirmed by additional research. At the same time, I believe that Aino represents a very typical Finnish/English bilingual whose L2 effects on her use of the L1 are likely to be typical.

The second research question was whether precisely the same L2 effects would show up in different types of language task. The present results show quite a bit of variability across data types: all 15 of the deviant structures were found in the natural-use data, but none of them were found in the more controlled film elicitation data. Aino's metalingual judgements, in turn, indicate that she does not recognise all of the deviant structures to be unacceptable in Finnish, and her self-report data further indicate that her implicit and explicit knowledge of Finnish are often at odds. What she knows to be unacceptable to Finns living in Finland does not always sound unacceptable to her personally. In some cases, the L2-influenced deviant structures sound more natural to her than do the corresponding conventional Finnish structures. Conversely, some L2-induced patterns show up in Aino's natural-use data and metalingual judgements even when she rejects them as incorrect in her self reports, and claims not to use them. To me, this highlights the importance of looking at multiple sources of data whenever investigating L2 effects, taking into consideration potential L2 effects in both the subject's implicit and explicit knowledge of the language. In the present study, L2 effects are most conspicuous in tasks that are spontaneous and rely relatively exclusively on implicit knowledge, whereas L2 effects are least conspicuous in tasks that are consciously controlled and rely more heavily on explicit knowledge (especially during production).

The third research question was whether L2 effects really are the result of restructured L1 competence, or whether they are merely a performance-level phenomenon. This is the most difficult question to answer because of the difficulty of distinguishing competence from performance (White, 1989: 18). It is probably true that all rule-like language behaviour is competence-driven; any patterns produced by a language user that can be shown to recur in regular and predictable ways are likely to represent that person's competence. If this is true, then all 15 of Aino's regularly-occurring deviant structures that have been the focus of this investigation must be assumed to be reflections of her language competence. The question is whether they reflect her L1 competence per se, or whether, as a performance-level phenomenon, she simply draws from her L2 English competence while using L1 Finnish (Nakuma, 1998). Although the latter possibility may be plausible in some cases, the results of the metalingual judgement task and Aino's self-report data indicate that her implicit knowledge of Finnish really has changed in some areas, influenced by the model of her L2 knowledge. I believe that this is true with respect to all of the items that she reported as sounding fine to her personally.

Finally, I will end by saying a few words about whether the changes in Aino's L1 knowledge represent L1 attrition. I have indicated throughout this paper that Aino does not fit the normal profile of L1 attrition found in the literature: immigrants with prolonged physical and emotional isolation from L1 speakers tied to the homeland (e.g. Jaspaert & Kroon, 1992; Kouritzin, 1999). Aino has maintained strong ties with Finnish speakers living in Finland, and has maintained what appears to be full fluency in Finnish. Although she does regularly produce L2-influenced deviant structures in her use of Finnish, these alternate with corresponding conventional structures (see Tables 5.1 and 5.2). Thus, Aino's L2-induced patterns do not seem to have replaced or led to a deterioration in her L1 knowledge, but instead seem to have been added to her L1 competence as additional options for expression. Thus, I believe that L2 influence in Aino's case is best described in terms of L1 maintenance instead of L1 attrition or loss. At the same time, I acknowledge that many cases of L1 attrition may begin in very similar ways: immigrants begin to incorporate L2-influenced options into their L1 knowledge, and eventually discontinue using the original L1-based alternatives. After this, the original L1-based alternatives may eventually become inaccessible, or lost (Batia Laufer, personal communication, April 24, 2001). For now, though, let me just say that questions concerning the role of L2 effects in both L1 maintenance and L1 attrition, as well as the psycholinguistic and sociocultural mechanisms through which these processes take place, should provide plenty of fodder for investigation well into the future.

## References

Andersen, R. (1982) Determining the linguistic attributes of language attrition. In R.D. Lambert and B.F. Freed (eds) *The Loss of Language Skills* (pp. 83–118). Rowley, MA: Newbury House.

Baker, C. (1996) *Foundations of Bilingual Education and Bilingualism* (2nd edn). Clevedon: Multilingual Matters.

Cook, V. (1991) The poverty of the stimulus argument and multi-competence. *Second Language Research* 7, 103–117.

Cook, V. (1992) Evidence for multi-competence. *Language Learning* 42, 557–591.

Cook, V. (1999) Going beyond the native speaker in language teaching. *TESOL Quarterly* 33, 185–209.

Ellis, R. (1994) *The Study of Second Language Acquisition*. Oxford: Oxford University Press.

Gass, S. and Selinker, L. (2001) *Second Language Acquisition: An Introductory Course*. Mahwah, NJ: Lawrence Erlbaum.

Halmari, H. (1998) Case-assignment and adverbials in Finnish–English bilingual sentences. In J. Niemi, T. Odlin and J. Heikkinen (eds) *Language Contact, Variation, and Change* (pp. 98–110). Joensuu: Faculty of Humanities, University of Joensuu.

Hirvonen, P. (1998) The Finnish–American language shift. In J. Niemi, T. Odlin and J. Heikkinen (eds) *Language Contact, Variation, and Change* (pp. 136–150). Joensuu: Faculty of Humanities, University of Joensuu.

Jarvis, S. (1998) *Conceptual Transfer in the Interlingual Lexicon*. Bloomington, IN: Indiana University Linguistic Club Publications.

Jarvis, S. and Pavlenko, A. (2000) Conceptual restructuring in language learning: Is there an end state? Paper presented at the Second Language Research Forum, Madison, WI, September.

Jaspaert, K. and Kroon, S. (1992) From the typewriter of AL: A case study in language loss. In W. Fase, K. Jaspaert and S. Kroon (eds) *Maintenance and Loss of Minority Languages* (pp. 137–147). Amsterdam/Philadelphia: John Benjamins.

Karttunen, F. (1977) Finnish in America: A case study in monogenerational language change. In B.G. Blount and M. Sanches (eds) *Sociocultural Dimensions of Language Change* (pp. 173–184). New York: Academic Press.

Kaufman, D. and Aronoff, M. (1991) Morphological disintegration and reconstruction in first language attrition. In H.W. Seliger and R.M. Vago (eds) *First Language Attrition* (pp. 175–188). Cambridge: Cambridge University Press.

Kecskes, I. and Papp, T. (2000) *Foreign Language and Mother Tongue*. Mahwah, NJ: Erlbaum.

Kokko, O. (1998) Loss and maintenance of linguistic features in language attrition. In J. Niemi, T. Odlin, and J. Heikkinen (eds) *Language Contact, Variation, and Change* (pp. 151–172). Joensuu: Faculty of Humanities, University of Joensuu.

Kouritzin, S. (1999) *Face[t]s of First Language Loss*. Mahwah, NJ: Lawrence Erlbaum.

Labov, W. (1972) *Sociolinguistic Patterns*. Philadelphia: University of Pennsylvania Press.

Lakoff, G. (1987) *Women, Fire, and Dangerous Things: What Categories Reveal about the Mind*. Chicago: Chicago University Press.

Nakuma, C. (1998) A new theoretical account of 'fossilisation': Implications for L2 attrition research. *International Review of Applied Linguistics* 36, 247–256.

Pavlenko, A. (1997) Bilingualism and cognition. PhD thesis, Cornell University.

Pavlenko, A. (1999) New approaches to concepts in bilingual memory. *Bilingualism: Language and Cognition* 2, 209–230.

Pavlenko, A. (2000) L2 influence on L1 in late bilingualism. *Issues in Applied Linguistics* 11 (2), 175–205.

Pavlenko, A. and Jarvis, S. (2001) Conceptual transfer: New perspectives on the study of cross-linguistic influence. In E. Németh (ed.) *Cognition in Language Use: Selected Papers from the 7th International Pragmatics Conference*, Vol. 1 (pp. 288–301). Antwerp: International Pragmatics Association.

Pavlenko, A. and Jarvis, S. (2002) Bidirectional transfer. *Applied Linguistics* 23, 190–214.

Poplack, S., Wheeler, S. and Westwood, A. (1989) Distinguishing language contact phenomena: Evidence from Finnish–English bilingualism. In K. Hyltenstam and L.K. Obler (eds) *Bilingualism across the Lifespan* (pp. 132-154). Cambridge: Cambridge University Press.

Selinker, L. (1992) *Rediscovering Interlanguage*. Harlow: Longman.

Selinker, L. and Lakshamanan, U. (1992) Language transfer and fossilisation: The multiple effects principle. In S.M. Gass and L. Selinker (eds) *Language Transfer in Language Learning* (rev. edn pp. 197–216). Amsterdam: John Benjamins.

Sharwood Smith, M. (1983) On first language loss in the second language acquirer: Problems of transfer. In S.M. Gass and L. Selinker (eds) *Language Transfer in Language Learning* (pp. 222–231). Rowley, MA: Newbury House.

Sharwood Smith, M. (1989) Crosslinguistic influence in language loss. In K. Hyltenstam and L.K. Obler (eds) *Bilingualism across the Lifespan* (pp. 185–201). Cambridge: Cambridge University Press.

Watson, G. (2001) Evidence of lexical re-borrowing in the spoken English of first generation Finnish-Australians. Paper presented at the 3rd International Symposium on Bilingualism, Bristol, April.

White, L. (1989) *Universal Grammar and Second Language Acquisition*. Amsterdam/Philadelphia: John Benjamins.

## Chapter 6

# English from a Distance: Code-mixing and Blending in the L1 Output of Long-Term Resident Overseas EFL Teachers

GRAEME PORTE

Van Els (1986) presents a perspective for research into language erosion and loss which attempts to relate what is lost to the language environment in which the loss is taking place. Four major attritional situations or categories are thus envisaged:

(1)  *L1 attrition in an L1 environment:* examples of these situations would be the non-pathological loss of language amongst old people, or the loss of a dialect in an environment where that dialect is spoken.

(2)  *L1 attrition in an L2 environment:* for example, when a migrant's mother tongue is lost during prolonged residence abroad or the loss of a dialect outside the environment where that dialect is spoken.

(3)  *L2 attrition in an L1 environment:* a common manifestation of this situation would be the loss of foreign languages that have been learned in a school or higher-education environment.

(4)  *L2 attrition in an L2 environment:* typically, an older migrant's foreign language is gradually lost during residence abroad.

This exploratory study was carried out in the context of potential L1 attrition in an L2 environment, and specifically focuses on a description of L1 output of long-term-resident EFL (English as a Foreign Language) teachers whose L1 loss or deviance may be further aggravated by the demands of their everyday working environment. Those who reside in foreign countries and who actively make use of their mother tongue in their work situations clearly have much to lose as a result of unattended, progressive L1 erosion. The resident EFL teacher is one such example. The interest generated in the teaching of EFL during the eighties and nineties produced a flood of newly-qualified native-speaker teachers, many of whom opted to exercise their profession in countries where demand, reward and/or the promise of prolonged sunshine proved attractive. It is hardly surprising that so many have stayed on long past the termination of their contractual duties, and have now become residents and parents in their adopted countries. In many cases, these erstwhile EFL teachers have since developed their individual careers and currently hold posts of considerable responsibility within the English-teaching profession in these countries. Whatever the direction chosen within the profession by these long-term residents, however, their continued suitability for such employment may no longer depend exclusively on their teaching expertise and paper qualifications, but rather on the acceptability of the authentic native model provided by them in all aspects of language proficiency. The long-term-resident EFL professional can find him or herself in a unique and unenviable position. He or she will be exposed to the inevitable erosion of the L1 consequent upon residence in the foreign country, and this already-alarming prospect may be further aggravated in everyday classroom situations wherein students' efforts at reproducing this target language are being formally evaluated by being matched for correctness or aptness against that of a potentially-deficient native-speaker teacher model.

Since L1 language attrition has been shown to be significantly related to length of residence in the foreign country (Olshtain & Barzilay, 1991; Major, 1992; Vilar Sánchez, 1995), it might be initially useful to try to visualise (and greatly simplify) the process of L1 attrition on a continuum along which various stages of maintenance and loss can be located – from 'intact' knowledge of the L1 at one end of the continuum to complete loss at the other. It follows that there would be various stages along this hypothetical continuum at which one would expect to find greater degrees of loss and/ or progressively more dominance of the L2. In practice, these would correspond to what content and amount of the first language is no longer readily accessed. Along the continuum, however, these stages might also be expected to relate to the amount of control consciously maintained by the speaker over the foreign and native languages. For example, L1 erosion might be encouraged by mixing or switching between languages, and it might later be manifested in occasional and momentary lapses of memory where the native-speaker might have a word or expression 'on the tip of the tongue' and remember it after some kind of internal or external prompting (Vilar Sánchez, 1995). Code-switching itself has a number of manifestations, such as when a person begins an utterance in one language and moves into another in mid-flow. The assumption is that the switch is made to a language that both interlocutors understand. It has also been seen as a rhetorical device or as a means of emphasis among fluent bilinguals (Fallis,

1976) and a fall-back strategy in children to handle momentary lapses in one of the two languages (Turian & Altenberg, 1991).

Prior to this stage, however, there may be other, more controlled, episodes of switching between languages (Kaufmann & Sridhar, 1986). Further along the continuum (and depending on a number of factors including the extent to which the native speaker consciously decides to maintain the L1 and/or the amount and nature of natural interference from the L2 on the L1), situations might be encountered where a lexical item, grammatical form, or feature of style can no longer be accessed in the L1 and where prompting succeeds only in retrieving something which, if not the L2 form itself, is more reminiscent of the L2 than the L1 (Dabhne & Moore, 1995).

While it is unlikely that one particular linguistic activity can be singled out as being a principal cause of L1 attrition, it has been suggested that certain practices in such periods of language flux might expose the already-weakened L1 of the long-term resident native-speaker to the more pernicious effects of erosion (Porte, 1999a). Two specific practices have been identified: code-mixing and code-blending. According to Kaufman and Aronoff (1991), code-mixing occurs when units such as the word, phrase or clause of one language are used together with similar (although not always corresponding) units of another language within one sentence. The phenomenon has been registered at various levels of language and hypothesised as demonstrating solidarity within a particular social group (Porte, 1999a). Code-blending occurs when morphemes from one language are produced alongside those of another language within a single word. The phonological characteristics of the word may combine features of the two languages or only one. In this chapter, I refer to code-mixing and code-blending generically as 'code-manipulation' to draw attention both to the protagonist and the object of his or her actions (i.e. that the interlocutors are working with their languages, and the languages used are themselves finally the object of such manipulation).

Recent work on code-manipulation has tended to focus on one of two traditions. The syntactic focus studies the particular linguistic principles underlying the form of code-manipulation (McSwan, 1999; Meisel, 1994). The pragmatic focus tries to relate linguistic form to communicative function in everyday discourse. In this tradition, talk is seen from the point of view of protagonists who communicate in the context of social groupings and who act and react to context-specific communicative needs (Auer, 1998; Clark, 1996). Code-manipulation then would serve a number of rhetorical functions, akin to stylistic variation in monolingual speech.

The present study is located within this latter area, and was prompted by the results of a previous survey carried out amongst 52 EFL teacher informants selected by invitation from private language schools and university faculties throughout Spain (Porte, 1999a). Results showed a trend towards incipient attrition perceived by the informants themselves: in particular, verbal – and occasionally written – code-manipulation was observed in the presence of family members (noticeably more frequent when addressing younger bilingual offspring) and work colleagues. Many expressed their anxiety that this kind of code manipulation was becoming much more prevalent than they would have wanted it to be, and that their inability to keep the phenomenon in check might be leading to the manifestation of occasional 'errors' in grammatical structure and lexical items. Eight informants even admitted that they would sometimes add Spanish past-tense suffixes to English verbs, or noun suffixes to similar English words. Many EFL professionals had also noted nouns and verbs with an academic bias entering their L1 output in the form of calques. Although the areas and examples of interference identified were almost exclusively perceived in their written work, they attributed the origin of many of these calques to their spoken code-mixing with colleagues or partners. Particular concern was expressed about the perceived effects of L1 erosion on the production and appraisal of L1 writing, wherein most informants were predominantly made conscious of L2 interference. Many confessed to recurrent doubts about the correctness of certain verb + preposition constructions, after a perceived levelling of English verb + preposition to *in* or *of*, following Spanish *en* and *de*. Spelling interference was cited frequently, with informants tending to reduce double consonants to single ones, and over half those surveyed commented on erroneous 'i/e' and 'i/y' substitutions in cognate words. A number of informants were disconcerted by other manifestations of L1 deterioration for which direct L2 influence was not evident and which were commonly assumed to have originated in carelessness or in self-generated extensions of the above tendencies to other words. Finally, teachers who regularly evaluated EFL students' written work repeatedly expressed concern that L1 deviance of this kind might be compounded by recurrent student errors that are no longer sufficiently raised in the teacher's consciousness to be immediately recognised as such. The teachers feared that such errors might actually be passing into their own performance. It was suggested that, rather than seek comprehensive solutions to the problem, further research might usefully focus on the output of a smaller group of similar professionals in an attempt to identify any potential sources or stimuli of L1 erosion (specific to a particular population and its everyday working context) that may require special attention.

The underlying assumption in this study is that certain elements of the L1 may be adversely affected, not only by the inevitable erosive consequences of L1 deprivation brought about as a result of long-term residence abroad, but also by certain features of the local everyday teaching and social context. Data from the previous study suggested that principal among these features or circumstances could be the context, content and frequency of any L1 language activity that the affected individual regularly carried out with colleagues and students from the closed community. Among other factors thought to determine how the local L2 environment impinges negatively on the L1 in such situations, Abdullah (1979) suggested that similarity of speech repertoires, shared personal experiences within a homogenous group, and subject topic could all be crucial. It was also proposed that L1 lexical accessibility may be impaired when a work-based task and/or subject matter that is naturally and/or often handled in the L1, is, nevertheless, also dealt with regularly in the L2 with native or non-native colleagues. In certain repeated scenarios (such as communication with an equally-attrited colleague and/or the lack of informed feedback on the correctness of the communication), a consequence of a momentary or more long-term lack of memory for the correct L1 item may be code-manipulation (Auer, 1998). The lack of corrective feedback means that the deviance can go unattended, potentially reinforcing its acceptability within the closed community. Thus, for example, many informants in the previous survey had commented that, following regular discussion in Spanish of student performance with the students themselves or with Spanish colleagues, they had noted how certain L2 terms referring to test performance, academic abilities and general administrative procedures would be slipped in to similar conversations with L1 native-speaker colleagues (Myers-Scotton, 1993a, 1993b). Indeed, the very nature of the participants in these regular contacts may facilitate this unmonitored code manipulation. Both native and non-native colleagues, if not bilingual, are sufficiently fluent in both languages to permit the acceptance, and perhaps even establish the challenge, of regular reciprocal code manipulation as a demonstration of solidarity and clubbiness amongst the protagonists (Milroy & Wei, 1995). It may be the frequency of these interactions and the consequent reinforcement of deviant forms that contributes considerably to an automatic use of language A's (i.e. L2) original or mixed terminology in language B's (L1) settings. This case study explores the idea that a group of individuals in the above circumstances might consciously or otherwise participate in the creation, sanction, and transmission of code-mixing and code-blending. I was also interested to discover how far such participation involved the toleration of deviance within the group during interaction. My interests centre on evidence of performance deviance and the discussion of possible causes and consequences of this, rather than testing for evidence of deeper, systematic attrition in L1 competence, for which few reliable testing procedures are available (Seliger & Vago, 1991).

## Subjects

Three senior lecturers in English as a Foreign Language at the University of Granada were invited to participate in the study. All three had taken part in the previous study and had previously communicated both their curiosity and anxiety about losing or forgetting certain elements of their L1. They were native speakers and currently long-term residents in Spain (15–24 years residence). The three were fluent speakers and readers of Spanish, and had undertaken only occasional trips to English-speaking countries in the last fifteen years, and these normally coincided with short attendance at conferences. All were well acculturated and integrated into Spanish society: they had Spanish spouses, and extended friendly relationships with Spanish-speaking individuals. All three had children of school age living with them at the time of the study. The teaching regularly undertaken by these subjects consisted of 10 contact hours per week lecturing on aspects of English literature and language, with classes customarily given in English. There was little social contact between them outside the work environment.

## Procedures

The observations below are based on data from three group conversations of 20–30 minutes, each obtained over three-month intervals during the 1999–2000 university year. So as not to arouse undue or atypical concern about L1 output, subjects were not informed about the real objectives of the study. They were told that recordings of native speakers conversing about subjects familiar to students were needed to build up a library of taped activities for the projected departmental multimedia centre. Two ten-minute 'mock' sessions were set up before recording commenced so that the participants would become accustomed both to the presence of tie-microphones and to the somewhat artificial situation of sitting round a table conversing about a set subject. The researcher prepared a prompt sheet for each of the three conversations in which questions were to be used to initiate (rather than guide) debate. The topics chosen were designed to stimulate use of language specifically directed towards familiar topics such as EFL teaching, university administration, student guidance and welfare, local social life, local and national government policies, and comparison between life in Spain and England. Beyond this, the objective was to provide as fluid a framework as possible to enable subjects both to initiate and participate in open conversation with colleagues, and to be as detailed or general as they liked, producing language in a typical interaction without any unnecessary interference from the researcher. In practice, conversation flowed fairly easily as a result of the individual and collective interest in topics of local interest to the participants.

## Analysis

All sessions were tape-recorded and then transcribed by the researcher. To allow for the differing contributions from each subject during the conversations, the total number of words in each conversation was calculated from the transcriptions, and an incidence rate of deviance calculated per 100 words. On the evidence of my own susceptibility to L1 code manipulation as a Spanish resident of more than twenty years, I decided to take no further part in analysis procedures. Transcriptions were analysed for features of deviance by one visiting British lecturer in English Language at a local university and another who lectures in Spanish language and literature and lives and works at a university in England.

## Results and discussion

Evidence of deviance was found mainly in the lexicon, where L2 nouns and nominal groups were typically inserted into an L1 syntactic environment. As suggested from the survey data on the perceived effects of erosion on L1 (writing) output, by far the greatest deviance was to be found in the form of Latinate nouns from the lexical field of education. All three subjects (S1, S2 and S3) indulged in similar code-mixing, some examples of which are illustrated below:

(1) **S1:** Most students wouldn't dream of coming to *tutorías* ('tutorial classes').

(2) **S2:** Years ago, of course, you'd find most lecturers doing *clases magistrales* ('master classes') all the time.

(3) **S3:** I do my three *prácticas* ('practical classes') in the language lab sometimes ... if I see it's worth it

(4) **S3:** I have three or four *actas* ('result sheets') to do in a week in June...
    **S2:** Yeah, when you have to work that quickly you're bound to make a mistake in one *acta* or another.

(5) **S1:** It rather depends on what you get in your *nómina* ('pay check') these days...

Nevertheless, the incidence of occurrence was not as great as I initially expected, given the length of residence of these subjects and the amount of daily exposure to the L2 as part of their working environment. Over the three conversations, the average rate of deviance amongst the subjects amounted to only 2 errors per 100 words, much of which was directed at code-mixing in the above field. There were individual differences observed, however, with S2 recording as many as 6 errors per 100 words in one of the conversations (see below), many of which showed evidence of code-blending. Across all three conversations, there were only nine examples recorded of code-mixing of nominal forms outside this particular lexical field. One explanation might be that these subjects tend mostly to code-mix what they are sure is familiar to their interlocutors. Indeed, this assumed familiarity may also explain the level of tolerance shown towards much of this deviance. In this reading, there would be tacit agreement about what can be code-mixed in the group and how, and the outcome of such code-mixing would not be subject to any critical address on the part of the protagonists. The hypothesis is that much of this code-mixing is done consciously and is constrained by the assumed shared knowledge and experience of the participants (see below).

There were many instances of loans from all three subjects, again mostly directed at the lexical field of education, and all subject to differing degrees of assimilation:

(6)  **S3:**  Most of these kids reach the age for Selectivity [*Selectividad* refers to the Spanish university entrance examination] without being mature enough to go on to university.

**S1:**  Exactly, and when they do the Selectivity exam it's always aimed at a particular degree they rarely end up reading anyway. If the *Selectividad* ever changes, God knows what we'll get in its place.

**S2:**  Mind you, even if you do get a good teacher who knows how to prepare them for Selectivity, there's no telling how the marking's going to be that year.

(7)  **S3:**  The jobs are always associated with oppositions [*oposición* refers to the public examinations to enter the Spanish Civil Service] for these kids ... they are brought up to see them as the ... way into a secure job ... In the first year they're already more worried about *oposiciones* than their course reading.

(8) **S2:** The new law might see them having to go back to try the *reválida* [Spanish *Reválida* is an examination taken at the end of secondary school, not specifically for university entrance].

    **S1:** But even the *reválida* result is going to be little use unless it's high.

(9) **S2:** Well, I mean they'd have to check it first with the Director [Spanish *Director*] of the department but directing is not a managerial thing in the department anyway.

(10) **S3:** You usually find only well, I'd say ... a maximum of ten students who are really able in each year's ... promotion [Spanish *promoción* refers to the final-year graduates]. I think if we had less to start with you'd get a *promoción* at the end that really had a chance of getting jobs.

(11) **S3:** You might have got someone famous in to give talk at a high-level *conferencia* on some subject, but the number of kids who would come to most conferences is always going to be limited, whoever's coming.

Given that most examples referred to highly-specific terms with no true L1 equivalents, it is not surprising that subjects may have resorted to these loans as an expedient communication strategy. Interestingly, however, several of these same terms were then accommodated grammatically in the subsequent conversation and further manipulated by the different protagonists in their own output. Thus, for instance, example (6) produced *the age for Selectivity, do the Selectivity exam,* and *prepare them for Selectivity,* while (8) saw *reválida* being used both nominally and adjectivally – see also example (9). A further feature of many of these loans was that they would often be juxtaposed with the correct L2 term within the same utterance – see examples (6), (7), (10) and (11). In his output, Subject 3 was particularly prone to this kind of alternation, whilst always maintaining the morphological and syntactical environment of the L1 (see Pavlenko, this volume). However, in all the examples, S3 would maintain the standard L2 pronunciation when expressing the true L2 word and assimilate the L2 word to a credible L1 pronunciation when expressing the loan. Thus, in (7) above, *oppositions* was pronounced /ɔpəˈzɪʃənz/ (Spanish /ɔpɔzɪˈθjɔnɪz/) and in (9) 'promotion' was pronounced /prəˈməʊʃn̩/ (Spanish /prɔmɔˈθjɔn/).

Examples of code-blending were few and restricted to the output of only two of the three subjects. These consisted exclusively of insertions into the L1 of L2 verbs which, in each case, were blended with an L1 bound morpheme. The outcome of these creations, however, was such that they came across more akin to deliberate demonstrations of language play than genuine unconscious examples of deviance or code-manipulation:

(12) **S2:**  I was really shocked when I first saw how molested (*molestar* 'to annoy') some teachers got at my criticising the system

(13) **S3:**  The difficult thing is accustoming yourself (*acostumbrarse* 'to get used to') to that kind of tradition.

(14) **S2:**  You'd rarely get invited (*invitar* 'to stand someone a drink') to a drink by your average professor [in England].

(15) **S3:**  Most of the beaches at home are much more contaminated (cf. Spanish: *contaminado* 'polluted') anyway, so there's not much difference there.

Interestingly, in all the cases registered, the L2 verb stem to which the bound morpheme was attached corresponds to an existing L1 form (e.g. *molest, accustom, invite* or *contaminate*). Perhaps there is a conscious desire here on the part of these language specialists to limit creations of this kind to the idiomatically plausible, if not the linguistically acceptable. Moreover, many examples were reminiscent of the kind of deviance mentioned in the original survey data as provoking most doubts when evaluating student output. It is conceivable that such blends find their origin, and perhaps their stimulus, in typical and familiar L1/L2 'false friend' errors produced in the kind of student L1 writing these staff regularly encounter as part of their regular duties. This said, there was little other evidence of the frequency of deviance that many informants in the previous survey feared had infiltrated their L1 output as a result of the defective input received from their students.

In their attempts to plan and execute a single L1 constituent in a single uninterrupted train of speech, speakers may often have to commit themselves to participating in turn-taking before they have the constituent sufficiently planned and accessed. These bilinguals could be presented with several – potentially confounding – levels to attend to, in particular those of L1/L2 word formation and L1/L2 phonetic segment formation. This would typically force them to stop, plan and try again to produce the constituent. For example, there were several occasions in Subject 1's output when (after having apparently decided on the meaning and approximate content word selection that the desired constituent should have) the subject's initial articulatory program seemed first to access the initial phonetic segments of the L2 item in the hierarchy of available units. Unlike typical L1 production errors in word selection, this did not only occur when there was a phonetic similarity between the target words. At this point, S1 would typically attempt to attend to the deviance, with varying degrees of success:

(16) **S1:** Spanish university departments don't work on that basis ... most dire ... directors (*Director* 'department head') ... of their departments ... the *catedráticos* I mean ... don't want to know.

(17) **S1:** That friend we used in the test last year ... in the *secreta* ... *secretaría* ... he knows what's going on.

(18) **S1:** Most of my students haven't got the econo..um..economy (Spanish *economía*) the means ... available. The economical means.

(19) **S1:** You get the biggest queues when students are ... matr...matriculating (Spanish *matricularse* 'register') ... putting in their *matrículas*.

Given the nature of this study, of particular interest here was not only the individual difficulty evinced, but also the immediate repercussion on that speaker's output, and the reactions from the protagonists. On a number of occasions, the consequence of such execution flaws would be an appeal for assistance in accessing the required term, an appeal that was not always successful:

(20) **S2:** Exactly ... that's the point ... so much of what people earn hereabouts is illegal ... in the ec ... um ... submerged isn't ... it's in a kind of submerged economy... In Spanish it's *economía submergida*.

**S1:** Yes, in English it's 'submerged', too.

**S3:** No, it's working in the black market ... no ... hang on ... working moonlighting, yeah.

(21) **S2:** You see, the government spends small ... relatively little on education ... of the ... PIB... (Spanish *Producto Interior Bruto*) what's that in English ... something with 'product'.

**S3:** Total national product.

**S2:** Yeah.

(22) **S1:** If it's a discipline problem, you are likely to see the ... *Rectorado*... [involved]?

**S2:** Rectorate.
**S3:** No, the rector is 'Vice-Chancellor' in English, ...the section [sic] itself is called the 'Registry'.

However, perhaps more worrying than its occurrence alone was the fact that most of the deviant output apparently went largely unmonitored by the protagonists themselves and unchallenged by the other participants in the conversations (cf. Bader & Mahadin, 1996). On the face of it, subjects might have felt such correction out of place in an intimate group, given the setting and the nature of their co-participants. However, the truth is that all three were producing conspicuously deviant output to a lesser or greater extent, and it is to be hoped that these lecturers in EFL were all aware of the erroneous nature of such forms! On the other hand, the level of tolerance shown for such deviance within this closed community might also indicate an acquired endorsement of the *practice* of such code-manipulation rather than tacit agreement on the acceptability of the resultant *form* itself. Other studies have indicated how widespread the practice is, but have suggested that manifestations of this kind may be considered by native speakers in other, non-teaching contexts as ill-mannered, ignorant, or even indicative of lack of imagination (Auer, 1998; Duran, 1994). One wonders, for example, how these same teachers would react to this kind of code-manipulation in the output of their own students' L1 speaking and writing. More insidiously, it may be that this code-manipulation and/or deviance within such a community *is* noticed. However, it is not commented upon because it has long lost its importance as a feature of incorrect L1 use since its collective use within this speech community has given it a kind of acquired recognition. Likewise, it may be that the feature *is* recognisable as non-standard L1 use, but it is not considered worthy of reproach on this occasion by the other interlocutor(s) because the feature's closeness to the easily-accessed or easily-imagined L2 equivalent give it an immediate shared acceptability for the interlocutors. In the long-term, the inherent danger of such tacit acceptance of deviance, as Ryan (1979) noted, is that such attitudinal fluctuations may eventually produce a relaxation of sociolinguistic and linguistic norms in the native-speaker teacher. Whatever apparent internal linguistic consistency and validity it may have for the user's underlying competence, the question remains in the present case as to how far the frequent, and unchallenged, practice of such verbal dexterity – for whatever reason – eventually makes the native-speaker's L1 more vulnerable to erosion.

It is pertinent to recall, at this point, the suggestion made in the light of the data received in the previous, nationwide, study. EFL teachers of writing may also have the effects of this lack of accurate L1 feedback from native-speaker colleagues exacerbated by their being obliged to receive constant 'counter-evidence' in the form of defective L1 production both in oral and more readily 'memorable' written student output. In such circumstances, the effects of unmonitored L1 deviance of this nature and origin can range from temporary uncertainty about correctness to an erosion in language competence and performance which may again profoundly affect error judgements (Porte, 1999b). Clearly, the present evidence does not allow one to suggest that this code-manipulation has its *origin* in such output. But it is plausible that some of the errors observed in the constant linguistic deviance received by these teachers in the course of their everyday duties are finding at least an echo in their own L1 output. Its use may be restricted to this kind of closed community who might share (and be prepared to tolerate) error production and dissemination within that group as a sign of membership of and/or solidarity with, that group. One might, however, hypothesise that lack of strict control on such output might provoke the kind of doubts when evaluating student output that were expressed by many informants in the previous study.

In such a scenario, there is clearly the potential for deviance to become a common feature of more than one individual's performance. Baetens Beardsmore (1982) suggested that, for such modifications in performance to be mutually tolerated in this way, at least two interlocutors must share the same pair of languages and tacitly sanction the use of code-manipulation by virtue of the fact that the situation, subject matter and participants are very familiar. Should only one of the two be a bilingual from this particular speech community, such use of certain code-modified output might on occasions lead to a temporary breakdown in communication – even if the language of the other interlocutor has suffered equal attrition. In other words, while at this stage on the attrition continuum regularity and/or systematisation may not be a marked feature of a specific speech community's eroding L1, one might still witness the setting up of different community-specific 'norms' about which kind of L1 elements are currently 'acceptably' modified.[1]

As might have been expected in an exploratory study such as this, these data provide more questions than answers about the individual practice of code-manipulation. Although all subjects code-mixed to some degree, there were individual differences as regards the way each went about his or her code-manipulation and management of perceived deviance. Subject 1, for example, would typically try to deal with any perceived deviance, whereas S2 and S3 seemed to experience more doubts in their output and were more likely to resort to loanwords. Again, S2 was responsible for nearly all the code-blending observed. One wonders – if code-manipulation of this kind does eventually expose the L1 to greater threats of attrition – whether some individuals are more at risk than others because of the way they go about manipulating their bilingualism in everyday interactions such as these. For example, it is not clear how far the present code-manipulation (at least at this stage on our hypothetical attrition continuum) is caused by momentary lexical inaccessibility due to the incipient effects of attrition, and how far it is down to more meditated responses to the interaction, such as a conscious decision by the speaker about the greater appropriateness of the L2 term. Other research has suggested that such behaviour may even respond to a momentary disinclination on the part of speaker to access the L1 term. Such disinclination might be because the speaker preferred the sound of the L2 term (Auer, 1998) or because it was more readily accessible, by virtue of its comparatively greater incidence in the linguistic input typically received by this speaker (Vilar Sánchez, 1995).

Similarly, some of the more surprising examples of code-blending found in S2's output seemed at times to reflect spontaneous expressions of linguistic invention more akin to language play between knowledgeable friends than to the unseen, incipient effects of L1 attrition. Thus, for example, there were a number of instances when words with distinctively English sounds were attached to typical Spanish endings:

(23) **S2**:  I was speakando with Steve the other day...

(24) **S2**:  Nothing better than going down the coast to sunbathar, eh?

Indeed, recent research in Spain has highlighted the increasing use of this practice among Spanish young people and, specifically, the increasing accommodation of English technological terms to the Spanish verbal system (Delgado Duatis, 1999). In the present case, it may be that such expressions are nothing more than transient phenomena that belong exclusively to the intimate atmosphere of a friendly conversation among similarly bilingual friends, and of little more importance. Indeed, to a certain extent, such verbal display is an inevitable (and desirable) by-product of one's own bilinguality. There may be an innate tendency in all those who communicate in a number of languages relatively frequently (specifically or non-specifically involved with the teaching of languages) to experiment with this capacity (Auer, 1995). It would be logical that such language play may manifest itself to an equal if not greater extent in those that must regularly engage in speaking or writing more than one language as part of their social and working lives. However, as they are obliged to rely on the accuracy and correctness of a potentially-defective L1 model in everyday life, these present native speakers may need to become more aware of the inclinations that precipitate this kind of linguistic act. Ironically, this may mean making more effort to keep their bilinguality in check at times, and perhaps actively trying to keep the two languages apart (Bhatia, 1989). For those teachers practising in their country of origin, the safeguard against any subsequent L1 attrition would be the corrective feedback continually provided by the same L1 context in which they live and work. When such monitoring is not available on a regular and/or satisfactory basis, or is provided with insufficient critical awareness on the part of the interlocutors, the result of such demonstrations of verbal dexterity may be rather more deleterious, perhaps predisposing the L1 to erosion.

## Conclusion

Despite the instances of code-manipulation (particularly code-mixing) in these data, there is no evidence that the L1 of these subjects has suffered significant attrition even after so many years of residence in Spain and the hypothesised negative effects on the L1 of their work and social environment. However, the suggestion has been made that the kind of code-manipulation shown here, and perhaps the implicit attitude towards biliguality that may trigger such production, could be instrumental in eventually predisposing the L1 to such effects by virtue of the diminished control and monitoring apparently being exercised over the L1 output. A further aspect of the hypothesis generated would be that, because of the lack of constant confirming evidence from reliable sources about the continued acceptable state of the individual's L1 in these circumstances, there remains implicit support for L1 erosion and, more insidiously, for it to become normalised within the closed speech community.

If the lack of accurate and critical feedback on the current state of the L1 is thought to be an important factor in predisposing the L1 to attrition, further research might usefully study the extent to which such subjects can themselves be trained to attend more to their own output and criticise their own performance using more formal criteria. Such awareness-raising might also help us to see how critically aware these speakers are of any contamination taking place. Episodes of interference tend to function at the subconscious level, and are intrusive because the speaker is unaware that he or she is producing features that do not align with established monoglot norms. The kind of code-manipulation seen here, however, might operate nearer the surface of consciousness in that it tends to manifest itself more in situations where it is meaningful to the interlocutor(s) (Myers-Scotton, 1993b). Similarly, to judge from the level of tolerance on the part of participants in this study, other protagonists in the closed community of long-term residents would also need to indulge in similar exercises to be continually made aware of such deviance in colleagues' output.

Finally, it would also be important to study whether or not these subjects behave differently in their production and tolerance of deviance when speaking to a native-speaker from outside this closed community. Two subjects from the same closed speech community here may feel at liberty to use such 'tolerated' deviance on the assumption that interpersonal communication may thereby be enhanced or facilitated. With the 'outsider', however, our same subject may feel that this 'authority' is missing and may attempt to maximise alignment on remembered norms by consciously reducing any deviant features to a minimum. If speakers from one such closed community are able to do this, it could be argued that they are at a less critical stage on the attrition continuum, where their L1 output can still be adapted and corrected to suit different circumstances and L1 protagonists by the exercise of greater control over deviant output than might at first seem apparent from some of the data in this study.

## Notes

1. One of the subjects had commented in the previous study how, on a visit to the expat community on the Spanish *Costa del Sol*, he had been initially unable to comprehend what a group of friends were referring to when they spoke of their houses having cost them *twenty to thirty mil* (i.e. twenty to thirty million pesetas) or that *there are ivas on everything in Spain*, in reference to *IVA* (an uncountable noun – 'Value Added Tax').

## References

Abdullah, P. (1979) Some observations on code-switching among Malay–English bilinguals. Paper presented at the 14th Regional Seminar, SEAMEO Regional Language Centre, Singapore, April.

Auer, J. (1995) The pragmatics of code-switching. In L. Milroy and P. Muyskens (eds) *One Speaker, Two Languages: Cross Disciplinary Perspectives on Code-Switching* (pp. 115–135). Cambridge: Cambridge University Press.

Auer, J. (1998) *Code-switching in Conversation: Language, Interaction, and Identity.* London: Routledge.

Bader, Y. and Mahadin, R. (1996) Arabic borrowings and code switches in the speech of English native speakers living in Jordan. *Multilingua* 15, (1) 35–53.

Baetens Beardsmore, H. (1982) *Bilingualism.* Clevedon: Multilingual Matters.

Bhatia, T. (1989) Bilinguals' creativity and syntactic theory: Evidence for emerging grammar. *World Englishes* 8 (3), 265–276.

Clark, H. (1996) *Using Language.* Cambridge: Cambridge University Press.

Dabhne, L. and Moore, D. (1995) Bilingual speech of migrant people. In L. Milroy and P. Muyskens (eds) *One Speaker, Two Languages: Cross Disciplinary Perspectives on Code-Switching.* Cambridge: Cambridge University Press.

Delgado Duatis, D. (1999) *Loan Words in Spanish and Catalan Computer Language.* Barcelona: Universitat Rovira I Virgili.

Duran, L. (1994) Toward a better understanding of code-switching and interlanguage in binguality. *The Journal of Educational Issues of Language Minority Students* 14, 69–88.

Fallis, G. V. (1976) Social interaction and code-switching patterns: A case study of Spanish/English alternation. In G.D. Keller, R. Teschner and S. Viera (eds) *Bilingualism in the Bi-centennial and Beyond* (pp. 53–83). New York: Bilingual Press.

Kaufman, D. and Aronoff, N. (1991) Morphological disintegration and reconstruction in first language attrition. In H. Seliger and M. Vago (eds) *First Language Attrition* (pp.175–188). New York: Cambridge University Press

Kaufman, D. and Sridhar, S. (1986) The process of becoming a bilingual: Simultaneous language loss and language acquisition. Paper presented at LSA/AAAL Annual Conference, New York.

Major, R. (1992) Losing English as a first language. *The Modern Language Journal* 76 (2), 190–208.

McSwan, J. (1999) *A Minimalist Approach to Intrasentential Code-switching*. New York: Garland Press.

Meisel, J. (1994) *Bilingual First Language Acquisition*. Amsterdam: John Benjamins.

Milroy, L. and Wei, Li (1995) A social network approach to code-switching. In L. Milroy and P. Muyskens (eds) *One Speaker, Two Languages: Cross Disciplinary Perspectives on Code-Switching* (pp. 136–157). Cambridge: Cambridge University Press.

Myers-Scotton, C. (1993a) Common and uncommon ground: Social and structural factors in codeswitching. *Language in Society* 22 (4), 475–503.

Myers-Scotton, C. (1993b) *Social Motivations of Code-switching*. Oxford. Clarendon Press.

Olshtain, E. and Barzelay, M. (1991) Lexical retrieval difficulties in adult language attrition. In H. Seliger and M. Vago (eds) *First Language Attrition* (pp. 139–150). New York: Cambridge University Press.

Porte, G.K. (1999a) English as a forgotten language: The perceived effects of language attrition. *English Language Teaching Journal* 53 (1), 28–35.

Porte, G.K. (1999b) Where to draw the red line: Error toleration of native and non-native EFL faculty. *Foreign Language Annals* 32 (4), 426–434.

Ryan, E. (1979) Why do low-prestige language varieties persist. In H. Giles and R. St Clair (eds) *Language and Social Psychology*. Oxford: Blackwell.

Seliger, H. and Vago, M. (1991) The study of first language attrition: An overview. In H. Seliger and M. Vago (eds) *First Language Attrition* (pp. 3–15). New York: Cambridge University Press.

Turian, D. and Altenberg, E. (1991) Compensatory strategies of child first language attrition. In H. Seliger and M. Vago (eds) *First Language Attrition* (pp. 207–226). New York: Cambridge University Press.

Van Els, T. (1986) An overview of European research on language attrition. In B. Weltens, K. de Bot and T. Van Els (eds) *Language Attrition in Progress* (pp. 3–18). Dordrecht: Foris.

Vilar Sánchez, K. (1995) For want of the standard educated variety of Spanish. *International Journal of the Sociology of Language* 116, 5–16.

*Chapter 7*

# Productivity and Lexical Diversity in Native and Non-Native Speech: A Study of Cross-cultural Effects

JEAN-MARC DEWAELE AND ANETA PAVLENKO

## Introduction

We all know highly talkative persons and very silent ones. Recent explorations in linguistics indicate that the degree to which one is talkative or silent is not only a matter of personality, topic or conversational context, but is also shaped by linguistic and cultural conventions (Lehtonen & Sajavaara, 1985; Sajavaara & Lehtonen, 1997). Scandinavians are less talkative than the Anglo speakers in the US. Sajavaara and Lehtonen (1997: 270) point out that in Scandinavian culture 'talkativeness is an indication of slickness, which serves as a signal of unreliability'. The silence of the Finns is disorientating for Americans and confusing for Arabs who are 'liable to think that something is definitely wrong' (Sajavaara & Lehtonen, 1997). Similarly, some people use a richer and more colourful vocabulary than others. The present study will investigate whether language and culture affect productivity and lexical diversity in the speech of monolinguals, and whether the degree of language proficiency and acculturation determines this variable in the speech of second language (L2) users. The study will compare productivity and lexical diversity in narratives elicited with the help of the same stimuli from Russian and American monolinguals, from Russian/English bilinguals speaking Russian, from Russian/English bilinguals speaking English as an L2 and from Russian/English bilinguals speaking English as a foreign language (FL).

## Literature Review

Productivity and lexical diversity have both been the subject of much investigation in psychology, applied linguistics and psycholinguistics. In what follows, we will discuss the definitions of the two constructs, and the key studies that illuminate the factors which may influence productivity and lexical diversity in the speech of monolingual and bilingual individuals.

## Productivity

Different authors use slightly different measures of 'productivity' in their work, depending in particular on whether they deal with the spoken or the written language. In the study of written discourse, Lauren (1987) defines productivity as the average length in words and/or the average number of sentences per essay. Since the focus of our work is on spoken language, we will limit our review to studies that deal with oral production. In the study of spoken discourse, productivity is often seen as a combination of three factors: the total number of lexical tokens produced by the individual, the number of different token types, and the type/token ratio of different word classes, which varies as a function of sample size (Carroll, 1960; Fielding & Fraser, 1978).

Whether measured in words, clauses or utterances, productivity measures are routinely included in oral language production tests (Vorster, 1980). Lennon (1995) chose three measures as indicators of productivity: total number of word tokens, number of T-units, and number of words per T-unit. T-units are commonly defined as 'the shortest possible units which are grammatically allowable to be punctuated as sentences. The T-unit can be described as one main clause plus whatever clauses, phrases and words happen to be attached to or embedded within it' (Larsen-Freeman, 1983: 288). We suggest that the total number of words is the best measure of productivity, as words are easier to define than T-units or utterances (Dewaele, 2000).

Over the years, studies conducted with monolingual and bilingual participants have established that productivity is related to a number of psychological, socio-biographical, and situational variables, some of which impact on productivity in both the L1 and L2. Among psychological variables, shyness, low sociability, introversion and anxiety were shown to influence productivity. Schmidt and Fox (1995) found that shy participants, and participants with low self-ratings on sociability, rated themselves significantly lower on amount of talking during the dyadic interaction and lower on extroversion when compared with the other participants. In some situations anxiety may have a disruptive effect on the interviewee's verbal fluency, leading to increased pauses and decreased speech rate (Markham & Darke, 1991). In other contexts, when the L2 speaker is not dealing with highly novel speech responses that require complex decision making, anxiety arousal tends to increase productivity and to accelerate speech rates (MacIntyre & Gardner, 1994).

Situational variables have also been linked to productivity. One such variable is the opportunity to plan one's contribution to the discourse. Comparing samples of unplanned spoken language (such as dinner table conversations) of two adult speakers of English with samples of their planned spoken language (class lectures and prepared talks), Danielewicz (1984) found that an opportunity to plan one's speech contributes favourably towards productivity and complexity (words, dependent clauses, coordinate clauses, nominalisations, attributive adjectives, and participles per idea unit).

A second situational variable shown to influence productivity, both in the L1 and in the L2, is the interlocutor's behaviour. In Siegman's (1980) study of L1 English, when a male interviewer was interviewing a female interviewee, interviewer warmth seemed to inhibit productivity, measured as the number of words per response. Similarly, Giles and Hewstone (1985) demonstrated that the relationship between the participants affects speech patterns evoked in L1 English. Thus, participants who like each other display more verbal productivity and self-disclosure; they also display less silent pausing than do people less positively predisposed towards each other.

L2 speech has also been shown to be affected by a number of socio-biographical factors, such as the level of proficiency in the L2, which determines productivity up to a certain point. Beginners are generally less productive but, once L2 users reach an intermediate level, their productivity becomes more independent of their proficiency level (Noyau *et al.,* in press). There is uncertainty, however, about the precise point at which the linear relation between proficiency and productivity fades. The studies by Lennon (1995) and De Lorenzo Rossello (2001) conducted with highly advanced learners revealed very different patterns. Lennon's (1995) sample consisted of four German learners of English who had learned English at school for periods ranging from 7 to 14 years and were majoring in English at university. Their scores on the British Council's English Language Battery (ELBA test) ranged from 78 to 92 out of a possible 120. Learners were asked to narrate the same picture story in English before and after a two-month period at Reading University. They were found to produce longer stories after having spent a period in England (see also Raupach, 1987; Towell, 1987). This increase in productivity (ranging from +3% to +50%) was linked to reduction in morphological, syntactical and lexical errors. De Lorenzo Rossello (2001) also used narrations of picture stories, but with a cross-sectional corpus, comparing productivity in the L1 with productivity in the L2. She found that advanced Spanish learners of

French and advanced French learners of Spanish produced longer stories in their L2 than in their L1.

The effect of cultural familiarity on productivity was demonstrated in van Hell *et al.* (in press) who found that children from Turkish and Moroccan origin living in the Netherlands produced longer stories about Ramadan than did monolingual and monocultural Dutch children, who in their turn produced longer stories about Carnival. No differences emerged between the groups in culturally 'neutral' stories (about the playground). The authors conclude that when speaking about a culturally familiar topic children 'can retrieve a richer constellation of concepts from memory (in terms of number and of covariances among concepts), which not only results in longer stories, but also enhances connectivity in discourse' (van Hell *et al.*, in press: 17). Low familiarity with the cultural context does not always affect the level of temporal resolution, however. The speaker can construct a global representation of the macro-event, containing a simple but complete succession of observed actions, without referring to background information, causes or intentions. The reverse is also true, as someone familiar with a culture-specific event may not feel the need to describe it in detail.

In sum, we can see that in both the L1 and the L2 productivity can be affected by psychological factors such as shyness, sociability, introversion and anxiety, and by situational factors such as the opportunity to plan one's contribution, and the behaviour of the interlocutor. In addition, in L2 speech, productivity may be influenced by socio-biographical factors such as the level of L2 proficiency and cultural familiarity with the topic.

## Lexical diversity

Lexical diversity, often linked to productivity, has also been studied under many guises and many forms. As with productivity, definitions of lexical diversity also differ in various studies. Most often, however, lexical diversity is measured through a type-token ratio (TTR), which compares the number of different words (types) with the number of total words (tokens). In both oral speech and writing, lexical diversity has been found to vary according to L1 background, L1–L2 proximity, age, L2 proficiency (Laufer, 1994; Laufer & Paribakht, 1998), FL or L2 learning context (Meara *et al.*, 1997), and also to the interaction of multiple cognitive, stylistic, situational and textual constraints (Dewaele, 1993). Many scholars emphasise the impact of lexical diversity in L1 on listeners' judgements about the speaker's personality and intellectual capacities (Bradac *et al.*, 1976; Bradac, 1982). Bradac and Wisegarver (1984) found that limited lexical diversity in native English speech extracts caused negative evaluations of the speaker's communicative competence and led the listeners to misjudge the speaker's socio-economic class. The researchers also observed that listeners quickly noticed above-average levels of lexical redundancy (i.e. low lexical diversity) in the speech extracts.

Recently, the phenomenon of lexical diversity has also attracted the attention of second language acquisition (SLA) researchers. One group of researchers based in the University of Paris X-Nanterre and led by Colette Noyau, has approached the phenomenon of lexical diversity and productivity in L1 and L2 from a perspective developed by Langacker (1987). Noyau and Paprocka (2000) analysed retellings of film extracts in Polish and French by six Polish learners of French. The authors focused on the organisation and the structure of micro-events that reflected the learners' perception, conceptualisation and formulation of the macro-event. In their analysis, they investigated two dimensions of lexical diversity which they termed the amount of granularity and the condensation of the information. Granularity, which can be temporal or lexical, is of particular interest for the present study. Temporal granularity is defined by Noyau *et al.* (in press) as a 'qualitative dimension which characterises the ways in which, in texts, a complex dynamic situation will be conceptualised'. A high degree of granularity entails the presentation of a detailed series of micro-events, while a low degree (reduced partitioning) presents the event from a macro perspective, where the different components are fused as either one single event, or a limited number of events. The authors explain that the linguistic means for choosing a specific degree of granularity are the lexical items for situations (states, activities, events, actions). Lexical granularity is reflected in productivity and lexical diversity values, as higher levels of resolution will result in longer and more fine-grained retellings with more specific (and low-frequency) words. From this perspective, the dynamic situation viewed in the extract (macro-event) can be reproduced in a sequence containing a variable number of micro-events. For example, a scene depicting a person entering a house can be described minimally as 'X entered', or maximally as 'X turned the doorknob, pushed against the door, stepped inside, closed the door behind him/her'. Similar resolution levels can be chosen lexically. A speaker may opt for specific words that provide extra detail rather than using high frequency words with a more generic meaning. Compare 'he looked at the trees' with 'X contemplated the eucalyptus and the pine trees in the garden'.[1]

Noyau and Paprocka (2000) note, as did researchers before them (Rosch, 1978), that both conceptual and linguistic factors may affect the resolution level. A gardener is more likely to give more detailed information because his/her expertise allows him to distinguish different types of trees.

Similarly, familiarity with the domain, which can be culturally determined, will affect resolution level, albeit not necessarily in a linear fashion. Of particular importance is the level of L2 proficiency. Comparing the retellings of Chaplin's *Modern Times* extracts in Polish L1 and French L2, Noyau and Paprocka (2000) discovered higher levels of lexical resolution in the L1 extracts, including a wide range of verbs of movement specifying manner and orientation of the movement. This finding confirms earlier research which found lower levels of lexical detail in L2 extracts compared with L1 extracts (Sanz, 1999; Schneider, 1999). Noyau *et al.* (in press: 2) suggest that 'the degree of granularity increases with the development of lexical items for expressing events in the L2, becoming in the more advanced stages a free variable giving the speaker greater leeway when faced with the situational constraints imposed by the particular communicative task'. The granularity curve levels out at more advanced stages because the speaker is better able to make use of condensation in order to produce more coherent texts.

There seems to be little doubt that beginners use a greater proportion of high- rather than low-frequency words (Laufer, 1991; Linnarud, 1986). A limited lexicon forces less proficient speakers to categorise processes in basic terms (*to do, to go*) and prevents them from offering great lexical detail in descriptions (Noyau & Paprocka, 2000). Advanced learners move more freely on the granularity continuum, and their choices will be determined by sociocultural background, task, interaction constraints and desired stylistic effects. This advanced group displays high levels of both inter-individual variation (Noyau & Paprocka, 2000) and intra-individual variation: less advanced speakers tend to stick to a certain degree of granularity and condensation from the beginning to the end of the extract (De Lorenzo Rossello, 1999).

Degree of granularity may also be affected by typological differences. Noyau *et al.* (in press) argue that Swedish is a more fine-grained language compared with French, where the structuring of narratives relies more on the ordering of events. A comparison of film-retellings in Swedish and French (Kihlstedt, 1998) revealed that the Swedish corpus contained twice as many connectors as the French corpus, despite being roughly equivalent in size. A similar comparison showed that Spanish learners of French used a lower degree of granularity than did a control group of native speakers of French, breaking their account down in fewer episodes, fewer utterances and fewer clauses. Noyau *et al.* (in press) argue that this difference is due to the Spanish speakers' focus on aspectual distinctions (perfective/imperfective) in the event structure of oral accounts, while French native speakers would prefer segmentation into sequences along the time axis (see also De Lorenzo Rossello, 2001). This transfer of granularity values was also found in the reverse direction, with French learners of Spanish using significantly higher degrees of granularity than did a control group of Spanish native speakers. Degree of granularity appears to be language-specific, and the language learner's aim must be 'to acquire the degree of granularity specific to the target language' (Noyau *et al.*, in press: 21). This culture-specific granularity will obviously always be context-specific and will vary from individual to individual. Given the dynamic nature of multi-linguals' linguistic systems (Herdina & Jessner, 2002; Cook, 1992), we may also expect changes in the degree of granularity of their output.

Psycholinguistic studies have shown that the choice of degree of granularity or lexical richness entails a clear cognitive cost. Scherer (1979), Roelofs (2002) and Roodenrys *et al.* (1994) found that processing longer words requires more effort both in terms of the demands made on cognitive processing (including naming latencies), and on the precision of articulation in speaking. Chincotta and Underwood (1998) found that within-language memory span was greater for short items than for long items, which the authors interpret as an indication that bilingual short-term memory capacity is sensitive to the effects of word length in both the dominant and the non-dominant language. This suggests there is a trade-off between fluency and lexical diversity. Dewaele (1993) found significant negative correlations between lexical richness scores and measures of fluency in the formal situation. He argued that when more cognitive resources are diverted to lexical searching, the speech production slows down, and filled pauses become more frequent. Dewaele and Furnham (2000) showed that introverts and extroverts make different choices in the trade-off between fluency and lexical diversity, but only in situations of stress. While no link was found between lexical diversity (measured with 'Uber') and extroversion in the informal situation, a significant negative relationship appeared in the formal situation. This suggested that when talking under pressure introverts use a much richer vocabulary (with longer low-frequency words), whereas extroverts opt for shorter high-frequency words and spend less time and energy on this task in the speech production process.

In sum, we can see why lexical diversity and, to a lesser degree, productivity have been considered to be extremely complex variables. The numerous lexical indices that have been proposed over the years testify to the difficulty, but also to the desire to capture this elusive variable. Because both productivity and lexical diversity have complicated relationships with different sociobiographical, linguistic, cultural, psychological, and situational variables, they present an irresistible challenge for researchers.

# The Research

## Design and methodology

Our corpus of film retellings in English and Russian produced by monolinguals and two types of bilingual was used to investigate cross-linguistic and cross-cultural effects (as well as possible gender effects) on productivity and lexical diversity.

The presence of monolingual controls, two populations of bilingual speakers, and equal proportions of male and female participants allow us to tackle questions that were previously unanswered.

Three-way univariate analyses of variance (ANOVAs) were used to test for statistical significance between means and for possible interaction effects. These analyses also yielded eta-squared values, which give a measure of effect sizes. Type of material was included as an independent variable in the design (see section on procedure) in order to verify that it did not unduly affect the dependent variables. Fisher's PLSD tests allowed us to compare the values of the bilingual groups with the two control groups of native speakers in Russian and English. The design permits us to check possible effects of the first language on the second, as well as effects of the second on the first.

## Participants

Two hundred and fifty-eight subjects (129 females and 129 males, aged between 18 and 31), participated in the experiment. All were middle-class urban adults, recruited in two universities, one in Russia and one in the US. The subjects were divided into five groups:

(1)   75 monolingual speakers of Russian (35 females and 40 males, aged between 18 and 26), students at the University of St Petersburg, St Petersburg, Russia.

(2)   80 monolingual speakers of English (40 females and 40 males, aged between 18 and 26), students at Cornell University, Ithaca, NY, United States.

(3)   36 L2 users of English (22 females and 14 males, aged between 18 and 31), students at Cornell University, Ithaca, NY, United States. All were L2 users, or late bilinguals, who learned their English post puberty (mean age of arrival 16); some came as immigrants, some as students. The amount of time spent in the US by these participants ranged between 1.5 and 14 years, the majority, however, spent between 3 and 8 years in the US. All students were fluent enough in English to be enrolled in regular undergraduate and graduate classes; none was

enrolled in the Intensive English Language Program. All the subjects in the study were administered a sociobiographical questionnaire in order to determine the frequency and degree of contact they had with the target language and culture – the variables that have been found to have significant effects on the level of sociolinguistic competence (Dewaele & Regan, 2001, 2002; Grabois, 1999). All of the subjects in this group were interviewed in English.

(4)   31 L2 users of English (16 females and 15 males, aged between 18 and 31), with the same profile as the group above, were interviewed in Russian (for a detailed description of this population see Pavlenko's chapter, this volume).

(5)   36 learners of English as a foreign language (FL learners) (16 females and 20 males, aged between 18 and 26). All subjects in this group had taken English at a high school level (3–5 hours a week) for up to 6 years, and then at the university level for up to 4 years. All were enrolled in advanced upper-level English classes at the University of St Petersburg, where they were recruited. None of the participants had ever visited an English-speaking country or had any long-term contact with native speakers of English.

## Linguistic material and procedure

The narratives in the study were elicited with the help of four 3-minute long films, made by the researcher (for a detailed description of the elicitation materials, see Pavlenko's chapter in this volume). Each participant was shown one film only. Then they were asked to retell what they saw, speaking directly into the tape recorder. The tape-recorded narratives were subsequently transcribed and coded at the word level.

Four 3-minute long films, with a sound track but no dialogue, were used for narrative elicitation purposes (see Pavlenko's chapter in this volume for a discussion of narrative elicitation as a method of data collection).

## The dependent variables

### Total number of words
This is the total number of word tokens produced in a speech extract.

### Lexical diversity
Measuring lexical diversity in extracts of different length is relatively difficult (Baayen & Tweedie, 1998; Cossette, 1994; Jarvis, 2001; Wimmer & Altmann, 1999). The length of the extract tends to be negatively correlated with lexical diversity (i.e. the longer extracts will have lower values for lexical diversity). Formulae that do not compensate for this effect, such as

the simple type/token ratio (TTR), are therefore of little use if extract length is not identical (Vermeer, 2000; Vorster, 1980). There are three solutions: first, using extracts of similar length (generally 1000 words), and applying the TTR (Biber, 1988); second, determining the proportion of low-frequency words in an extract (Laufer, 1994; Laufer & Nation, 1995; Meara & Bell, 2001); third, using formulae that provide a close fit with the TTR curve. The most popular formulae are Herdan's index C, Guiraud's index R, Zipf's Z, Malvern and Richard's D and Dugast's Uber (see Jarvis, 2001 for an in-depth discussion).

In the present study, lexical diversity was measured with Dugast's (1980, 1989) Uber formula, which is an algebraic transformation of TTR:

$$Uber\ index = U = \frac{(\log tokens)^2}{\log tokens - \log types}$$

This formula provides a relatively accurate measure of lexical variation (Dewaele, 1993, Tweedie & Baayen, 1998). Vermeer (2000), however, argues that, although the Uber index is an adequate measure for early stages of vocabulary acquisition, it loses its validity from 3,000 words upwards. She suggests that more effective measures of lexical diversity should be based, not on the distribution of or the relation between the types and tokens, but on the degree of difficulty of the words used, as measured by their (levels of) frequency in daily language input.

The careful methodological study by Jarvis (2001) suggests that Uber is sufficiently valid for the type of analysis we wish to pursue. He compared the accuracy of five lexical diversity measures in terms of their ability to model the TTR curves of written texts (ranging from 70 to 420 words) in native and non-native English. The corpus in his study consisted of narratives written by the participants after viewing an 8-minute segment of Chaplin's silent film *Modern Times*. Participants included 140 Finnish and 70 Finland/Swedish adolescent learners of English living in Finland, and another 66 native English-speaking adolescents living in the US. After lemmatising the words in each narrative, Jarvis calculated and recorded TTR ratios at 20 evenly spaced measurement points. In order to smooth the curve, he averaged the TTR values at each measurement point with the TTRs of the two immediately preceding and the two immediately following token points (Jarvis, 2001: 67). Goodness of fit was then calculated between the TTR curves of each text and the curves of the five formulae using the chi-square function for non-linear least-squares curve fitting (Jarvis, 2001: 70). The rankings produced by the D (Malvern & Richards, 1997) and U formula are the most similar (Jarvis, 2001: 70), and turned out to be the most accurate (Jarvis, 2001: 71) with rejection rates of less than 5%. Considering other properties of both formulas, Jarvis (2001: 72) concludes that Uber 'may be a better overall index of lexical diversity than D is'. Uber may also be best suited for relatively small samples, whereas the D measure is especially useful when dealing with very large samples (McKee *et al.*, 2000).

## Hypotheses

(1)  Productivity and lexical diversity are independent dimensions.

(2)  Productivity:
(a) Lexical productivity in our film-retellings is subject to cross-linguistic and cross-cultural lexical differences.
(b) Factors such as gender and type of material may also affect productivity.
(c) If L1 and L2 values for productivity differ systematically, co-existence of two languages in one mind may bring them closer together.

(3)  Lexical diversity:
(a) Lexical diversity in our film-retellings is subject to cross-linguistic and cross-cultural lexical differences.
(b) Factors such as gender and type of material may also affect lexical diversity.
(c) If L1 and L2 values for lexical diversity differ systematically, co-existence of two languages in one mind may bring them closer together.

## Results

### Hypothesis 1: The independence of productivity and lexical diversity

To check the robustness of our Uber measure, we correlated total number of words per narrative with the Uber values. No such correlation appeared: $r(257) = 0.01$, $p = $ ns. It can therefore be assumed that in our data Uber values are not influenced by narrative length.

### Hypothesis 2: Productivity

In order to see whether factors such as speaker group, gender, and type of material may have affected the number of words produced in the retellings, we performed a three-way ANOVA. This also allowed us to check for any interaction effects. The complete set of results is presented in Table 7.1

**Table 7.1** Results of the three-way ANOVA on number of words produced

| Source | Degrees of freedom | F | p | $\eta^2$ |
|---|---|---|---|---|
| Gender | 1 | 0.06 | 0.799 | 0 |
| Material | 3 | 1.05 | 0.372 | 0.014 |
| Group | 4 | 3.11 | 0.016 | 0.053 |
| Gender * Material | 3 | 1.17 | 0.321 | 0.016 |
| Gender * Group | 4 | 1.02 | 0.400 | 0.018 |
| Material * Group | 11 | 0.76 | 0.675 | 0.037 |
| Gender * Material * Group | 11 | 0.28 | 0.989 | 0.014 |

$R$-squared = 0.140

The results suggest that neither gender nor type of material is linked to productivity. A significant effect did emerge for speaker group. However, the strength of this effect (the eta-squared value, $\eta^2$) is modest, as it accounts for 5.3% of the variance in the data. No interaction effects exist between the independent variables. The global R Squared value of 0.14 suggests the existence of a medium effect size (Cohen, 1992).[2]

A look at the means for the different groups shows that the extracts of the Americans (and especially the males) were the longest (see Figure 7.1).

A post-hoc analysis of variance (Fisher's PLSD) for speaker group confirmed that there are significant mean differences between American monolinguals and monolingual Russians ($p < 0.012$), the L2 users speaking Russian ($p < 0.012$), the FL users speaking English ($p < 0.010$), but not the L2 users speaking English ($p$ = ns). This suggests that the latter group has moved close to American norms. The analysis of the mean differences also allows us to compare the position of the bilinguals speaking Russian with that of the monolingual Russians. It appears that the mean difference between both groups is –9.52 which is not significantly different. A comparison of the values of bilinguals speaking Russian and the bilinguals speaking English is equally non-significant although the mean difference is larger (–29.1).

## Hypothesis 3: Lexical diversity

Following the same procedure as before, we performed a three-way ANOVA in order to determine whether factors such as speaker group, gender and type of material may have affected the lexical diversity in the retellings. The complete set of results is presented in Table 7.2.

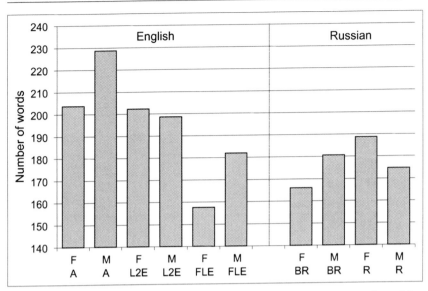

**Figure 7.1** Mean number of words in English and Russian produced by female (F) and male (M) speakers in the five speaker groups

A = American monolinguals, L2E = English Second Language speakers, FLE = English Foreign Langage speakers, BR = Bilinguals speaking Russian, R = Russian monolinguals)

**Table 7.2** Results of the three-way ANOVA on values of Uber

| Source | Degrees of freedom | F | p | $\eta^2$ |
|---|---|---|---|---|
| Gender | 1 | 3.92 | 0.049 | 0.018 |
| Material | 3 | 1.72 | 0.162 | 0.023 |
| Group | 4 | 26.87 | 0.000 | 0.328 |
| Gender * Material | 3 | 0.59 | 0.619 | 0.008 |
| Gender * Group | 4 | 0.42 | 0.793 | 0.008 |
| Material * Group | 11 | 0.75 | 0.682 | 0.037 |
| Gender * Material * Group | 11 | 1.22 | 0.27 | 0.058 |

$R$-squared = 0.413

The results suggest that gender and speaker group are significantly linked to lexical diversity. Type of material failed to reach statistical significance. The effect size for gender is limited, as it accounts for less than 2% of the variance in the data. The effect for speaker group is much stronger, accounting for more than a third of the variance. No interaction effects exist between the independent variables. The global $R$-squared value of 0.41 indicates a very large effect size (Cohen, 1992).

A comparison of the means of the different groups shows that lexical diversity values for the extracts in English are lower than for those in Russian (see Figure 7.2).

A post-hoc analysis of variance (Fisher's PLSD) of the effect of speaker groups confirmed that there are significant ($p < 0.0001$) mean differences between the different groups except between the American monolinguals and the English L2 speakers.

The difference between the FL and the L2 users interviewed in English was significant ($p < 0.010$), with the L2 speakers being closer to the American monolingual value and the FL speakers being further away from both the American L1 and the Russian L1 values. The difference between monolingual and bilingual Russians speaking Russian was not significant ($p = $ ns).

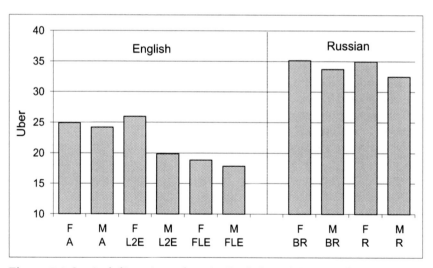

**Figure 7.2** Lexical diversity values in English and Russian for female (F) and male (M) speakers in the five speaker groups

A = American monolinguals, L2E = English Second Language speakers, FLE = English Foreign Langage speakers, BR = Bilinguals speaking Russian, R = Russian monolinguals

## Discussion

As lexical diversity is difficult to measure intrinsically (i.e. without referring to external sources such as frequency lists), our first hypothesis
concerned the methodological robustness of Uber, our lexical diversity
measure. To make sure that this measure was not unduly influenced by
extract length, we correlated it with number of words. The Pearson 'r' was
close to zero, thereby establishing the fact that in the present corpus our
measures of productivity and lexical diversity are independent.

Earlier, we have shown that productivity and lexical diversity are
affected by a large number of independent variables (personality, culture,
language and situation). In the present study, one such variable may have
been the type of material, but the ANOVAs revealed that this factor did not
affect either productivity nor lexical diversity.

Gender was not linked to productivity, but emerged as a significant but
weak effect in the analysis of lexical diversity. The finding that female
speakers across the different groups tended to provide more lexical detail is
interesting, but should not be overstated. A similar difference emerged in
the analysis of the emotion vocabulary of 40 monolingual speakers of
English and 40 monolingual Russians – but not the 34 bilinguals – in a part
of the present corpus (Dewaele & Pavlenko, 2002). Monolingual female
speakers were found to use a wider variety of emotion words and to
produce them in greater numbers. One possible explanation is that the
female participants found the film extracts, which in all four cases had
female protagonists, more interesting, prompting them to retell them in
greater detail. When the whole corpus was considered, the strongest
difference was observed among the English L2 speakers, followed by the
Russian monolinguals.

Of the factors considered in the present study, speaker group emerged as
the strongest. It appeared to be linked to both productivity and lexical
diversity. The strong differences between the monolingual Russian and
American control groups allowed us to investigate possible L1 effects on
the L2, and vice versa in the bilingual groups. The American monolinguals
in the study produced significantly longer extracts than did the Russian
monolinguals. Interestingly, the Russian bilinguals speaking English as an
L2 approximated the values of the Americans – suggesting that they have
internalised culture-specific values that regulate productivity in English in
the context in question – while the Russian bilinguals speaking Russian as
an L1 approximated the values of the Russian monolinguals. This suggests
that the process of second language socialisation had not altered their
productivity in Russian. In other words, there was no obvious effect of the

L1 on the L2, nor any visible effect of the L2 on the L1. The low productivity values of the Russian FL speakers could be an indication that they are unfamiliar with cultural requirements regulating productivity in American English. The values could also be indicative of a lower level of proficiency in English (Dewaele, 2001; Hyltenstam, 1988; Laufer, 1991).

It thus seems that as far as productivity is concerned there is no L2→L1 effect in our study and that our bicultural study participants follow different rules when speaking different languages.

A similar pattern emerged in the analysis of lexical diversity. Here again the Russian and American monolinguals stand clearly apart. Russian bilinguals speaking Russian as an L1 approximate the values of the Russian monolinguals (hence no L2 effect on the L1), and the acculturated Russian bilinguals speaking English as an L2 approximate the values of the Americans (hence no L1 effect on the L2). The lower lexical diversity values of the FL speakers (below those of the Americans and the L2 speakers) might again point to low proficiency and a limited lexicon. Dewaele and Pavlenko (2002) found that these English FL speakers produced a more limited range of emotion words than did the English L2 speakers and the English L1 speakers.

We see the statistical differences uncovered in the output as reflections of pragmatic and conceptual differences at a higher level. While it is possible that the Americans were more interested in the films (which, in turn, increased their productivity), it is much more likely that American subjects – and Russians assimilated to the L2 community – may have a different interpretation of a retelling task and thus of Grice's (1975: 45) maxim of quantity i.e. 'Make your contribution as informative as is required (for the current purposes of the exchange). Do not make your contribution more informative than is required', i.e. a judgement about the appropriate amount of information in retelling the film. The possibility that cultural factors influence speakers' interpretation of Grice's maxim with regard to context was initially introduced by Hall (1976). He distinguished low-context situations, where communication is explicit and overt, and facts are stated exactly and in detail, from high-context situations where communication is implicit, and information is conveyed more by the context than by the verbal expression. Hall introduced this concept primarily to distinguish different types of cultures (e.g. American and Northern European cultures are typically low-context, while Mediterranean and Eastern cultures are high-context). While we disagree with the level of oversimplification present in such assumptions, we believe that Noyau's conceptual framework (Noyau & Paprocka, 2000; Noyau *et al.*, in press) offers a new and interesting approach to the study of the effect of morphosyntactic and cultural factors on the resolution level (in other words, the amount of information provided by the speaker and its specificity). Clearly, to confirm the findings of the present study, a series of cross-linguistic comparisons needs to be carried out in a variety of contexts and a range of genres.

With regard to lexical diversity, the differences between monolingual Russians and monolingual Americans could be related to typological differences between the languages. Pavlenko (2002) showed that, owing to different conceptualisations of emotions in the two languages and cultures, Russian monolinguals provided more fine-grained descriptions of emotions through a wide range of adjectives rather than through a small number of verbs as Americans did. Further research may enquire whether some cross-linguistic differences between English and Russian, whether in encoding of emotions or in tense and aspect or verbs of motion, may lead to differences in granularity in particular areas. A complementary explanation for the differences in lexical diversity could be a different interpretation of Grice's (1975: 46), maxim of formulation 'Be perspicuous. Avoid obscurity of expression. Avoid ambiguity. Be brief (avoid unnecessary prolixity)' (i.e. a judgement about the appropriate formulation of information in retelling the film). Here again one could argue that linguistic and cultural conventions regulate the expected formulation of information (i.e. lexical diversity or granularity) produced in specific circumstances. Since the Russians outperformed the Americans in terms of lexical granularity, we can hypothesise that, in this particular situation, linguistic and cultural conventions called for different levels of specificity in the two cultures.

With regard to a more general monolingual/bilingual comparison, our results suggest that bilinguals do not surpass monolinguals in terms of quantity in a film-retelling task. This seems to contradict findings that bilinguals are more productive because they are able to make a greater number of connections between concepts and lemmas in two languages (Baker, 2000; Cook, 2001). On the other hand, it is quite possible that the short and focused task with no planning time did not encourage creativity. The present findings add a new dimension to Pavlenko's (1999) findings on cultural competence. She found that in the process of second language socialisation, Russian L2 users of English may transform their conceptual representations and internalise new concepts and linguistic frames. As a result, at times their linguistic performance in L1 is subject to L2 influence. In contrast, it appears that the productivity and lexical diversity values of our bicultural study participants have been modified in English but not in Russian, suggesting that these features may not be subject to change in the way that conceptual representations are.

## Conclusion

To sum up, it appears that acculturated L2 users can approximate native-speaker values in productivity and lexical diversity in the target language without losing the original values in their L1. This means that in the process of second language socialisation conceptual restructuring is taking place, as Pavlenko (this volume) demonstrated, but that some areas of pragmatic knowledge are either unaffected or less affected by L2 influence. This may give an original view of Cook's idea of multi-competence, namely that 'L2 users' knowledge of the second language is not the same as that of the native speaker' (Cook, 2001: 195). An individual's multi-competence is not a fixed, ideal end-state. It is in a constant state of flux both within and between individuals (two persons will never have isomorphic multi-competence). Metaphorically one could compare the languages in contact in the individual's mind to two liquid colours that blend unevenly, i.e. some areas will take on the new colour resulting from the mixing, but other areas will retain the original colour, while yet others may look like the new colour, but a closer look may reveal a slightly different hue according to the viewer's angle. Multi-competence should be seen as a never-ending, complex, non-linear dynamic process in speaker's mind. This does not mean that parts of the system cannot be in equilibrium for a while; but a change in the environment, i.e. a change in the linguistic input, may cause widespread restructuring with some 'islands' remaining in their original state (see also Larsen-Freeman, 2002). The lack of L2 effects on the L1 in the present study suggests that, as far as productivity and lexical diversity are concerned, original colours may survive in their new environment.

## Acknowledgement

We would like to thank Vivian Cook and Scott Jarvis for their excellent feedback on an earlier version of this paper.

## Notes

1. Resolution levels are independent of the chronological sequence and the events may be narrated in or out of sequence.
2. According to Cohen (1992), squared partial correlation values between 2 and 12.99% suggest small effect sizes, values between 13 and 25.99% indicate medium effect sizes, and values of 26% and greater suggest large effect sizes.

## References

Baker, C. (2000) *A Parents' and Teachers' Guide to Bilingualism* (2nd edn). Clevedon: Multilingual Matters.

Baayen, R.H. and Tweedie, F.J. (1998) Sample-size invariance of LNRE model parameters: Problems and opportunities. *Journal of Quantitative Linguistics* 5, 145–154.

Biber, D. (1988) *Variation across Speech and Writing*. Cambridge: Cambridge University Press.

Bradac, J.J. (1982) A rose by another name: Attitudinal consequences of lexical variation. In E.B. Ryan and H. Giles (eds) *Attitudes toward Language Variation* (pp. 99–115). London: Edward Arnold.

Bradac, J.J., Konsky, C.W. and Davies, R.A. (1976) Two studies of the effects of lexical diversity upon judgments of communicator attributes and message effectiveness. *Communication Monographs* 43, 70–90.

Bradac, J.J. and Wisegarver, R. (1984) Ascribed status, lexical diversity and accent: Determinants of perceived status solidarity, and control of speech style. *Journal of Language and Social Psychology* 3, 239–255.

Carroll, J.B. (1960) Vectors of prose style. In T.A. Sebeok (ed.) *Style in Language*. Cambridge, MA: MIT Press.

Chincotta, D. and Underwood, G. (1998) Non-temporal determinants of bilingual memory capacity: The role of long-term representations and fluency. *Bilingualism: Language and Cognition* 1 (2), 117–130.

Cohen, J. (1992) *Statistical Power Analysis for the Behavioral Sciences*. New York: John Wiley.

Cook, V. (1992) Evidence for multi-competence. *Language Learning* 42 (4), 557–591.

Cook, V. (2001) *Second Language Learning and Language Teaching* (3rd edn). London: Arnold.

Cossette, A. (1994) *La richesse lexicale et sa mesure*. Paris: Champion–Slatkine.

Danielewicz, J. (1984) The interaction between text and context: A study of how adults and children use spoken and written language in four contexts. In A.D. Pellegrini and T.D. Yawkey (eds) *The Development of Oral and Written Language in Social Contexts* (pp. 243–260). Norwood, NJ: Ablex.

De Lorenzo Rossello, C. (1999) La variabilité des degrés de granularité et condensation comme critère conceptuel d'évaluation du niveau de développement des lectes post-basiques. Paper presented at the Ninth EUROSLA Conference, University of Lund, June.

De Lorenzo Rossello, C. (2001) Les relations temporo-aspectuelles entre les procès dans le récit oral en français et en castillan, langues premières et langues étrangères. Unpublished PhD thesis, University of Paris X.

Dewaele, J-M. (1993) Extraversion et richesse lexicale dans deux styles d'interlangue française. *ITL Review of Applied Linguistics* 100, 87–105.

Dewaele, J-M. (2000) Saisir l'insaisissable? Les mesures de longueur d'énoncés en linguistique appliquée. *International Review of Applied Linguistics* 38, 31–47.

Dewaele, J-M. (2001) Interpreting Grice's maxim of quantity: Interindividual and situational variation in discourse styles of non-native speakers. In E. Németh (eds) *Cognition in Language Use: Selected Papers from the 7th International Pragmatics Conference* (Vol. 1, pp. 85–99). Antwerp: International Pragmatics Association.

Dewaele, J-M. and Furnham, A. (2000) Personality and speech production: A pilot study of second language learners. *Personality and Individual Differences* 28, 355–365.

Dewaele, J-M. and Pavlenko, A. (2002) Emotion vocabulary in interlanguage. *Language Learning* 52 (2), 265–324.

Dewaele, J-M. and Regan, V. (2001) The use of colloquial words in advanced French interlanguage. In S. Foster-Cohen and A. Nizegorodcew (eds) *EUROSLA Yearbook 2001* (pp. 51–68). Amsterdam: John Benjamins.

Dewaele, J-M. and Regan, V. (2002) Maîtriser la norme sociolinguistique en interlangue française: Le cas de l'omission variable de *ne*. *Journal of French Language Studies* 12 (2), 131–156.

Dugast, D. (1980) *La Statistique Lexicale*. Genève: Slatkine.

Dugast, D. (1989) Le vocabulaire du théâtre de Shakespeare. Sur l'appréciation de la richesse lexicale et le rôle de la fréquence moyenne. *Cahiers de Lexicologie* LV, II, 135–165.

Fielding, G. and Fraser, C. (1978) Language and interpersonal relations. In I. Markova (ed.) *The Social Context of Language* (pp. 217–232). Chichester: J. Wiley.

Giles, H. and Hewstone, M. (1985) Cognitive structures, speech, and social situations: Two integrative models. In A. Furnham (ed.) *Social Behaviour in Context* (pp. 240–269). Boston: Allyn and Bacon.

Grabois, H. (1999) The convergence of sociocultural theory and cognitive linguistics: Lexical semantics and the L2 acquisition of love, fear, and happiness. In G. Palmer and D. Occhi (eds) *Languages of Sentiment: Cultural Constructions of Emotional Substrates* (pp. 201–233). Amsterdam/Philadelphia: John Benjamins.

Grice, H.P. (1975) Logic and conversation. In P. Cole and J.L. Morgan (eds) *Syntax and Semantics: Speech Acts* (pp. 41–58). New York: Academic Press.

Hall, E.T. (1976) *Beyond Culture*. New York: Anchor Press.

Herdina, P. and Jessner, U. (2002) *A Dynamic Model of Multilingualism. Perspectives of Change in Psycholinguistics*. Clevedon: Multilingual Matters.

Hyltenstam, K. (1988) Lexical characteristics of near native second language learning. *Journal of Multilingual and Multicultural Development* 9, 67–84.

Jarvis, S. (2001) Short texts, best-fitting curves, and new measures of lexical diversity. *Language Testing* 19 (1), 57–84.

Kihlstedt, M. (1998) La référence au passé dans le dialogue. Etudes de l'acquisition de la temporalité chez des apprenants dits avancés de français. PhD thesis, University of Stockholm.

Langacker, R.W. (1987) Nouns and verbs. *Language* 63, 53–99.

Larsen-Freeman, D. (1983) Assessing global second language proficiency. In H. Seliger and M. Long (eds) *Classroom-Oriented Research in Second Language Acquisition* (pp. 287–305). Rowley, MA: Newbury House.

Larsen-Freeman, D. (2002) Language acquisition and language use from a Chaos/Complexity Theory perspective. In C. Kramsch (ed.) *Language Acquisition and Language Use: An Ecological Perspective* (pp. 33–46). London: Continuum.

Laufer, B. (1991) The development of L2 lexis in the expression of the advanced learner. *Modern Language Journal* 75, 440–448.

Laufer, B. (1994) The lexical profile of second language writing: Does it change over time? *RELC Journal* 25, 21–33.

Laufer, B. and Nation, P. (1995) Vocabulary size and use: Lexical richness in L2 written production. *Applied Linguistics* 16, 307–322.

Laufer, B. and Paribakht, T.S. (1998) The relationship between passive and active vocabularies: Effects of language learning context. *Language Learning* 48, 365–391.

Lauren, U. (1987) The linguistic competence of mono- and bi-lingual pupils in Swedish in the Finland-Swedish school. *Journal of Multilingual and Multicultural Development* 8, 83–94.

Lehtonen, J. and Sajavaara, K. (1985) The silent Finn. In D. Tannen and M. Saville-Troike (eds) *Perspectives on Silence* (pp. 193–201). Norwood, NJ: Ablex,

Lennon, P. (1995) Assessing short-term change in advanced oral proficiency: Problems of reliability and validity in four case studies. *ITL Review of Applied Linguistics* 109–110, 75–109.

Linnarud, M. (1986) *Lexis in Composition: A Performance Analysis of Swedish Learners' Written English.* Malmö: Liber Förlag.

MacIntyre, P.D. and Gardner, R.C. (1994) The subtle effects of language anxiety on cognitive processing in the second language. *Language Learning* 44, 283–305.

Malvern, D. and Richards, B. (1997) A new measure of lexical diversity. In A. Ryan and A. Wray (eds) *Evolving Models of Language: Papers from the Annual Meeting of the British Association for Applied Linguistics Held at the University of Wales, Swansea, September 1996* (pp. 58–71). Clevedon: Multilingual Matters.

Markham, R. and Darke, S. (1991) The effects of anxiety on verbal and spatial task performance. *Australian Journal of Psychology* 43, 107–111.

McKee, G., Malvern, D. and Richards, B. (2000) Measuring vocabulary diversity using dedicated software. *Literary and Linguistic Computing* 15, 323–338.

Meara, P. and Bell, H. (2001) P_Lex: A simple and effective way of describing lexical characteristics of short L2 texts. *Prospect* 16 (3), 5–19.

Meara, P., Lightbown, P.M. and Halter, R.H. (1997) Classrooms as lexical environments. *Language Teaching Research* 1, 28–47.

Noyau, C. and Paprocka, U. (2000) La représentation de structures événementielles par les apprenants: granularité et condensation. *Roczniki Humanistyczne* XLVIII, 5 (Lublin).

Noyau, C., De Lorenzo, C., Kihlstedt, M., Paprocka, U., Sanz, G. and Schneider, R. (in press) Two dimensions of the representations of complex event structures: Granularity and Condensation. Towards a typology of textual production in L1 and L2. In H. Hendricks (ed.) *The Structure of Learner Varieties.* Berlin: Mouton de Gruyter.

Pavlenko, A. (1999) New approaches to concepts in bilingual memory. *Bilingualism: Language and Cognition* 2, 209–230.

Pavlenko, A. (2002) Emotions and the body in Russian and English. *Pragmatics and Cognition* 10 (1/2), 201–236.

Raupach, M. (1987) Procedural learning in advanced learners of a foreign language. In J. Coleman and R. Towell (eds) *The Advanced Language Learner* (pp. 123–156). London: CILT.

Roelofs, A. (2002) Syllable structure effects turn out to be word length effects: Comment on Santiago *et al.* (2000). *Language and Cognitive Processes* 17 (1), 1–13.

Roodenrys, S., Hulme, C., Alban, J. and Ellis, A. (1994) Effects of word frequency and age of acquisition on short-term memory span. *Memory and Cognition* 22 (6), 695–701.

Rosch, E. (1978) *Cognition and Categorisation.* Hillsdale, NJ: Erlbaum.

Sajavaara, K. and Lehtonen, J. (1997) The silent Finn revisited. In A. Jaworski (ed.) *Silence: Interdisciplinary Perspectives* (pp. 263–283). Berlin: Mouton de Gruyter.

Sanz, G. (1999) Schèmes de lexicalisation dans le récit en espagnol et en français langues maternelles et étrangères. PhD thesis, University Paris X and Universidad Autonoma Madrid.

Scherer, K.R. (1979) Personality markers in speech. In K.R. Scherer and H. Giles (eds) *Social Markers in Speech* (pp. 147–209). Cambridge: Cambridge University Press.

Schmidt, L.A. and Fox, N.A. (1995) Individual differences in young adults shyness and sociability: Personality and health correlates. *Personality and Individual Differences* 19 (4), 455–462.

Schneider, R. (1999) L'expression des procès dans les récits d'un enfant bilingue. *AILE* Special issue: *La personne bilingue* 9, 63–82.

Siegman, S. M. (1980) Interpersonal attraction and verbal behaviour in the initial interview. In R.N. St. Clair and H. Giles (eds) *The Social and Psychological Contexts of Language* (pp. 73–99). Hillsdale, NJ: Lawrence Erlbaum.

Towell, R. (1987) Approaches to the analysis of the oral language development of the advanced language learner. In J. Coleman and R. Towell (eds) *The Advanced Language Learner* (pp. 157–182). London: CILT.

Tweedie, F.J. and Baayen, R.H. (1998) How variable may a constant be? Measures of lexical richness in perspective. *Computers and the Humanities* 32, 323–352.

van Hell, J., Wiggers, I. and Stoit, J. (in press) The influence of children's cultural background knowledge on story telling. In J-M. Dewaele, A. Pavlenko and R. Schrauf (eds) *New Directions in the Study of Bilingual Memory.* Special issue of *The International Journal of Bilingualism.*

Vermeer, A. (2000) Coming to grips with lexical richness in spontaneous speech data. *Language Testing* 17, 65–83.

Vorster, J. (1980) *Manual for the Test of Oral Language Production* (T.O.L.P.) Pretoria: South African Human Sciences Research Council.

Wimmer, G. and Altmann, G. (1999) Review article: On vocabulary richness. *Journal of Quantitative Linguistics* 6, 1–9.

## Chapter 8

# L2 Influence on L1 Linguistic Representations

VICTORIA A. MURPHY AND KAREN J. PINE

## Introduction

The focus of this chapter is on how knowledge of a second language (L2) might influence the way in which first language (L1) linguistic knowledge is represented in bilingual children. We will present data from three preliminary pilot studies that explore how explicitly bilingual children represent their L1 knowledge. We will be drawing from two different, but related, theoretical models that speak to the issue of how knowledge of language, and the representation of that knowledge, develops. The first model is Karmiloff–Smith's (1992) *Representational Redescription* model (the RR model). This is a model that describes the nature of development in all cognitive domains, and thus can also be applied to the development of linguistic knowledge. The second model we will be discussing (and in relation to the RR model) is Bialystok's (1991, 2001) *Analysis/Control* framework (the A/C model), which addresses linguistic knowledge representation in the bilingual mind, in addition to specific cognitive skills that bilingual children have.

The particular issue we are focusing on in this chapter concerns the extent to which knowledge of language is rendered more explicit in children who have learned more than one language. Bialystok (1991, 1999, 2001) has reported that, in general, bilinguals are not different from monolinguals in terms of how explicitly their knowledge of language is represented. They do manifest some advantages, however, in terms of attentional skills in performing different kinds of metalinguistic tasks. Karmiloff-Smith's RR model predicts, however, that as individuals progress through learning in a particular cognitive domain, knowledge of that domain becomes increasingly explicit in its representation. We believe that these two models, when considered together, are useful in helping us to appreciate how representing multiple linguistic systems will influence not only the way knowledge of language (both L1 and L2) is represented, but also the interaction between different cognitive processes (such as attention) and linguistic representation.

In Experiment 1, we present some data that suggest that bilingual children behave like older monolingual children in generalising their knowledge of inflectional morphology. Furthermore, the bilinguals demonstrate use of a multi-representational system as described by the RR model. In Experiment 2, we present some research that demonstrates how, in performing a reading task, bilinguals are better at ignoring distracting contexts. Interestingly, these bilinguals, while behaving like older monolingual children, are slower at performing the task. This finding suggests that (a) they do indeed have better attentional skills than monolinguals of a similar age, and (b) they are using more explicit processes, as their speed of processing is slower. Finally, in Experiment 3, we report on some data comparing adult monolinguals and bilinguals in learning an artificial linguistic paradigm. These adults had to learn about new inflectional forms under either salient or non-salient conditions. The preliminary evidence indicates that rendering linguistic features more salient during learning allowed the monolingual adults to perform more like bilinguals on a later grammaticality-judgement task. This finding indicates that attention during learning is a crucial component in forming explicit representations, and also in allowing monolinguals to manifest superior attentional skills in later linguistic tasks.

Before we discuss these three pilot studies in more detail, however, we will provide the necessary background to both the RR and the A/C models. Then we will present each of the three studies with brief discussions for each. We will close our chapter by discussing some of the implications of our preliminary research, particularly with respect to the relationship between attentional processes and developing explicit representations of language.

## The Representational Redescription Model

The Representational Redescription (RR) model describes how representations across all domains, including language, change from an implicit, non-conscious format to become increasingly available for conscious access and, in some cases, explicitly available for verbal report. In the 1970s, cognitive psychologists identified two modes of knowledge representation in adult thinking, implicit and explicit, but Karmiloff-Smith (1992) extended this notion from a developmental perspective in three distinct ways:

## Implicit knowledge is the starting point for development

In a variety of domains, knowledge begins as implicit, consciously inaccessible, procedurally-coded representations. These give rise to successful data-driven output (e.g. mastery of a spatial skill or linguistic form), without any explicit understanding of the rules underlying such success.

## Development involves a process of making implicit knowledge explicit

According to the model, the implicitly represented knowledge gradually becomes more explicit, via a number of representational redescriptions. The first redescription is from the *Implicit level (I)* to the *Explicit level E1*, an abstract, theory-driven code, but one that is still consciously inaccessible and not available for verbal report. Next, redescription occurs from level *E1* to *E2*, a format that is consciously accessible but still not verbalisable. The final redescription is to level *E3*, when full explicit knowledge is available for conscious access and verbal report.

## The cognitive system is multi-representational

As the RR drive is for understanding and flexibility of use, rather than cognitive economy, earlier implicit representations are not overwritten and supplanted by more explicit formats but continue to be represented and may be accessed for different tasks.

Evidence for the process of Representational Redescription occurring in the linguistic domain is seen in studies of metalinguistic awareness (Karmiloff-Smith, 1986). As in other cognitive domains, Karmiloff-Smith claims, children go beyond behavioural mastery as they acquire language. They are not satisfied with just producing the correct words and structures, but spontaneously engage in metalinguistic reflection. This, she argues, involves the cognitive system exploiting the linguistic knowledge already stored at the implicit level to produce, via representational redescription, more flexible and accessible linguistic representations (Karmiloff-Smith, 1992: 32). Here we shall be asking whether this process is heightened in children who are dealing with two linguistic systems, and whether bilingual children show an increased tendency to analyse their linguistic representations and to attend to structural patterns in language. In terms of the RR model, bilingual children may need to construct more stable and robust representations about the components of their linguistic input in order to build theories about how each language functions as a system. However, according to the model, the earlier implicit level representations will still exist for rapid input/output computations.

## The Analysis/Control Framework

The Analysis/Control (A/C) framework describes changes in mental representations that result in increasingly explicit use of language in children (Bialystok, 2001). There are two processing components of this model that are argued to be responsible for the development of these mental representations. The first processing component is 'analysis' which refers to '... the ability to represent increasingly explicit and abstract structures' (Bialystok, 2001: 131). The second component is 'control' which refers to '... the ability to selectively attend to specific aspects of a representation' (Bialystok, 2001: 131). One can see right away how the 'analysis' component of the A/C framework relates to the RR model, as both are concerned with describing increasingly explicit representations of knowledge. In the present context, it is concerned with explicit representations of linguistic knowledge. Somewhat surprisingly perhaps, Bialystok does not elaborate on the RR model, other than to recognise that the RR model is a theory that describes cognitive development in terms of representational redescription. One facet of both models that Bialystok does mention is the notion of explicitness as resting on a continuum. However, she does not delve further into the RR model, nor how it relates to her A/C model in particular, or the development of linguistic representations in bilingual children in general.

### Evidence for the A/C model

Bialystok (1991, 2001) has discussed the importance of task demands as drawing differentially upon both the analysis and the control/processing components. That is, different tasks require more or less analysis and/or control. For example, Bialystok (1999, 2001) describes a version of a grammaticality judgement (GJ) task that illustrates differing burdens upon analysis and control. A sentence that is both grammatical and meaningful (*Why is the dog barking?*) places minimal demands on either analysis or control. Sentences that are ungrammatical but meaningful (*Why the dog is barking?*) place a greater emphasis on analysis, because the children have to use their knowledge of language more actively to identify the ungrammaticality. Sentences that are anomalous place greater demands on control, (i.e. selective attention), as children must ignore the semantic anomaly and focus only on the grammatical structure of the sentence (*Why the cat is barking?*). Bialystok (1999, 2001) reports that a consistent finding of research that compares monolinguals and bilinguals on tasks that tease apart these two components is that

> ... bilingual children perform better than their monolingual peers in tasks that demand high levels of control, but there is no bilingual

advantage in tasks for which the solution relies primarily on high levels of analysis of representational structures.(Bialystok, 1999: 636)

Bialystok (2001) reports on a number of different investigations that manifest this pattern of a bilingual advantage on tasks requiring higher levels of control. Studies have examined children's concept of word labels (Bialystok, 1988; Ricciardelli, 1992), levels of phonological awareness (Bruck & Genesee, 1995; Campbell & Sais, 1995) and syntactic awareness (Bialystok, 1988; Galambos & Goldin-Meadow, 1990). In reviewing the evidence, Bialystok (1987, 1988, 2001) does stress, however, that there is no blanket advantage for bilinguals, indicating that different tasks will draw differentially on different skills. This also reminds us of the complexity of the factors and tasks that result in a bilingual advantage.

In terms of how this A/C approach relates to the RR model, one would expect that bilinguals should be at the same level as monolinguals in terms of representation (i.e. I, E1, E2 or E3). This conclusion stems from Bialystok's (1991, 1999, 2001, and other) research, which suggests that bilinguals tend not to show any advantage over monolinguals in terms of analysis. Since analysis refers to the level of explicitness of linguistic knowledge, and the research suggests that overall bilingual and monolingual children are similar in terms of analysis, then it follows that bilinguals and monolinguals should be at the same phases of development as described by the RR model.

If the RR model can be considered a model of 'analysis' in the A/C model's terms, then the next question is how 'control' (i.e. selective attention) relates to the development of increasingly explicit representations. Bialystok (1999) has claimed that the availability of more explicit representations (i.e. better analysis) *permits* execution of higher levels of control. In other words, greater control over the allocation of attention is necessary when there are greater levels of representational complexity (Bialystok, 2001). This implies that explicit representations (i.e. greater analysed knowledge) *precedes* the execution, or perhaps even the development) of skills in selective attention. As Bialystok has said ' ... increases in levels of analysis precede increases in levels of control. Put another way, increases in control occur in response to increases in analysis' (Bialystok, 2001: 133).

This relationship (i.e. explicit representations allowing greater control) raises some interesting questions about the research cited above. Bialystok (1991, 1999, 2001) has reported no bilingual advantage in tasks requiring greater analysis (more explicit representations). However, bilinguals do tend to show an advantage in their skills at focusing their attention to the necessary linguistic feature(s) in completing a task. If analysis precedes (or permits the execution of) control, then one would also expect that, given their superior attentional control, bilinguals should have more analysed or explicit knowledge representations than monolinguals have. In other words, how could bilinguals manifest superior attentional skills if their linguistic representations were not more explicit? The RR model might be helpful here. It could be that bilinguals are further along the RR continuum in terms of how their knowledge of language (or certain features of language) is represented. That is, they may indeed have more analysed knowledge than the monolinguals have.

The overall aim of the preliminary research we describe below is to investigate the influence (or at least, one effect) of learning an L2 on the way L1 knowledge is represented in bilingual children. One of the goals of this research is to determine where along the developmental continuum bilingual children will be relative to differing age groups of monolinguals, when the language of the monolinguals is the L1 of the bilinguals. In the light of our interest in exploring the RR model as it relates to bilingual language representation, we felt it was important to situate bilingual children along the developmental continuum.

The focus of Experiment 1 was to ascertain whether bilinguals really are at the same level as monolinguals in terms of the RR model, as Bialystok's work would suggest. We were also interested in investigating the notion of a multi-representational system, as described by the RR model. Thus, in addition to comparing bilinguals against different ages of monolinguals, we were looking for evidence that bilingual children would draw upon differentially represented knowledge depending upon the task demands.

In Experiment 2 we were interested in exploring the issue of attentional control in bilingual and monolingual children. Bialystok's research indicates that bilinguals have superior attentional skills than monolinguals in that they are better at focusing on the relevant feature of language to perform a particular task. Bialystok (1999, 2001) has also suggested that these superior attentional skills derive from having more analysed or explicitly represented language. As in Experiment 1, one of the aims of Experiment 2 was to situate a group of bilingual children along the developmental continuum on a task which required them to ignore a distracting context in order to accomplish the task.

In Experiment 3 we were interested in exploring whether attention during learning itself would lead to the kind of patterns reported in the literature regarding superior attentional skills in performing different tasks. Both the RR and A/C models are models of development. Karmiloff-Smith (1992) has argued that the principles of development as instantiated in the RR model are relevant for learning any new domain, at any time of life. Thus we should find evidence for these multi-representational systems in adult language learning as well. Bialystok's A/C model has not systematically been applied to the adult learning context. Experiment 3, therefore, is an adult L2 (artificial grammar) learning experiment where bilingual and monolingual adults had to learn a new inflectional paradigm in which attention to the linguistic form was manipulated during learning.

## Experiment 1

This study explored whether bilingual children show evidence of having multiple representations of a linguistic component when compared with monolingual children and whether, when their knowledge of a particular linguistic form is at level E1, this representation is more pronounced than in their monolingual peers.

### Analogies from studies of cognitive development

According to the RR model, language learning undergoes many of the processes seen during children's cognitive development. To illustrate this, before presenting the language data, we will outline studies which have been carried out in the domain of children's problem solving. It will then be argued that these processes are analogous to those in the linguistic domain.

As mentioned, the RR model proposes a gradual process of representational change through several levels of representation. Karmiloff-Smith and Inhelder (1974) studied children's behaviour on a balance-beam task and these findings were later invoked as an example of how children exhibit the various levels in the RR model (Karmiloff-Smith, 1992; Pine & Messer, 1999).

The task involves the child balancing wooden beams on a simple support, or fulcrum. The beams are not unlike a wooden ruler and are either symmetrical, with a wooden block at each end, or asymmetrical, with a block or two at one end only. The symmetrical beams balance on the fulcrum at their mid-point. The asymmetrical beams have to be placed off-centre on the fulcrum to balance. Many young children (4–5 years) can balance both types of beam successfully, but are unable to explain their success or to explain any of the rules underlying the concept of balance. They are, according to the RR model, at the Implicit level. They have achieved behavioural mastery, but have no accessible or verbalisable knowledge about their successful procedures.

From these implicit procedures the cognitive system detects regularities, or a central tendency, in order to begin building an abstract knowledge system. From the Implicit (I) knowledge a theory or rule is abstracted, and this is evident in the first explicit level of the RR model, level E1. On the balance-beam task level E1 behaviour is seen in most 6–7 year old children. They are successful at balancing the symmetrical beams, but are unable to balance asymmetrical beams. They place them onto the fulcrum at their mid-point and, when they fail, often dismiss them as 'impossible to balance'. These children have abstracted a rule that 'all things balance in the middle' and they over-apply this rule to all instances, leading them to fail on the asymmetrical beams (Karmiloff-Smith & Inhelder, 1974). Studies point to the robustness of this finding; for example Pine & Messer (1999) found that of 168 5–9 year olds tested on the balance-beam, 80 children held a 'centre theory' as described by the model and over-generalised it to asymmetrical beams. The RR model states that this level is still non-conscious, does not give rise to verbal report and is followed by redescription to more explicit levels.

After Level E1, Karmiloff-Smith (1992) claims, the representations are redescribed again, this time into Level E2 format, when knowledge becomes consciously accessible but is not yet coded in a linguistic format. Her model offers little empirical support for this level but, she argues, consciousness should not be defined by verbal reportability. Knowledge can exist that is visually or spatially encoded and available to consciousness but which may be difficult to explain verbally. That is why, according to Karmiloff-Smith (1992: 22), 'We often draw diagrams of problems we cannot verbalise'.

The final level in the model is level E3. This is characterised by behavioural success with understanding and the ability to produce verbal explanations. On the balance-beam task children who have reached this level can balance both types of beam on the fulcrum and can also explain how they balance and show that they understand the compensatory function of the weight and distance variables. This type of E3 representation also allows greater flexibility (Implicit level procedures, though successful, are context-bound and inflexible) and the transfer of knowledge to other domains.

### Past-tense overgeneralisation and the RR model

According to the RR model, the phenomenon of young children overgeneralising the *–ed* past-tense ending to irregular verbs would be explained as level E1 behaviour. This type of error, like the 'centre' error on the balance-beam task, suggests that the children have analysed their Implicit-level representations that have built up in response to input, and have begun to build an abstract theory system about language. This is a naturally-occurring phenomenon in all children's development that can give rise to U-shaped development and production errors.

The errors derive from having abstracted a rule that captures a general principle of the instances represented at the Implicit level and applying it, indiscriminately and in a top-down manner, to all past-tense verbs whether regular or irregular. Hence children produce past-tense forms such as *taked, breaked, catched* or *falled,* errors that can offer insight into the learning mechanisms and representations underlying the linguistic system.

Although this redescription to level E1 is seen in all children, we do see children with more robust level E1 representations. These children are more error-prone and may have been exposed to particular experiences that cause them to attend more closely to regularities in their environment (e.g. the linguistic input). Bilingual children may be such a case. Their exposure to two languages may have heightened their sensitivity to linguistic regularities and resulted in their having a greater degree of awareness and a stronger E1 representation. Thus we hypothesised that bilingual children may show evidence of more over-regularisation of past-tense verb endings than their monolingual peers.

According to the RR model, the children should still have their implicit level representations available for certain tasks. The model is not one based on cognitive economy, earlier representations are not supplanted by newer ones but continue to exist and may operate under particular circumstances. For example, Karmiloff-Smith and Inhelder (1974) found that children at level E1 could still balance all types of beams when they were asked to close their eyes. This seemed to prompt them to fall back on their implicit level representations.

To test this notion, our study included measures of explicit language production and also a recognition task, since recognition is thought to access earlier, more implicit representations. So by giving children different tasks to elicit their knowledge of past-tense verb endings, it is possible that different representations may be accessed for each task.

### Do bilingual children over-regularise more than their monolingual peers?

The participants in this study were 70 children, comprising three groups of monolingual children, aged 5, 7 and 9 and a group of bilingual children aged 6–7. The bilingual children attended a European School in Oxfordshire. They had English as an L1 and at least one other language – which was also spoken in the home. They were following the National Curriculum in English. The monolinguals were recruited from a school in Hertfordshire that had comparable SAT (Scholastic Achievement Test) scores to those of the European School. All children took part in a WUG-like test (Prasada & Pinker, 1993) where they were presented with non-words that were phonologically similar to real verbs. The task for the children on half of the stimuli was to generate the past tense of the non-word (Production Task). For example, the children heard, 'This is Graham. Graham is plinking. Yesterday he ........?' For the remaining stimuli the children heard the sentence but, instead of generating the past tense, they were given a choice of two past tenses and asked which one they thought was appropriate (Forced Choice Task).

Examples of the production and forced-choice stimuli can be seen in Figure 8.1.

This is Michael.
Michael knows how to spling
He is splinging.
Yesterday he _____.

**Production version**

This is Michael.
Michael knows how to spling.
He is splinging.
Yesterday he splinged.
OR
Yesterday he splung.

**Forced-choice version**

**Figure 8.1**  Production and forced-choice stimuli

We found that, as monolingual children get older, they produced more regular verb endings when the phonological stem of the non-word was analogous to a real regular verb: *blip* → *blipped* (analogous to *flip, sip*, etc.). They also over-regularised the -ed verb ending more as they got older, i.e. they were increasingly likely to add -*ed* as a verb ending, even if the phonological stem of the non-word was analogous to a real irregular verb *spling/ splinged* (even though *spling* rhymes with *sing*). So the 9-year-old monolingual children were less likely to produce the analogous irregular verb ending. Figure 8.2 shows the mean number of suffixes produced for regular and irregular verbs across all groups.

As can be seen from Figure 8.2, as children get older they add -*ed* more to regular verb endings, but produce fewer irregular verb forms. This is because, as they develop more knowledge about language, the pattern for

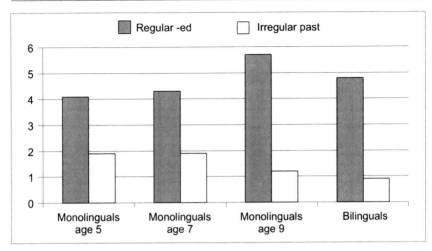

**Figure 8.2** Mean number of suffixes for regular and irregular verbs (all groups) for monolingual and bilingual children

adding *-ed* to a verb stem is reinforced, thus becoming more explicit and hence more likely to be overgeneralised. Consequently, performance worsens with age on irregular verbs: the downward trend from 5 to 7 to 9 is clear to see. However, the children in the bilingual group, who should be performing at around the level of the 5–7 year olds, are actually more similar to the 9 year olds, or even slightly more advanced. This suggests that their ability to notice regularities far exceeds that of their same-age peers.

We also investigated the effects of the task demands on the different groups of children. On the production task, bilingual children were found to over-regularise more than monolinguals do. As Figure 8.3 shows, on the production task they were producing far fewer analogous irregular past-tense forms than the monolingual children did. Analysis of the type of answers given revealed that these children were likely to produce a regular *-ed* verb ending even when the phonological cue suggested an irregular verb form. They produced significantly fewer of these forms than did monolingual children from all age groups. The bilingual group showed the largest discrepancy in scores on the two tasks, producing 25% more regularised forms on the production task for irregular verbs than on the forced choice task.

However, when given a forced choice test where they had to choose between an irregular verb ending (the 'correct' form) and an over-regularised *-ed* ending (not suggested by the phonological cue in the stem),

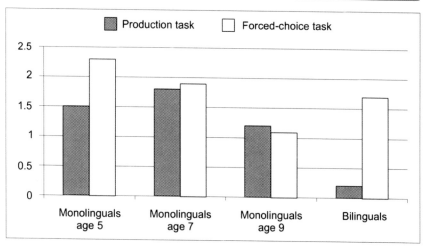

**Figure 8.3** Mean number of irregular suffixed past-tense forms produced by children across monolingual and bilingual groups for each task

the bilingual children's performance did not differ significantly from the performance of the other, monolingual, children across all age groups.

Is this evidence for stronger E1 representations in bilinguals? The discrepancy in performance between the two task types in bilinguals but not in monolinguals suggests that bilinguals are accessing different representations for different tasks. This supports the claims of the RR model that multiple representations co-exist as knowledge develops, and suggests the existence of more robust level E1 representations in bilingual children. The forced choice task may prompt access to the implicit linguistic representations and allow recognition of the correct verb ending.

In the forced choice task, the child is prompted only by the phonological cue in the verb stem, and this inhibits activation of the implicit representation. Since children with Level E1 representations are likely to ignore external input cues and respond according to their own abstracted representation, the bilingual children over-regularise the *-ed* verb ending. In production, their E1 representation is the strongest representation, which 'wins out' over others.

## Discussion of Experiment 1

In the context of the RR model, the children all show evidence of rule-based behaviour, fitting with level E1. However, the data presented here suggest an increased tendency in bilinguals to attend to the past-tense endings for verbs and to notice and over-extend the use of regular forms.

This results in a stronger E1 representation for the stem/suffix pattern. The discrepancy in task performance by the bilingual children is further evidence for a multi-representational linguistic system, since they were able to access implicit representations for the recognition task. This produced fewer over-regularisations, although the children were unable to justify their choice verbally. Overall these data suggest that dealing with a second language makes children better language processors and analysers. This may go some way towards explaining why bilingual children are more advanced than monolingual children on a range of metalinguistic problems, particularly those requiring high levels of control.

## Experiment 2

As in Experiment 1, the focus of Experiment 2 was on comparing a group of bilingual children against different ages of monolingual children. In Experiment 2, however, the task placed significant demands on the children's skills in selective attention. The main question of Experiment 2 was whether the bilinguals would be better at ignoring a distracting context than monolinguals of a similar age. This prediction stems from Bialystok's (1991, 1999, 2001) research, which indicates that bilinguals are indeed better than monolinguals at tasks requiring superior levels of attentional control. Experiment 2, however, allows us to determine how bilingual children fare against different ages of monolinguals.

The task of Experiment 2 was a basic reading task. An important feature of learning to read is phonological awareness (Adams, 1990). Being able to segment words into their phonological units has been argued to be a predictive factor in emerging literacy in a number of different languages (Liberman & Liberman, 1990). Children who are not given practice with phonics (segmenting words into their phonological components) do not make the same progress in word recognition and spelling as do children who are given phonic training (Bruck *et al.*, 1998). We felt that phonological awareness would be an interesting feature to examine in the light of the claim that bilingual children generally are more metalinguistically aware than monolingual children. With regard to reading, Bialystok and Herman (1999) report that bilinguals have an advantage over monolinguals on some measures of phonological awareness. Furthermore, Campbell and Sais (1995) have also reported that bilingual children develop enhanced awareness and control of phonological structures. If phonological awareness is an important factor in reading, and if bilinguals are better than monolinguals at tasks placing greater demands on attentional control, then we would predict that the bilingual children will be more accurate at reading words in distracting contexts than are monolinguals of a similar age.

There were four groups of children in Experiment 2 consisting of one group of bilinguals and three different age groups of monolinguals. The bilingual children were the same as those recruited for participation in Experiment 1 ($n = 18$, see above for details). There were three groups of English monolingual children, aged 5 ($n = 15$), 7 ($n = 13$) and 9 ($n = 12$) years respectively. An F-test and Tukey post hoc test confirmed that each of these three groups was statistically different in terms of their age. The monolinguals were recruited from a school in Hertfordshire with SAT (Scholastic Achievement Test) scores that were comparable to those of the bilingual participants' school.

The study incorporated the use of line drawings of common objects, aural presentations of the object's label, and visual word stimuli, all of which were presented via a laptop computer. The visual word stimuli were either real words or nonsense words. The real words corresponded to both the picture and the aural stimuli. The non-words were similar to the items represented by the picture and the aural presentation, however, either the first or last letter was changed to make it a non-word.

In this way then, the presentation of the non-words elicited a distracting context, as the visual non-word presentation was similar to the object represented in the line drawing and the aural presentation. The motivation of changing either the beginning or final letter to generate a non-word was to vary the different kinds of non-words to which participants were exposed. These items are presented in Table 8.1.

**Table 8.1** Stimuli used in Experiment 2

| Real words | Non-words (first letter changed) | Non-words (last letter changed) |
|---|---|---|
| phone | drush (from brush) | stap (from star) |
| spoon | ning (from ring) | tij (from tin) |
| tree | vag (from bag) | ped (from pen) |
| sledge | mun (from sun) | glap (from glass) |
| fence | lish (from dish) | cul (from cup) |
| pear | sey (from key) | dret (from dress) |
| kite | pock (from sock) | cal (from car) |
| broom | plock (from clock) | swad (from swan) |
| hat | | rak (from rat) |
| hand | | leat (from leaf) |
| | | comp (from comb) |

The task was structured as follows. A picture and a word appeared simultaneously on the computer screen. At the same time, the children heard a spoken word over the computer's speaker. If the word on the screen was a real word, then there was perfect correspondence between the visual and aural presentations (non-distracting context). If the word on the screen was a non-word, however, it rhymed with the aurally presented real word and was different only by virtue of a change to either the first or the last letter of the word (see Table 8.1). This was the distracting context, as the children had to ignore the spoken word (which was a real word), ignore the drawing (which corresponded to the spoken word) and focus only on the visually presented word. The stimuli remained on screen until the children made their response.

The children's first task was to press a key (one of two keys marked on the keyboard, one for 'yes', another for 'no') if they recognised the word on the screen (the visual word) as a real word or not. Both their key press (accuracy) and their reaction times were recorded. After their response to the LD, the children were asked to read the word out loud and their accuracy in doing so was recorded.

## Accuracy on lexical decision task

The bilinguals were more accurate than the 5-year-old monolinguals in the lexical decision task for both types of non-word, but there were no differences between them for the real words, as seen in Figure 8.4. There were no differences between the bilinguals and the 7-year-old monolinguals in their accuracy in the lexical decision task on any of the three types of word. However, the bilinguals were less accurate than the 9-year-old monolinguals on their lexical decision on all three types of word.

## Reaction time on lexical decision task

The main findings of the reaction time (RT) data show that the monolinguals were not different from each other, but were faster than the bilinguals at making their lexical decisions. Overall, it took the children less time to respond to the real words than to the non-words. This RT effect is illustrated in Figure 8.5.

## Accuracy at reading the words

The findings for the measure of accuracy at reading the words are illustrated in Figure 8.6. The bilinguals were more accurate at reading the non-words than the 5-year-old monolinguals were, but there was no difference between them on the real words. The bilinguals and 7-year-old monolinguals were not different in their accuracy at reading any of the three categories of word. And finally, the 9-year-old monolinguals were more accurate than the bilinguals were at reading all three types of word.

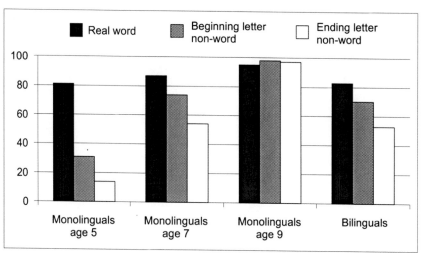

**Figure 8.4** Mean per cent accuracy on the lexical decision task for monolingual and bilingual children

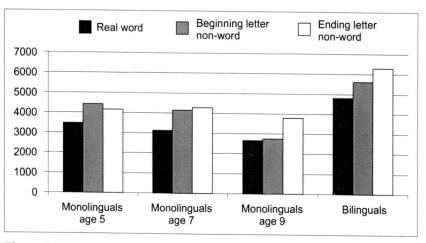

**Figure 8.5** Mean reaction time on the lexical decision task for monolingual and bilingual children

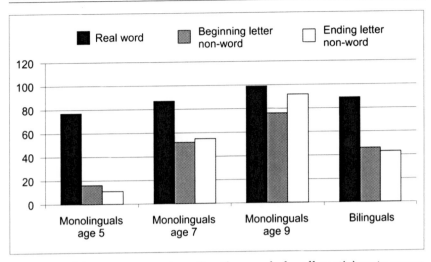

**Figure 8.6** Mean accuracy at reading the words for all participants across categories of words

## Discussion of Experiment 2

The focus of Experiment 2 was on identifying whether bilingual children were better than monolingual children at ignoring a distracting context, and to determine how bilinguals performed on this task relative to different ages of monolinguals. We can see that indeed bilinguals' performance on accuracy in the lexical decision task (Figure 8.4) and accuracy at reading the words (Figure 8.6) was comparable to that of monolinguals who were statistically older (7 years). This finding supports previous research arguing that bilinguals are better than monolinguals at tasks that require greater control over their attentional skills (Bialystok, 2001). But interestingly, we see in this study where the bilingual advantage fits relative to the performance of monolinguals of different ages. This finding is important, as it suggests that the bilinguals are further along a developmental continuum in their skills at reading English words and non-words, and at selectively focusing their attention on the relevant features of a task.

In terms of the Analysis/Control model, Experiment 2 confirms the claim that bilinguals have superior attentional skills. We can see from Experiment 2, however, that bilinguals are not simply better than all monolinguals at control, but rather, behave more like monolinguals who are approximately one year older (7 year olds). One can also infer from the bilinguals' accuracy scores on the lexical decision (LD) and reading tasks that their representations of the phonological structure and the phoneme–

grapheme correspondences in English are also more explicit. In order to be able to accurately read the words (and perform the LD task), these participants need to have a certain degree of phonological awareness, which is a critical factor in reading skills (Adams, 1990). The finding that the bilingual children are like older monolinguals on this reading task suggests that they are also further along the developmental continuum in this respect. These results would imply, therefore, that the bilinguals not only have attentional skills that are superior to those of monolinguals of their age, but also have more explicit representations (in the RR framework) or 'analysis' (in the A/C framework).

A further finding to support the assertion that the bilinguals do indeed have more explicit representations than the monolinguals is their RT on the lexical decision task. Unlike their profile on the accuracy measures, the bilinguals were reliably slower to perform the lexical decision task than the monolinguals. Slower processing suggests more 'effortful' or controlled processing, which in turn suggests processing of more explicit representations (Hasher & Zacks, 1979, 1984; Schneider & Shiffrin, 1977; Shiffrin & Schneider, 1977; Turner & Fischler, 1993). The results of Experiment 2 corroborate the findings of Experiment 1 which suggest that the bilinguals have more explicit representations of language than do monolinguals of a similar age. These experiments together suggest that not only do bilinguals have better skills at attentional control (as Bialystok and others would claim), but that they also have more 'analysed' knowledge (in the A/C framework) or more explicitly represented knowledge (in the RR framework).

Certainly what is undisputed is the finding that bilinguals consistently show superior attentional control to that of monolinguals, both in the research presented in Experiment 2 and the research discussed in Bialystok (1991, 1999, 2001). What is not clear, however, is the exact relationship between the development of these attentional skills and more 'analysed' or explicitly represented knowledge. Bialystok (2001, and elsewhere) suggests that bilinguals are no different from monolinguals in terms of analysis. However, she claims that more explicit representations must precede superior attentional control. This assertion, and the evidence regarding the bilinguals' performance in Experiments 1 and 2, does suggest that bilinguals in fact have more analysed knowledge than was previously thought. The issue of the relationship between attention and explicit representations then becomes increasingly important. A weakness from much of the research on these issues is that implications about development are being based on discrete tasks – tasks measuring some linguistic skill or knowledge at some point along the developmental continuum. To supplement some of this research, however, it would be useful to have a sense of the role of attention during learning, when the representations are being developed. The picture that one gets from the research is that, once these representations are developed and analysed/explicit, then attentional control comes into play. It could be the reverse, however. Attention could be the catalyst to more explicit representations. Experiment 3 was developed to investigate the role of attention during learning.

## Experiment 3

The focus of Experiment 3 was on exploring whether/how differences in attentional focus would influence later performance on linguistic tasks. A considerable amount of research has argued that attention to linguistic form, either in the form of instruction or feedback in classroom L2 learning (Lightbown & Spada, 1990, 1994) or through some experimental manipulation in the laboratory (Williams, 1999; Murphy & Ellis, 1999), does result in more accurate performance on formal linguistic tasks. Perhaps the bilinguals in the research described above manipulate their attention differently during learning, either by virtue of different language-learning contexts (i.e. instruction or 'naturalistic' exposure) or as some concomitant 'side-effect' of having to store multiple linguistic systems in memory. To properly test this possibility, one would need to carry out a number of fully controlled experiments that compared bilinguals and monolinguals of various ages on different kinds of learning tasks, and controlled for the way in which the bilinguals learned their languages, and the potential transfer of skills and knowledge from one language into another. We certainly cannot do this in one experiment. Nonetheless, as a starting point we felt it would be interesting to compare monolinguals with bilinguals in an artificial learning task, where we could manipulate attention to the linguistic form during learning. After learning, we tested the participants on a grammaticality judgement (GJ) task, formulated in the same manner as Bialystok's paradigm where differential focus is on either analysis or control. If attention during learning is a crucial component, then monolinguals in an attentionally focused condition should perform like bilinguals on these kinds of tasks.

Forty undergraduate psychology students participated in this study. Twenty of these were monolingual (their language was English) and their mean age was 21.35 years. The remaining twenty were a heterogeneous group of bilinguals varying in their L1s and the way in which they learned English (their L2). Their mean age was 22.25 years.

These adults were required to first learn the meaning and form of a set of

Old English noun stems. After which, they learned the plural morphology of these nouns. In this way, a set of nouns and their corresponding plurals were developed. These can be seen in Table 8.2.

**Table 8.2** Stimuli for Experiment 3

| Noun stem | Plural form | Meaning |
|---|---|---|
| benn | bennum | wound |
| fugol | fugolum | bird |
| blaed | blaedum | leaf |
| tun | tunum | village |
| fetel | fetelum | belt |
| daru | dara | mistake |
| ac | aec | tree |
| stol | stola | seat |
| ent | entas | giant |
| gefera | geferan | friend |

The students first learnt the noun stem forms, then learned about the plural forms of these nouns by seeing them in Modern English sentential contexts. The key experimental manipulation here, however, was that half the participants learned about the plurals in a 'salient' condition, where the plural element of the noun was in block caps (e.g. *bennUM*). The other half, however, were in a 'non-salient' condition where all words appeared as normal (e.g. *bennum*). After the students had finished both the stem learning and the plural training phase, they were given a GJ task. The sentences for this task were like Bialystok's described above, where some were grammatical and meaningful (*The little boy got bennum from falling down*), some were grammatical and anomalous (*The stola are a great starter*), some were ungrammatical and meaningful (*He the fetelum tightened his trousers*), and the others were ungrammatical and anomalous (*The dara the car drove*). Therefore, the grammaticality factor tested 'analysis' and the anomalous factor tested 'control'.

The main results of this pilot study can be seen in Figure 8.7. This figure shows that the bilinguals in the 'non-salient' group exhibit the characteristic advantage on the 'control' sentences. Interestingly, the bilinguals in the 'salient' condition exhibited the reverse pattern, i.e. they performed better on the 'analysis' sentences. More interesting perhaps is to compare the

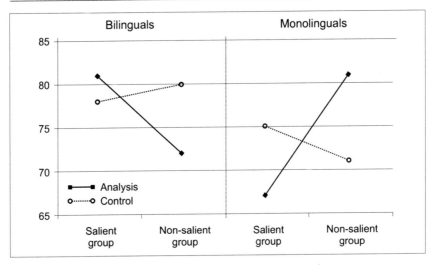

**Figure 8.7** Accuracy on grammaticality judgement task

'non-salient' bilinguals with the 'salient' monolinguals'. What we see there is that the 'salient' monolinguals exhibit the same pattern of performance as the 'non-salient' bilinguals, i.e. an advantage over control. This interaction is only marginally reliable ($p < 0.06$), so we must treat these results with some caution. It is compelling, nonetheless, that there is such a strong effect given the small number of items, and only ten adults participating in each cell of the design. In any case, these pilot results show an interesting pattern, namely, that by increasing attention during learning, monolinguals can exhibit the same superior performance on the 'control' sentences.

**Discussion of Experiment 3**

The purpose of Experiment 3 was to manipulate attention during learning and to compare bilinguals and monolinguals in either attentionally focused or less-focused conditions when learning about new linguistic items. Experiment 3 is a pilot study, and there are a few problems associated with it (such as small numbers of participants, heterogeneity of participants and small number of items). Consequently, we must be careful in the conclusions we draw from the results. Nonetheless, the pattern of results in this study is interesting and points to future research that should prove more conclusive.

Specifically, we found that learning about language under more attentionally focused conditions (i.e. the salient groups) allows participants to fare better (relative to the non-salient groups) on those tasks that demand more attentional control (i.e. the anomalous sentences). Figure 8.7 illustrates that the 'salient' monolinguals exhibit the same pattern of performance on the GJ task as the 'non-salient' bilinguals. Thus, attention during learning helps on later tasks requiring control. These findings also imply that the bilinguals 'naturally' direct their attention to the appropriate structural properties when learning about language, hence the non-salient bilinguals' characteristic advantage on the 'control' sentences.

## General Discussion

The research we have presented in this chapter has focused on the nature of language representation in bilinguals, and in particular, on the effect that being bilingual has on the nature of L1 linguistic representations. Experiments 1 and 2 were motivated by the need to contextualise the performance on linguistic tasks of bilinguals relative to monolinguals of different ages. In particular, these bilingual children were using English, which for all of them was (one of) their L1s, and their performance was compared to that of English monolinguals. The monolinguals were from backgrounds of high socio-economic status and from schools where the performance on the SATs tests are comparable to those of the bilinguals' school. Thus we feel that, despite the constraints (such as the lack of appropriately age-matched monolinguals, and the significant heterogeneity within the bilingual sample), this research is worthy of pursuit.

The main findings of Experiments 1 and 2 were that the bilinguals' performance was similar to that of a group of (statistically) older monolinguals. This was the case for the past-tense generalisation task of Experiment 1, and for the accuracy to the lexical decision task and reading the words in Experiment 2. These findings suggest to us that these bilingual children are further along the developmental continuum as described by Karmiloff-Smith's RR model (1992). Bialystok (1991, 1999, 2001) has reported that bilinguals do not display an advantage over monolinguals (of similar ages) in terms of how explicitly their knowledge of language is represented, but our research implies that in fact bilinguals do have more explicitly represented knowledge of language than do monolinguals of a similar age. However, this finding does fit with other claims that Bialystok has made, since she has also argued that the bilingual advantage of control over attention arises out of more complex representations (Bialystok, 1999, 2001). If, as Bialystok claims, bilinguals have superior attentional control, then they should also have more complex linguistic representations. What is at issue is whether the bilinguals' complex linguistic representations are *more* complex than those of monolinguals. Our research would suggest that these representations are more complex than those of monolinguals of similar ages in terms of how explicitly they are represented. Experiment 2 indicated that the bilingual children did have more advanced skills at 'control', as their ability to read the non-words (i.e. distracting context) was again like that of monolinguals who are a year older. Thus, we feel that our research shows that, when elements of both models are taken together, we have a theoretical approach that offers the most explanatory power. Specifically, the 'control' component of the A/C framework, in conjunction with the development of increasingly explicit linguistic representations from the RR model, allows us to understand both the nature of linguistic development and the cognitive skills (attention) that further promote the development of those representations.

Further evidence suggesting that our bilingual sample was working with more explicit representations stems from the RT differences in Experiment 2. The bilinguals were slower than the monolinguals to make their lexical decisions, as illustrated in Figure 8.5. As has been widely reported in the cognitive literature, processing of explicit representations operates within conscious awareness (Maybery *et al.*, 1995) and consequently is slower than automatic processing (Hasher & Zacks, 1979, 1984; Schneider & Shiffrin, 1977; Shiffrin & Schneider, 1977; Turner & Fischler, 1993). The slower reaction time in Experiment 2 does not unequivocally imply explicit representations, however. The difference could have resulted from the nature of being bilingual, i.e. that the children have two languages to deal with. This raises the question, however, as to what it is about being bilingual that could slow them down on these tasks that is not due to more explicit representations. This is definitely an avenue of further research.

Being bilingual does seem to influence one's attentional skills. This notion certainly fits in well with Bialystok's model. It could be that bilinguals become adept at solving the puzzle of language by focusing in on its structure differently, perhaps more explicitly, than monolinguals do. Using their attentional skills in a more focused and directive way might trigger representational redescription, resulting in greater metalinguistic awareness. These speculations are made even more compelling by the pattern of results found in Experiment 3. The bilingual adults who were in the 'non-salient' condition displayed the same pattern of results as the 'salient' monolinguals. This finding could be preliminary evidence that bilinguals naturally focus their attentional skills on linguistic structure *during learning* (and not just in task performance). Focus of attention could both be a result of, and further develop, more explicitly represented linguistic knowledge. The fact that the participants in Experiment 3 were adults also further supports the RR model. Karmiloff-Smith (1992) has argued that representational redescription happens throughout cognitive development. That is, it is not a phenomenon of childhood, but a phenomenon of learning, even if that learning is taking place in adulthood.

Certainly more research is needed to systematically explore the exact influence that becoming bilingual has on the nature of L1 linguistic representations. A number of issues need to be addressed within this future research. For example, one constraint on the research reported in this chapter concerns the heterogeneity of the bilingual sample. There could be many differences between the bilinguals themselves in terms of how they have learned their second languages, what the actual second languages are, how balanced they are in terms of their proficiency in their languages, etc. Further research should control, as much as is possible, the bilingual and monolingual samples to ensure that they are as matched as possible. Another interesting comparison would be between bilingualism and L2 learning. In our research, the bilinguals could be considered to be L2 learners, as many of them have an identifiable first language relative to their second. It would be interesting to explore these ideas within children who were developing multiple L1s.

Our research indicates that the most profitable route forward would be to explore the issue of attention and language learning, in particular, to investigate the developing attentional skills of bilinguals (or L2 learners) and the way these skills influence the development of increasingly explicit linguistic representations. We would agree with Bialystok (2001: 143) that 'Bilingualism itself is insufficient to fundamentally change the path of metalinguistic development'. However, what needs to be explored further is the interaction between different factors that do influence linguistic development within a broader theoretical framework. Factors such as the specific linguistic feature being investigated (i.e. knowledge of words, morphology, syntax, phonology?), the context of learning (in classrooms? in the home?), the influence of language transfer, age of the learners and so on, all need to be rigorously and systematically explored in order to further understand the factors that interact with each other and change the path of metalinguistic development. In general terms, however, we believe that the A/C framework will be useful in helping us understand the attentional skills of bilinguals and L2 learners and the extent to which different tasks place differential demands on these skills. We also believe that the RR model will be a useful theoretical framework for understanding how knowledge of language becomes increasingly explicit. Taking these two issues together (i.e. attention and the development of increasingly explicit knowledge of language), will help us uncover how the bilingual child both develops and uses superior attentional skills to more explicitly represent linguistic knowledge that will ultimately lead to greater metalinguistic awareness.

## Acknowledgements

We would like to thank our colleague, Christina Schelletter, and our students, Carol Collins, Helen Smithies and Helena Karageorgis, for their help in conducting this research.

## References

Adams, M.J. (1990) *Beginning to Read: Thinking and Learning about Print*. Cambridge, MA: MIT Press.

Bialystok, E. (1987) Words as things: Development of word concept by bilingual children. *Studies in Second Language Acquisition* 9, 133–140.

Bialystok, E. (1988) Levels of bilingualism and levels of linguistic awareness. *Developmental Psychology* 24, 560–567.

Bialystok, E. (1991). Metalinguistic dimensions of bilingual language proficiency. In E. Bialystok (ed.) *Language Processing in Bilingual Children* (pp. 113–140). Cambridge: Cambridge University Press.

Bialystok, E. (1999) Cognitive complexity and attentional control in the bilingual mind. *Child Development* 70, 636–644.

Bialystok, E. (2001) *Bilingualism in Development: Language, Literacy and Cognition*. Cambridge: Cambridge University Press.

Bialystok, E. and Herman, J. (1999) Does bilingualism matter for early literacy? *Bilingualism: Language and Cognition* 2, 35–44.

Bruck, M. and Genesee, F. (1995) Phonological awareness in young second language learners. *Journal of Child Language* 22, 307–324.

Bruck, M., Treiman, R., Caravolas, M., Genesee, F. and Cassar, M. (1998) Spelling skills of children in whole language and phonics classroom. *Applied Psycholinguistics* 19, 669–684.

Campbell, R. and Sais, E. (1995) Accelerated metalinguistic (phonological) awareness in bilingual children. *British Journal of Developmental Psychology* 13, 61–68.

Galambos, S.J. and Goldin-Meadow, S. (1990) The effects of learning two languages on levels of metalinguistic awareness. *Cognition* 34, 1–56.

Hasher, L. and Zacks, R.T. (1979) Automatic and effortful processes in memory. *Journal of Experimental Psychology: General* 108, 356–388.

Hasher, L. and Zacks, R.T. (1984) Automatic processing of fundamental information: The case of frequency of occurrence. *American Psychologist* 39, 1372–1388.

Karmiloff-Smith, A. (1986) From metaprocesses to conscious access: Evidence from children's metalinguistic and repair data. *Cognition* 23, 95–147.

Karmiloff-Smith, A. (1992) *Beyond Modularity: A Developmental Perspective on Cognitive Science*. Cambridge, MA: MIT Press.

Karmiloff-Smith, A. and Inhelder, B. (1974) If you want to get ahead, get a theory. *Cognition* 3, 195–212.

Liberman, I.Y. and Liberman, A. (1990) Whole language versus code emphasis: Underlying assumptions and their implications for reading instruction. *Annals of Dyslexia* 40, 51–76.

Lightbown, P.M. and Spada, N. (1990) Focus on form and corrective feedback in communicative language teaching: Effects on second language learning. *Studies in Second Language Acquisition* 12, 429–448.

Lightbown, P.M. and Spada, N. (1994) An innovative program for primary ESL students in Quebec. *TESOL Quarterly* 28, 563–579.

Maybery, M., Taylor, M. and O'Brien-Malone, A. (1995) Implicit learning: Sensitive to age but not IQ. *Australian Journal of Psychology* 47, 8–17.

Murphy, V.A. and Ellis, N.C. (1999) Attention and L2 learning of inflectional morphology. Paper presented to AAAL conference, Stamford, NY.

Pine, K.J. and Messer, D.J. (1999) What children do and what children know: Looking beyond success using Karmiloff-Smith's RR framework. *New Ideas in Psychology* 17, 17–30.

Prasada, S. and Pinker, S. (1993) Generalisation of regular and irregular morphological patterns. *Language and Cognitive Processes* 8, 1–56.

Ricciardelli, L.A. (1992) Bilingualism and cognitive development in relation to threshold theory. *Journal of Psycholinguistic Research* 21, 301–316.

Schneider, W. and Shiffrin, R.M. (1977) Controlled and automatic human information processing: I. Detection, search, and attention. *Psychological Review* 84, 1–66.

Shiffrin, R.M. and Schneider, W. (1977) Controlled and automatic human information processing: II. Perceptual learning, automatic attending, and a general theory. *Psychological Review* 84, 127–190.

Turner, C.W. and Fischler, I.S. (1993) Speeded tests of implicit knowledge. *Journal of Experimental Psychology: Learning, Memory and Cognition* 19, 1165–1177.

Williams, J.N. (1999) Memory, attention and inductive learning. *Studies in Second Language Acquisition* 21, 1–48.

## Chapter 9

# Cross-linguistic Influence of L2 English on Middle Constructions in L1 French

PATRICIA BALCOM

## Introduction

Cook (1991, 1992, 1993) discussed the question of ultimate attainment in L2 acquisition under the rubric of what he called *multi-competence*, that is, 'the compound state of a mind with two grammars' (Cook, 1991: 112). He proposed that the internalised grammars of native-like learners were not the same as those of monolingual native speakers, although their linguistic performance might be similar, and hypothesised that the differences could be due to the L1 and the L2 influencing one another.

The influence of the L1 in L2 acquisition has a long and sometimes contentious history in the field of SLA (second language acquisition), and I can only skim the surface here. (See Gass, 1996 and Kellerman, 1995 for overviews; Gass & Selinker, 1994 and Kellerman & Sharwood-Smith, 1986 for collections of articles on the topic, and Jarvis, 2000 for a discussion of methodological issues.) Contrastive analysis viewed interference from the L1 as the prime cause of errors in the L2, and a major obstacle to successful mastery (Lado, 1957). Somewhat later, the creative construction hypothesis (Dulay & Burt, 1975 and subsequent work) viewed the influence of the L1 as insignificant: it was merely one of many cognitive strategies employed by L2 learners. Influence of the L1 re-emerged as a significant factor in L2 acquisition under principles and parameters (P & P) theory. There is some evidence that the L1 setting of a syntactic parameter is transferred at the initial stages of L2 acquisition, although it may subsequently be reset (see White, 1994, 1996). Similarly, research into the L2 acquisition of the lexicon has shown that learners may initially transfer a lexical parameter or rule from the L1, but they are able to re-set the parameter or acquire a lexical rule in the L2 that does not exist in the L1 (Juffs, 1996; Wang, 1995). And finally, SLA researchers working within the Minimalist Program (MP) have found that the L1 values of functional categories are transferred to the L2 at the initial stage of L2 acquisition, and may continue to play a role at subsequent stages. (See Hawkins, 2001 and Herschensohn, 2000 for recent overviews.)

As mentioned above, Cook (1993) suggested that the enhanced meta-linguistic awareness possessed by bilinguals might influence knowledge of both the L1 and L2. Influence of the L2 on the L1 has been studied extensively in the code-switching literature (for overviews see Grosjean, 1982; MacSwan, 2000; Romaine, 1995). However, code-switching is rarely discussed in SLA – Dulay *et al.* (1982: 112–119) and Bhatia & Ritchie (1996) are notable exceptions – although code-switchers represent the culmination of L2 acquisition, that is, fluent bilingualism. Yet apart from the other articles in this volume, there has been little research in SLA on the issue of influence of the L2 on the L1.

Since the multi-competence hypothesis is based on the P & P framework (Chomsky, 1981; Chomsky & Lasnik, 1993), it is possible to modularise the research question. Cook (1993) suggested that the linguistic competence of bilinguals should be examined in the various components of the grammar to see in which components the two grammars influenced each other. Satterfield (1999) showed that knowledge of English as an L2 caused increased use of overt pronouns in non-emphatic contexts in L1 Spanish by Spanish/English bilinguals. Cenoz (2002) found that with request strategies there was a bi-directional interaction between English and Spanish in the pragmatic component of Spanish/Basque L1 speakers. Arcay-Hands (1998) demonstrated that taking an advanced course in English L2 writing had a beneficial effect on students' writing skills in the L1, and Kecskes (1998) reported similar findings with Hungarian L1 speakers learning English, French or Russian. With regard to the lexicon, Pavlenko (2000) discussed the transfer of L2 concepts from American English to Russian L1 with bilinguals who lived in an English-speaking environment, but not by bilinguals in a foreign-language context. Thus, there is some evidence that the L2 can influence the L1 in the morpho-syntactic, pragmatic and lexical components of the grammar.

This chapter makes a contribution to the study of the influence of the L2 on the L1 by examining the influence of the L2 on L1 lexico-syntactic rules and representations for verbs that undergo middle formation. According to Kemmer (1993), in traditional grammar the middle voice is viewed as being situated halfway between the active and the passive voice. It is a very broad category, and includes reflexives (*John hit himself*), reciprocals (*John and Mary kissed each other*), and events in which the action described by the verb appears to occur spontaneously (*The bomb exploded*). More recently, within theories of lexical semantics, middle constructions are viewed as generic statements that attribute properties to entities (*Politicians bribe easily. Polyester washes well*). In other words, they are generalisations that specify the ease with which an action or process can be performed on an entity. The relevant characteristics of middle constructions will be described in the next section.

I chose to study middle constructions for several reasons. First of all, Balcom (1995) showed that, while very advanced Francophone learners of English had native-like performance and judgements for several different verb classes, the greatest divergence between the Francophones and native speakers of English was with middle constructions. Similarly, Connors and Ouellette (1993, 1994) showed that very advanced Francophone learners of English and very advanced Anglophone learners of French had difficulties with middle constructions, as did the very advanced Anglophone learners of French in Birdsong's (1992) study. The multi-competence hypothesis would suggest that these results could be due to the two languages influencing each other. A second reason to study middle constructions is that, as is demonstrated in the next section, middle constructions in English and French contrast in several different ways, with English having a much more constrained grammar in this regard, allowing the issue of L2 influence on the L1 to be addressed in a very specific way.

The chapter is organised as follows. The following section gives certain differences between French and English middle constructions, and then these differences are set within theories of lexical semantics. Next I describe a study I conducted to compare the intuitions of grammaticality for middle constructions in French of bilingual and monolingual Francophones, and present the results of the study. Finally, I discuss the results in light of the questions raised by the multi-competence hypothesis: that is, do bilinguals have the same mentally represented grammars in their L1 as monolinguals do, and are the differences found due to L2 influence?

## Some Differences Between French and English Middles

English and French middle constructions are similar in that, (as in passive constructions), in both the logical object is the grammatical subject, although in neither is there passive morphology. Moreover, in both languages middle constructions are interpreted as having an implicit Agent, and generally require some kind of adverbial modification. Nevertheless, Fellbaum and Zribi-Hertz (1989) delineated a number of differences between French and English middle constructions. First of all, French middle constructions have a clitic pronoun (*se*), as in (1a), while English middles do not have its equivalent (*-self*), as in (1c).

(1)(a) Le grec <u>se</u> traduit facilement.
  (b) Greek translates easily.
  (c) *Greek translates <u>itself</u> easily. (Fellbaum & Zribi-Hertz, 1989: 4).

A second difference is that middles in French can occur with a wide variety of adverbials of time, place and manner, while English middles can occur only with a limited number of adverbials of manner (called adverbials of facility), such as *easily, with difficulty, quickly, badly.* Adverbials of facility describe the ease or difficulty with which an action is 'doable' to an entity (Pinker, 1989). Thus the French sentence (2a) is grammatical, while the English equivalent (2b) is not, because there is no adverb of facility, *easily* for example, as in (1b).

(2)(a) Le grec se traduit avec un dictionnaire.
  (b) *Greek translates with a dictionary. (Fellbaum & Zribi-Hertz, 1989: 10).

Thirdly French, unlike English, allows impersonal Subjects with middle constructions, so that (3a) is grammatical, while the English equivalent (3b) is ungrammatical.

(3)(a) Il se traduit facilement beaucoup de textes grecs dans cette université.
  (b) *There translate easily many Greek texts at this university. (Fellbaum & Zribi-Hertz, 1989: 12).

A fourth characteristic distinguishing the two languages is that the grammatical Subject in French middles does not have to be affected. Affectedness refers to a change to an entity that is apparent or visible, often as a result of its being moved or altered. Fellbaum and Zribi-Hertz defined affectedness as follows:

> An argument of a verb is affected by the action or process referred to by the verb if the referent of the argument exists prior to the action or process taking place, and if its inherent properties are modified by the action or process. (Fellbaum & Zribi-Hertz, 1989: 28)

In (1b) for example, *Greek* is affected because by the process of translation it becomes another language.

Thus the French sentence (4a) is grammatical, while the English equivalent (4b) is not, since the grammatical Subject, the *Eiffel Tower,* is not affected, that is, changed or modified by the action of the verb.

(4)(a) La Tour Eiffel se voit facilement de ma fenêtre.
  (b) *The Eiffel Tower sees easily from my window. (Fellbaum & Zribi-Hertz, 1989: 11)

Although Fellbaum and Zribi-Hertz asserted that neither language allows middle constructions with an overt Agent in a *by*-phrase, Authier and Reed (1996) provided data that show that some varieties of Canadian French do allow such constructions as in (5a), while the English translation is ungrammatical (5b).

(5)(a) Ce costume traditionnel se porte surtout <u>par les femmes</u>.
   (b) *This traditional costume wears mostly by women. (Authier & Reed, 1996: 4).

## Conceptual framework

This study adopts as its conceptual framework recent models of lexical semantics (Jackendoff, 1987, 1990 and Levin & Rappaport, 1995) that are situated within theories of generative syntax. In very general terms, researchers in lexical semantics assume that a verb's lexical entry consists of semantic elements as well as what is often called its subcategorisation frame (i.e. obligatory nominals and adverbials that complement the verb). A lexical entry encoding the information presented in the last section is given in (6) below.

(6) Lexical entry for verbs undergoing middle formation in French

$$[[[_{\text{Event}} x_{\text{Arb}} \text{ DO SOMETHING}][_{\text{Event/State}} y \text{ BECOME/BE STATE}]] [<\text{by } x>]]$$
$$[\text{AFFECT } [x,<y>]]$$

(Adapted from Levin & Rappaport Hovav, 1995 and Jackendoff 1987, 1990)

Lexical entries for verbs undergoing middle formation include an Agent ($x$) with arbitrary reference – having no antecedent (Chomsky, 1981: 24) – which is interpreted generically as 'people' or 'one'. The fact that in Canadian French a middle verb can optionally subcategorise for a *par*-phrase is indicated by putting the phrase within <angle brackets>, Jackendoff's (1987) notation for an optional argument. Jackendoff (1987, 1990) added an additional level of lexical representation – the action tier – which encodes affectedness. The optionality of the affected argument in French is indicated by enclosing it in <angle brackets>. (This would not be the case in English, where the argument must be affected.) Because an adverbial of facility is not obligatory in French, it does not appear in the lexical entry, although it would in English.

Within P & P theory the lexicon has a vital role, since syntax is projected from the lexicon (Chomsky, 1981; 1986; Chomsky & Lasnik, 1993). The lexicon is equally important in the Minimalist Program (Chomsky, 1995;

2000) since 'the lexical entry provides, once and for all, the information required for further computations' (Chomsky, 1995: 239), and 'derivations make a one-time selection of a *lexical array* LA from Lex [the lexicon], then map LA to expressions ...' (Chomsky, 2000: 100). Figure 9.1 gives a representation of the model of the grammar in the MP.

Under the MP, the lexicon contains both lexical categories (e.g. Noun, Verb) and functional categories (e.g. Tense, Clitic). From the lexicon, derivations select a lexical array that includes both functional and lexical categories. This lexical array enters the Computational System where the operations Agree, Merge and Move apply to lexical items to generate syntactic expressions. Spell-Out is the input to Phonological Form (PF) and Logical Form (LF), the interfaces to the articulatory-perceptual system and the conceptual-intentional system respectively.

A verb undergoing middle formation enters the Computational System with all the syntactically relevant information from its lexical entry (as in (6) above), including the number of arguments it takes (i.e. *x* and *y*, the Agent and Object respectively), with the Agent being arbitrary. *Se-moyen* is a clitic, a functional category selected from the lexicon and inserted under I(nflection) in the syntax (Belletti, 1982; Bruhn de Garavito, 1999; Fagan, 1992; Vinet, 1987). To account for impersonal constructions in French middle constructions, following Alexiadou and Anagnostopoulou (2001), I suggest that if there is an expletive (impersonal *il*) in the lexical array it can fill the subject position (in their terms, check the E(xternal) A(rgument) feature and merge with it); otherwise, the Object moves to the subject position (in technical terms, to check its Case and EA feature).

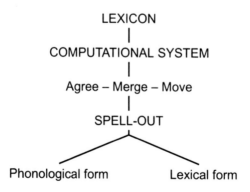

**Figure 9.1** The Minimalist Program model of grammar

## The Study

### The research question

Based on the differences between middle constructions in English and French described earlier, it is possible to pose the research question. If L2 lexico-syntactic rules and representations influence the L1, bilingual Francophones should:

- Judge middle constructions in French with no *se-moyen* to be grammatical, since there is no clitic pronoun in comparable English constructions, as shown in (7):

  (7) (a)  Les barbecues (*<u>se</u>) vendent bien pendant l'été.
      (b)  Barbecues sell well during the summer months.

- Reject middle constructions with a variety of adverbials in French, since verbs in middle constructions in English strictly subcategorise for adverbials of facility, which are optional in French, as in (8):

  (8) (a)  Un tricot de laine se lave <u>à l'eau froide</u>.
      (b)  *A wool sweater washes <u>in cold water</u>.

- Reject middle constructions with impersonal Subjects in French since they are ungrammatical in English, as shown in (9):

  (9) (a)  L'année prochaine, <u>il se traduira</u> beaucoup de textes acadiens à l'Université de Moncton.
      (b)  *Next year, <u>there will translate</u> many Acadian texts at l'Université de Moncton.

- Adhere to the affectedness constraint in French middle constructions since this constraint forms part of the verb's lexical entry in English, as in (10):

  (10)(a)  La musique de Mozart <u>s'entend</u> merveilleusement bien au théâtre Capitol.
      (b)  *Mozart's music <u>hears</u> marvellously well at the Capitol Theatre.

- Reject *by*-phrases in middle constructions in French since they are ungrammatical in English, as shown in (11):

  (11)(a)  Ce costume traditionnel se porte surtout <u>par les femmes</u>.
      (b)  *This traditional costume wears mostly by women.

Moreover, in their corrections to sentences they judge ungrammatical, bilinguals should correct grammatical sentences in French using constructions influenced by English.

## Participants

All participants were students at l'Université de Moncton, a Francophone university in Moncton, New Brunswick, Canada's only officially bilingual province. According to the 1996 Census (Statistics Canada, 2001), 32.6% of the population of New Brunswick is Francophone. This population is concentrated in two Francophone regions of the province (the northeast and northwest, which are more than 90% Francophone and where there is little contact with English) and in two areas in which Francophones represent a large minority and where there is extensive contact with English (the north-central region and the southeast, which are roughly 40% Francophone) (Blanc, 1993; Castonguay, 1998). The bilingual Francophones in this study were from the southeast, while the monolingual Francophones were from either the northeast or the northwest.

The bilingual Francophones (henceforth referred to as bilinguals) were seven females and five males with a mean age of 21.3. Both parents were Francophones, and the primary language in the home, at university and during social, cultural and athletic activities was French. Participants were excluded from the study if they had studied in English schools and/or if they used more English than French in their daily lives, so all were French dominant. (The language-use questionnaire is in the Appendix to this chapter.) With regard to their English proficiency, all had been placed in an advanced English course on the basis of near-native fluency of expression in an oral interview, a writing sample in English (which had to be nearly error-free) and their Grade 12 English marks (A or B+ in the bilingual track in ESL). The bilingual (B) track is the ESL programme in the province of New Brunswick for students who have had considerable contact with Anglophones outside the classroom and are already fluent in spoken English before they start school (Ministère de l'Éducation, 1992).

The 13 monolingual Francophones (henceforth monolinguals) were eight females and five males with a mean age of 19, all of whom were high-beginner or low-intermediate learners of ESL, as close to monolingual as one is likely to find in Canada. Again, both parents were Francophones, and the primary language in the home, at university and during social, cultural and athletic activities was French. Their high-school ESL was in the A track, which is for students who have had no experience with English before starting school, and little contact with English outside the classroom.

## Experimental task

The research reported here is part of a larger study that examined grammaticality judgements of middle constructions in English and French by bilingual Anglophones and Francophones, and by monolingual Anglophones and Francophones. There were two tasks, an English one and a French one; both of these were administered to the two groups of bilinguals, and one to the monolinguals. Some of the results of the larger study are reported in Balcom (1999).

There was a total of 28 sentences on the French task, all of which are grammatical according to the description of middle constructions given above, with the exception of six sentences with no clitic *se-moyen*. The equivalents of all except those with no *se-moyen* are ungrammatical in English. Examples of each type are shown in (12).

(12) Examples of test sentences

(a) *No clitic pronoun*
Les barbecues vendent bien pendant l'été.
'Barbecues sell well during the summer months.'

(b) *No adverb of facility*
Un tricot de laine se lave à l'eau froide.
'A wool sweater washes in cold water.'

(c) *Impersonal Subject*
L'année prochaine, il se traduira beaucoup de textes acadiens à l'Université de Moncton.
'Next year, there will translate many Acadian texts at l'Université de Moncton.'

(d) *Grammatical Subject not affected*
La musique de Mozart s'entend merveilleusement bien au théâtre Capitol.
'Mozart's music hears marvellously well at the Capitol Theatre.'

(e) *Par-phrase*
Ce costume traditionnel se porte surtout par les femmes.
'This traditional costume wears mostly by women.'

Participants were asked to mark sentences as grammatical or ungrammatical, or to put a question mark (?) if they were uncertain. Because subjects may reject sentences for a variety of reasons (Birdsong, 1989; Klein, 1995; Zobl, 1994), the participants in this study were asked to correct the sentences they considered ungrammatical so that the basis of their judgements was clear. These corrections proved to be an additional source of data that was useful in providing insights into participants' mental rules and representations.

## Results

### Preliminary analysis

A preliminary analysis of the responses indicated that looking exclusively at the participants' judgements would obscure the matter under study, since participants marked sentences as ungrammatical and made a variety of changes while maintaining the sentence structure of the original. For example the original sentence in (13) below was marked ungrammatical and the adverb changed, but the phrase *par les femmes* 'by women' was maintained. (The original and amended adverbs are underlined.)

(13)  *Original:*
      Ce costume traditionnel se porte <u>surtout</u> par les femmes.
      'This traditional costume wears <u>mostly</u> by women.'

      *Correction:*
      Ce costume traditionnel se porte <u>généralement</u> par les femmes.
      'This traditional costume wears <u>generally</u> by women.'

Another type of correction was to change the preposition, as in (14), where the phrasal preposition *à partir de* ('as of') was changed to *dès* ('as of'), while the impersonal construction *il ne se vendra plus* ('There won't sell any more') was not changed.

(14)  *Original:*
      <u>À partir du</u> premier mars, il ne se vendra plus de cigarettes dans des pharmacies en Ontario.
      '<u>As of</u> the first of March, there won't sell cigarettes in pharmacies in Ontario any more.'

      *Correction:*
      <u>Dès</u> le premier mars, il ne se vendra plus de cigarettes dans des pharmacies en Ontario.
      '<u>As of</u> the first of March, there won't sell cigarettes in pharmacies in Ontario any more.'

Since these types of corrections maintained the structure under study (*par*-phrases and impersonal Subjects in the examples), they were counted as 'grammatical' responses.

### Results in the grammaticality judgement task

Table 9.1 shows the number and percentage of sentences judged 'grammatical' by monolinguals and bilinguals, broken down by sentence type.

Recall that all sentences, with the exception of those with no *se-moyen*, are grammatical according to the description of French given earlier. The salient results are shown graphically in Figure 9.2.

**Table 9.1** Judgements by sentence type (monolingual $n = 13$, bilingual $n = 12$)

| Sentence Type | Group | Grammatical | | Ungrammatical | | Not sure | | Total |
|---|---|---|---|---|---|---|---|---|
| | | n | (%) | n | (%) | n | (%) | n |
| No *se-moyen* | Monolingual | 6 | (8) | 71 | (91) | 1 | (1) | 78 |
| | Bilingual | 2 | (3) | 69 | (96) | 1 | (1) | 72 |
| No adverb of facility | Monolingual | 69 | (66) | 22 | (21) | 13 | (13) | 104 |
| | Bilingual | 61 | (64) | 34 | (35) | 1 | (1) | 96 |
| Impersonal Subject | Monolingual | 30 | (58) | 18 | (35) | 4 | (7) | 52 |
| | Bilingual | 15 | (31) | 33 | (69) | 0 | (0) | 48 |
| Unaffected | Monolingual | 46 | (88) | 3 | (6) | 3 | (6) | 52 |
| | Bilingual | 35 | (73) | 11 | (23) | 2 | (4) | 48 |
| Par-phrase | Monolingual | 39 | (50) | 37 | (47) | 2 | (3) | 78 |
| | Bilingual | 24 | (33.3) | 48 | (66.6) | 0 | (0) | 72 |
| TOTAL | Monolingual | 190 | (52) | 151 | (41) | 23 | (7) | 364 |
| | Bilingual | 137 | (41) | 195 | (58) | 4 | (1) | 336 |

The monolinguals were significantly more likely to judge sentences to be grammatical than the bilinguals: 52% grammatical for the monolinguals and 41% grammatical for the bilinguals. These overall differences between the two groups are significant ($\chi^2 = 26.21$, 2 d.f., $p < 0.001$). Because there was a fairly large number of 'Not sure' responses on the part of the monolinguals (7% of the total), another $\chi^2$ (chi-squared) test was performed excluding these responses, and the differences were still highly significant ($\chi^2 = 14.05$, 1 d.f., $p < 0.001$). If the different types of sentences are examined separately, significant differences are seen between the groups in their judgements of three types of sentences: those with an impersonal Subject (58% grammatical for the monolinguals, 31% for the bilinguals, $p < 0.005$); those with an unaffected grammatical Subject (88% grammatical for the

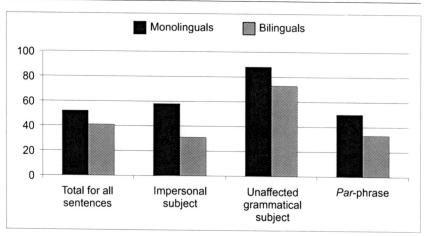

**Figure 9.2** Percentage of four sentence types judged grammatical by monolinguals and bilinguals

monolinguals, 73% for the bilinguals, $p < 0.025$); and those with a *par*-phrase (50% for the monolinguals, 33.3% for the bilinguals, $p < 0.025$). In all cases the monolinguals were more likely than the bilinguals to judge such sentences as grammatical, as can be seen in Figure 9.2. There were no significant differences in sentences with no adverb of facility (monolinguals 66%, bilinguals 64%) or those with no *se-moyen* (8% and 3%).

## Major types of corrections

In (15) below I have given examples of the major types of correction that participants made to sentences they judged ungrammatical, underlining the relevant portion of the correction.

(15) Examples of corrections to sentences participants considered ungrammatical

(a) *Correction with a passive sentence.* These all incorporated some form of the verb *être* 'to be' and the past participial form of the verb.

*Original:*
Un tricot de laine <u>se lave</u> à l'eau froide.
'A wool sweater <u>washes</u> in cold water.'

*Correction:*
Un tricot de laine <u>devrait être lavé</u> à l'eau froide.
'A wool sweater <u>should be washed</u> in cold water.'

(b) *Correction with a referential SVO sentence.* These involved sentences in which impersonal subjects were replaced by referential Subjects (i.e. pharmacies).

*Original:*
À partir du premier mars, <u>il</u> ne se vendra plus de cigarettes dans des pharmacies en Ontario.
'As of the first of March, <u>there</u> won't sell cigarettes in pharmacies in Ontario any more.'

*Correction:*
À partir du premier mars <u>les pharmacies en Ontario</u> ne vendront plus de cigarettes.
'Starting the first of March, <u>pharmacies in Ontario</u> won't sell cigarettes any more.'

(c) *Correction with a non-referential SVO sentence.* In these sentences an impersonal subject was replaced by an indeterminate generic noun or pronoun Subject, *les gens* 'people' or *on* 'one'.

*Original:*
La France est le pays où <u>il</u> se consomme le plus de vin chaque année.
'France is the country where <u>there</u> consumes the most wine every year.'

*Correction:*
La France est le pays où <u>les gens/ l'on</u> consomme(nt) le plus de vin chaque année.
'France is the country where <u>people/one</u> consume(s) the most wine every year.'

(d) *Correction with a middle construction.* Here the original sentence structure was maintained, but the verb in the original was replaced by a synonym:

*Original*:
Les maisons préfabriquées <u>se bâtissent</u> rapidement par les charpentiers.
'Prefabricated houses <u>build</u> rapidly by carpenters.'

*Correction:*
Les maisons préfabriquées <u>se construisent</u> rapidement par les charpentiers.
'Prefabricated houses <u>construct</u> rapidly by carpenters.'

The monolinguals made a total of 152 corrections (range 5–71; median 23; mean 31 per sentence type; mean 11.7 per subject). Since the bilinguals judged more sentences to be ungrammatical, they made more corrections, a total of 201 (range 14–72; median 34; mean of 40.2 per sentence type; mean 16.75 per subject).

The frequencies and percentages of the different types of correction that participants made to sentences they considered ungrammatical are given in Table 9.2. 'Other' corrections were those using structures not included in the three major types: their number was small and the types of corrections varied. I will discuss them in more depth later in the chapter.

**Table 9.2** Corrections by sentence type by monolinguals and bilinguals

| Sentence Type | Group | Passive | | SVO | | Middle | | Other | | Total |
|---|---|---|---|---|---|---|---|---|---|---|
| | | *n* | *(%)* | *n* | *(%)* | *n* | *(%)* | *n* | *(%)* | *n* |
| No *se-moyen* | Monolingual | 9 | (13) | 0 | (0) | 62 | (87) | 0 | (0) | 71 |
| | Bilingual | 7 | (10) | 1 | (1) | 63 | (87.5) | 1 | (1) | 72 |
| No adverb of facility | Monolingual | 14 | (61) | 4 | (17) | 1 | (4) | 4 | (17) | 23 |
| | Bilingual | 28 | (82) | 1 | (3) | 0 | (0) | 5 | (15) | 34 |
| Impersonal Subject | Monolingual | 8 | (44) | 8 | (44) | 1 | (6) | 1 | (6) | 18 |
| | Bilingual | 19 | (58) | 13 | (39) | 0 | (0) | 1 | (3) | 33 |
| Unaffected | Monolingual | 0 | (0) | 2 | (40) | 2 | (40) | 1 | (20) | 5 |
| | Bilingual | 2 | (14) | 7 | (50) | 3 | (21) | 2 | (14) | 14 |
| *Par*-phrase | Monolingual | 26 | (68) | 8 | (21) | 1 | (3) | 3 | (8) | 38 |
| | Bilingual | 42 | (88) | 2 | (4) | 0 | (0) | 4 | (8) | 48 |
| TOTAL | Monolingual | 57 | (38) | 19 | (12) | 66 | (44) | 9 | (6) | 151 |
| | Bilingual | 98 | (49) | 23 | (11) | 66 | (33) | 14 | (7) | 201 |

The results are represented graphically in Figure 9.3. Of particular interest in this figure is the almost complete mirror image in the percentage of responses of two groups for corrections using passive and middle constructions, while the percentages of other types of corrections are almost exactly the same.

In their corrections bilinguals used the passive voice more frequently than did the monolinguals (49% and 38% respectively), while using middle

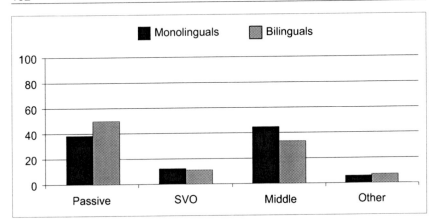

**Figure 9.3** Percentage of different types of correction by monolinguals and bilinguals

constructions less (33% and 44%, respectively). These differences are significant ($\chi^2$ = 12.03, 3 d.f., $p$ < 0.005). However, although the bilinguals used middle constructions in their corrections significantly less frequently than did the monolinguals, in their corrections of sentences with no *se-moyen* the responses of the two groups were almost exactly the same (87.5% of the bilinguals and 87% of the monolinguals used a middle construction to correct sentences with no *se-moyen*). Both groups used almost the same percentage of SVO constructions in their corrections (12% for the monolinguals, 11% for the bilinguals), although the monolinguals used almost the same number of referential and non-referential Subjects while the bilinguals preferred non-referential Subjects by a ratio of greater than 3 to 1. These differences are probably due to the types of sentences the two groups chose to correct and the ease with which non-referential Subjects could be used in the corrections. For example the bilinguals judged impersonal constructions to be ungrammatical more often than did the monolinguals, and corrected them frequently with non-referential Subjects, as was shown in (15c).

## Other corrections

Due to the fact that most sentences are grammatical according to the description of middle constructions given in Section 2, there were not always a large number of corrections, so the responses could not be analysed statistically. In (16) I have given examples of the types of 'Other' corrections.

(16) Other corrections

(a) *Correction with Se faire ('make') causative*

*Original:*
Les maisons préfabriquées <u>se bâtissent</u> rapidement par les charpentiers.
'Prefabricated houses <u>build</u> rapidly by carpenters.'

*Correction:*
Les maisons préfabriquées <u>se font bâtir</u> rapidement par les charpentiers.
'Prefabricated houses <u>make build</u> quickly by carpenters.'

(b) *Correction with Facile/difficile à + Infinitive ('Easy/hard to V')*

*Original:*
Ce genre de nourriture <u>se digère mal</u> par les malades.
'This kind of food <u>digests poorly</u> by invalids.'

*Correction:*
Ce genre de nourriture <u>est difficile à digérer</u> pour les malades.
'This kind of food is <u>hard to digest</u> for invalids.'

(c) *Correction with an adjective*

*Original:*
La tour Eiffel <u>se voit</u> clairement de la fenêtre de mon hôtel.
'The Eiffel Tower <u>sees</u> clearly from the window of my hotel.'

*Correction:*
La tour Eiffel <u>est très visible</u> de la fenêtre de mon hôtel.
'The Eiffel Tower <u>is very visible</u> from the window of my hotel.'

(d) *Correction with a synonymous verb with different argument structure*

*Original:*
L'argent brasilien <u>se dévalue</u> de semaine à semaine.
'Brazilian currency <u>devalues</u> from week to week.'

*Correction:*
L'argent brasilien <u>perd de la valeur</u> de semaine à semaine.
'Brazilian currency <u>loses value</u> from week to week.'

Table 9.3 shows that the bilinguals used the same range of resources as did the monolinguals in their corrections of sentences that they considered ungrammatical.

**Table 9.3** Number of 'Other' corrections by monolinguals and bilinguals

| *Type* | *Monolingual* | *Bilingual* |
|---|---|---|
| *Se faire* + **Infinitive** | 1 | 5 |
| *Facile/difficile à* + **Infinitive** | 1 | 2 |
| **Adjective** | 2 | 2 |
| **Synonymous verb with different argument structure** | 3 | 3 |
| **Other** | 2 | 1 |
| **TOTAL** | 9 | 13 |

## Discussion

### Judgements

The research question presented earlier is partly supported by the data, since bilinguals judged three types of grammatical sentences to be ungrammatical significantly more frequently than did the monolinguals: sentences with impersonal Subjects, sentences with *par*-phrases and sentences with unaffected grammatical Subjects. Since all these sentence types are ungrammatical in English, the results suggest that the bilinguals' knowledge of L2 English affected their judgements in L1 French, leading them to be more conservative in their judgements. They further show that the L2 has an influence on various aspects of the mental lexicon: functional categories (impersonal *il*), sub-categorisation frames (*par*-phrases) and semantic elements (affectedness).

However there were no significant differences between the groups in their judgements of (ungrammatical) sentences with no *se-moyen*, although it was expected that bilinguals would accept these more frequently, since the equivalent sentences are grammatical in English. In (17), I have repeated (7) here for the reader's convenience.

(17)  (a)  Les barbecues (*se)vendent bien pendant l'été.
     (b)  Barbecues sell well during the summer months.

Yet 96% of the time, the bilinguals judged French sentences such as (17) to be ungrammatical, and in 87.5% of their responses they corrected them by adding *se-moyen*. In Connors and Ouellette's (1994) study, Francophone bilinguals interpreted the clitic *se* in ambiguous sentences as reflexive and reciprocal rather than as *se-moyen* because of 'a bias in favour of (referential) argument readings' (p. 20). They concluded that subjects performed poorly because *se-moyen* is non-referential. However, despite its lack of argument status in middle constructions, and despite its non-occurrence in English, *se-moyen* is clearly a functional category with the appropriate features in the lexicons of the bilinguals in this study.

Moreover, there were no significant differences between the groups in their judgements of sentences with no adverb of facility, although if direct transfer from English were involved we would expect bilinguals to reject sentences such as (8a) – which I have repeated as (18) – more frequently than monolinguals, because middles in English typically require an adverb of facility.

(18)  (a)  Un tricot de laine se lave à l'eau froide.
      (b)  *A wool sweater washes in cold water.

However, this was not the case; nor did bilinguals correct such sentences they judged ungrammatical by adding an adverbial of facility (*A wool sweater washes easily/well in cold water*). This suggests that the obligatoriness of an adverbial in English middle constructions has not been transferred to the lexical entry for verbs undergoing middle formation in French. The results of the judgement task show, therefore, that there is L2 influence on the L1, but that it is not across the board.

The monolinguals had more 'Not sure' responses than the bilinguals (7% and 1% respectively). This is somewhat surprising, since research has shown that a similar population (Francophone secondary-school graduates from south-eastern New Brunswick, in a minority situation) manifested greater linguistic insecurity in both a questionnaire and an oral interview than did their peers from regions of the province where Francophones are in the majority (Boudreau & Dubois, 1992, 1993). The lack of linguistic insecurity of the bilinguals in this study may be due to the nature of the task, a change in attitudes during the six-year period between the two studies, or the fact that all participants in this study were French-dominant.

### Corrections

In their corrections to sentences they judged as ungrammatical, the bilinguals used significantly more passives than did the monolinguals, which can again be attributed to influence from L2 English. Delisle (1993) noted that the passive is used in both English and French, but it is considerably more frequent in English. Over-use of the passive is therefore common when translating the passive from English into French, and translators have to be trained to resist this natural tendency (Delisle, 1993; Spilka, 1979; Vinay & Darbelnet, 1995). This is not surprising since in the translation tasks both languages must be fully activated and translators are in bilingual mode. However, the bilinguals in this study were in monolingual mode throughout the experiment: they were on campus at a Francophone university, the research assistant spoke to them exclusively in French, and the instructions and task were in French. It can be assumed that only the L1 would be highly activated in such an environment, although the L2 would be on standby. The bilinguals' corrections are thus not due to real-time interference from the L2: the passive is grammatical in French, but it is not as frequent as it is in English. Its frequency in English has altered the mentally represented grammars of the bilinguals, leading them to use passives rather than the other means that French has for suppressing the Agent (that is, *se-moyen*).

The other types of corrections indicate that the bilinguals are able to use a range of linguistic resources to express different aspects of middle constructions. Within P & P theory and the MP, grammatical constructions no longer exist per se: they are now viewed as artifacts of the interaction of principles of Universal Grammar (UG) with parameters set at a particular value (Chomsky, 1995: 170). In MP terms, it can be said that the bilinguals and the monolinguals in this study possess the same types of lexical items: (1) synonymous verbs with or without the same argument structure as shown in (15d) and (16d); (2) non-referential Subjects such as *on* 'one' and *les gens* 'people'; (3) adjectives and their subcategorisation frames; (4) *se faire* 'make' causatives; and (5) *facile à* 'easy to' constructions. These interact with the principles of UG to produce the same diversity in terms of alternate means of paraphrasing sentences containing middle constructions. The functional category of *se-moyen* is robust, and even though bilinguals accept expletive *il* in impersonal constructions less readily than monolinguals do, it is clearly a functional category in their mental lexicons.

### General discussion and conclusion

The bilingual participants in this study are in a minority language situation (Boudreau & Dubois, 1992, 1993). In such a situation, bilingualism is often seen as negative: the L2 somehow takes away from the linguistic resources in the L1 ('subtractive bilingualism' Weinreich, 1968). Seliger (1996: 605) defined language attrition as: 'The loss of aspects of a previously fully acquired primary language resulting from the acquisition of another language', and suggested that attrition can be reflected in grammaticality judgements that differ from those of monolingual native speakers. One way in which Seliger suggests that their judgements differ is that they would 'correct' grammatical sentences. The bilinguals in this study clearly have different judgements of grammaticality than the monolinguals have: they were less likely to judge sentences as grammatical and, since they judged the sentences to be ungrammatical, they corrected more sentences. Furthermore, they used more passives and fewer middle constructions in their corrections. However, there is other evidence which suggests that, although their judgements are different, they have not lost anything in the L1. First of all, they were much more certain of their judgements than the monolinguals, who gave significantly more 'not sure' responses. Second, in their corrections the bilinguals used the same linguistic resources as the monolingual native speakers did.

These differences may be due to the environment in which the L1 and L2 are used: in many studies of language attrition the attriters have immigrated to a new country and use the L1 in limited situations. The participants in the present study, although in a linguistic minority situation and fluently bilingual, still use the L1 more than the L2. The divergence from previous work in attrition may also be due to the area of the grammar – lexico-syntactic rules and representations rather than type/token ratios of content words in production.

In an article that examined regional variation in North American French, Roberge and Rosen made the following observation:

> Our claim is that in a contact situation it is possible that *que*-deletion ... has been reinterpreted in some NAF [North American French] varieties as an indication that prepositions are obligatory case-assigners thereby allowing for the emergence of English-type stranded prepositions. In this sense, NAF has not 'borrowed' the construction. Instead, contact with English may have stirred the change in a direction not attested across-the-board in Popular French. (Roberge & Rosen, 1999: 165)

Although more research is necessary before strong conclusions can be drawn, the present study suggests that a similar phenomenon is taking place with passives in the French of the bilingual participants in this study. In a contact situation with English, the L1 grammars of individuals are 'stirred' in a certain direction (more use of passives) under the influence of the L2. In the future this increased use of the passive may spread to monolingual speakers. Interestingly, a similar phenomenon occurred in Chinese. According to Norman (1988: 165), in the past, the *bei* passive was 'for the most part restricted to verbs of an unfavourable meaning or to verbs denoting disposal or separation'. However, in modern written Chinese it is much more frequent, owing to the influence of translations from Russian and English.

These results support Cook's (1992: 580) suggestion that with bilinguals there is a 'mutual interaction' between their knowledge of L1 and L2, and that multi-competence is a 'distinct state of mind' (Cook, 1992: 585).

However, this mutual interaction between the two mentally represented grammars does not take away from the L1: although the linguistic competence of the bilinguals in this study diverges from that of the monolinguals, they are not 'losers' or 'attriters'. Their mentally represented grammars are different, but they are not deficient.

## Acknowledgements

This study was supported by research grant #004109 from the Faculté des Études supérieures et de la recherche, Université de Moncton, for which I am grateful. I would like to thank my research assistants Gilles Cormier and Vanessa Michalik for their help in executing this study. *Un gros merci* to my colleagues Annette Boudreau, Lise Dubois and Mathieu LeBlanc for sharing with me a questionnaire regarding language use and materials regarding translating the passive from English to French. I would like also to thank Marcel Guisset and Rick Hudson for providing access to Anglophone participants. And finally, many thanks for their questions and comments to the participants at the Workshop on the Effects of the L2 on the L1 held at Wivenhoe House, University of Essex.

## Appendix 1: Language use questionnaire

Please note that Francophone participants were given this questionnaire in French, but what follows is the English questionnaire (which was translated from the French one) for those readers who do not read French. Questions 1 to 12 asked for general information about age, sex, language background, etc, which is in The Participants section of this chapter.

*Circle the response which most closely reflects your language use*

13. When I am at home, I speak French:

    never        seldom        about half the time        usually        always

14. When I am at home, I speak English:

    never        seldom        about half the time        usually        always

15. When I am with my family, I speak French:

    never        seldom        about half the time        usually        always

16. When I am with my family, I speak English:

    never        seldom        about half the time        usually        always

17. During social, cultural or sports activities, I use French:

    never        seldom        about half the time        usually        always

18. During social, cultural or sports activities, I use English:
    never     seldom     about half the time     usually     always

19. When I express my personal feelings, I use French:
    never     seldom     about half the time     usually     always

20. When I express my personal feelings, I use English:
    never     seldom     about half the time     usually     always

21. When I assemble an item I have bought, I read the instructions in French:
    never     seldom     about half the time     usually     always

22. When I assemble an item I have bought, I read the instructions in English:
    never     seldom     about half the time     usually     always

23. When I am shopping, I speak to the salespeople in French:
    never     seldom     about half the time     usually     always

24. When I am shopping, I speak to the salespeople in English:
    never     seldom     about half the time     usually     always

## References

Alexiadou, A. and Anagnostopoulou, E. (2001) The subject-in-situ generalization and the role of Case in driving computations. *Linguistic Inquiry* 32, 193–231.

Arcay-Hands, E. (1998) Written academic texts: A multidimensional analysis of students' essays. Paper read at the 29th Annual Conference of the Canadian Association of Applied Linguistics, Trends in Second Language Teaching and Learning, Carleton University, Ottawa.

Authier, J-M. and Reed, L. (1996) Un analyse microparamétrique des moyens dans les langues romanes. In J.R. Black and V. Motapanyane (eds) *Micro-parametric Syntax and Dialect Variation* (pp. 1–23). Amsterdam: John Benjamins.

Balcom, P. (1995) Argument structure and multi-competence. *Linguistica atlantica* 17, 1–18.

Balcom, P. (1999) These constructions don't acquire easily: Middle constructions and multi-competence. *Canadian Journal of Applied Linguistics* 2, 5–20.

Belletti, A. (1982) Morphology, passive and pro-drop: The impersonal construction in Italian. *Journal of Linguistic Research* 2, 1–34.

Bhatia, T.K. and Ritchie, W.C. (1996) Bilingual language mixing, universal grammar, and second language acquisition. In W.C. Ritchie and T.K. Bhatia (eds) *Handbook of Second Language Acquisition* (pp. 627–688). San Diego: Academic Press.

Birdsong, D. (1989) *Metalinguistic Performance and Interlinguistic Competence*. Berlin: Springer.

Birdsong, D. (1992) Ultimate attainment in second language acquisition. *Language* 68, 706–55.

Blanc, M. (1993) French in Canada. In C. Sanders (ed.) *French Today: Language in its Social Context* (pp. 239–256). Cambridge: Cambridge University Press.

Boudreau, A. and Dubois, L. (1992) Insécurité linguistique et diglossie: Étude comparative de deux régions de l'Acadie du Nouveau-Brunswick. *Revue de l'Université de Moncton* 25, 3–22.

Boudreau, A. and Dubois, L. (1993) Je parle pas comme les Français de France ben c'est du français pareil. J'ai ma own petite langue. In M. Francard (ed.) *L'insécurité linguistique dans les communautées francophones périphériques* (pp. 147–168). Louvain-La-Neuve: Cahiers de l'Institut de Linguistique de Louvain, 19.

Bruhn de Garavito, J. (1999) The syntax of Spanish multifunctional clitics and near-native competence. PhD thesis, McGill University, Montréal.

Castonguay, C. (1998) The fading Canadian duality. In J. Edwards (ed.) *Language in Canada* (pp. 36–60). Cambridge: Cambridge University Press.

Chomsky, N. (1981) *Lectures on Government and Binding*. Dordrecht: Foris.

Chomsky, N. (1986) *Knowledge of Language: Its Nature, Origin and Use*. New York: Praeger.

Chomsky, N. (1995) *The Minimalist Program*. Cambridge, MA: MIT Press.

Chomsky, N. (2000) Minimalist inquiries: The framework. In R. Martin, D. Michaels, and J. Uriagereka (eds) *Step by Step: Essays on Minimalist Syntax in Honor of Howard Lasnik* (pp. 89–155). Cambridge, MA: MIT Press.

Chomsky, N. and Lasnik, H. (1993) The theory of principles and parameters. In J. Jacobs, A. von Stechow, W. Sternefeld and T. Vennemann (eds) *Syntax: An International Handbook of Contemporary Research* (pp. 506–568). Berlin: de Gruyter.

Connors, K. and Ouellette, B. (1993) Meaning and grammaticality in the awareness of native speakers and advanced learners. Paper read at the 10th AILA World Congress, Amsterdam.

Connors, K. and Ouellette, B. (1994) The meanings of pronominal-verbal constructions for speakers and learners of French. *Linguistica Atlantica* 16, 1–24.

Cook, V.J. (1991) The poverty of the stimulus argument and multi-competence. *Second Language Research* 7, 103–17.

Cook, V.J. (1992) Evidence for multi-competence. *Language Learning* 42, 557–91.

Cook, V.J. (1993) Wholistic multi-competence: Jeu d'esprit or paradigm shift? In B. Kettemann and W. Wieden (eds) *Current Issues in European Second Language Acquisition* (pp. 3–8). Tubingen: Gunter Narr Verlag.

Delisle, J. (1993) *La traduction raisonée*. Ottawa: Les presses de l'Université d'Ottawa.

Dulay, H. and Burt, M. (1975). Creative construction in second language learning. In M. Burt and H. Dulay (eds) *New Directions in Second Language Learning, Teaching, and Bilingual Education* (pp. 21–32). Washington, DC: TESOL.

Dulay, H., Burt, M. and Krashen, S. (1982) *Language Two*. Oxford: Oxford University Press.

Fagan, S. (1992) *The Syntax and Semantics of Middle Constructions*. Cambridge: Cambridge University Press.

Fellbaum, C. and Zribi-Hertz, A. (1989) *The Middle Construction in French and English: A Comparative Study of its Syntax and Semantics*. Bloomington, IN: Indiana University Linguistics Club.

Gass, S. (1996) Second language acquisition and linguistic theory: The role of language transfer. In W.C. Ritchie and T.K. Bhatia (eds) *Handbook of Second Language Acquisition* (pp. 317–348). San Diego: Academic Press.

Gass, S. and Selinker, L. (eds) (1994) *Language Transfer in Language Learning* (rev. edn). Amsterdam: John Benjamins.

Grosjean, F. (1982) *Life with Two Languages. An Introduction to Bilingualism.* Cambridge, MA: Harvard University Press.

Hawkins, R. (2001) *Second Language Syntax: A Generative Introduction.* Oxford: Blackwell.

Herschensohn, J. (2000) *The Second Time Around: Minimalism and L2 Acquisition.* Amsterdam: John Benjamins.

Jackendoff, R. (1987) The status of thematic relations in linguistic theory. *Linguistic Inquiry* 18, 369–411.

Jackendoff, R. (1990) *Semantic Structures.* Cambridge, MA: MIT Press.

Jarvis, S. (2000) Methodological rigor in the study of transfer: Identifying L1 influence in the interlanguage lexicon. *Language Learning* 50, 245–309.

Juffs, A. (1996) *Learnability and the Lexicon.* Amsterdam: John Benjamins.

Kecskes, I. (1998) The state of L1 knowledge in foreign language learners. *Word* 49, 321–340.

Kellerman, E. (1995) Crosslinguistic influence: Transfer to nowhere? *Annual Review of Applied Linguistics* 15, 125–150.

Kellerman, E. and Sharwood-Smith, M. (eds) (1986) *Cross-linguistic Influence in Second Language Acquisition.* Oxford: Pergamon Press.

Kemmer, S. (1993) *The Middle Voice.* Amsterdam: John Benjamins.

Klein, E.C. (1995) Second versus third language acquisition: Is there a difference? *Language Learning* 45, 419–465.

Lado, R. (1957) *Linguistics across Cultures: Applied Linguistics for Language Teachers.* Ann Arbor: University of Michigan Press.

Levin, B. and Rappaport Hovav, M. (1995). *Unaccusativity: At the Syntax-Lexical Semantics Interface.* Cambridge, MA: MIT Press.

Ministère de l'Éducation, Nouveau-Brunswick (1992) *Anglais Langue Seconde: Programme d'Études Voie B.* Fredericton, N-B: Ministère de l'Éducation.

MacSwan, J. (2000) The architecture of the bilingual language faculty: Evidence from intrasentential code switching. *Bilingualism: Language and Cognition* 3, 37–54.

Norman, J. (1988) *Chinese.* Cambridge: Cambridge University Press.

Pavlenko, A. (2000) New approaches to concepts in bilingual memory. *Bilingualism: Language and Cognition* 3, 1–5.

Pinker, S. (1989) *Learnability and Cognition: The Acquisition of Argument Structure.* Cambridge, MA: MIT Press.

Ritchie, W.C. and Bhatia, T.K. (eds) (1996) *Handbook of Second Language Acquisition.* San Diego: Academic Press.

Roberge, Y. and Rosen, N. (1999) Preposition stranding and QUE-deletion in North American French. *Linguistica Atlantica* 21, 153–168.

Romaine, S. (1995) *Bilingualism* (2nd edn). Oxford: Blackwell.

Satterfield, T. (1999) *Bilingual Selection of Syntactic Knowledge: Extending the Principles and Parameters Approach.* Dordrecht: Kluwer Academic.

Seliger, H. (1996) Primary language attrition in the context of bilingualism. In W.C. Ritchie and T.K. Bhatia (eds) *Handbook of Second Language Acquisition* (pp. 605–626). San Diego: Academic Press.

Spilka, I. (1979) La traduction du passif anglais en français. *Meta* 24 (2), 240–252.

Statistics Canada (2001). *1996 Census, Nation Tables: Mother Tongue.* On-line document: http://www.statscan.ca.

Vinay, J-P. and Darbelnet, J. (1995) *Comparative Stylistics of English and French.* Amsterdam: John Benjamins.

Vinet, M-T. (1987) Implicit arguments and control in middles and passives. In D. Birdsong and J-P. Montreuil (eds) *Advances in Romance Linguistics* (pp. 427–437). Dordrecht: Foris.

Wang, C. (1995) Semantic structure theory and L2 learning of English adjectival participles. In D. MacLaughlin and S. McEwan (eds) *Proceedings of the 19th Annual Boston University Conference on Language Development (BUCLD) Vol. 2* (pp. 655–666). Somerville, MA: Cascadilla Press.

Weinreich, U. (1968) *Languages in Contact*. The Hague: Mouton.

White, L. (1994) Universal grammar: Is it just a new name for old problems? In S.M. Gass and L. Selinker (eds) *Language Transfer in Language Learning* (rev. edn) (pp. 217–232). Amsterdam: John Benjamins.

White, L. (1996) The tale of the ugly duckling (or the coming of age of second language acquisition research). In A. Stringfellow, D. Cahana-Amitay, E. Hughes and A. Zukowski (eds) *Proceedings of the 20th Annual Boston University Conference on Language Development (BUCLD) Vol. 1* (pp. 1–17). Somerville, MA: Cascadilla Press.

Zobl, H. (1994) Grammaticality intuitions of monolingual and multilingual non-primary language learners. In S.M. Gass and L. Selinker (eds) *Language Transfer in Language Learning* (rev. edn) (pp. 176–192). Amsterdam: John Benjamins.

## Chapter 10

# Effects of the L2 on the Syntactic Processing of the L1

VIVIAN COOK, ELISABET IAROSSI, NEKTARIOS STELLAKIS AND
YUKI TOKUMARU

## Introduction

Not only second language acquisition researchers but also linguists
have tended to treat the monolingual native speaker as the norm and to see
the L2 user as an approximation to a native speaker. In this view the first
language of someone who speaks a second language holds no particular
interest. However, in the multi-competence view, at some level the
languages form a complex single system in one mind, of which the first
language forms part (Cook, 2002). Until this volume, the effects of the
second language on the first language have rarely been documented. The
two exceptions are Kecskes (1998) who found a beneficial effect on the
development and use of mother tongue skills with regard to structural
well-formedness in Hungarian students of modern languages, and Balcom
(1995) who found different acceptability judgements of French passive
sentences in Francophone speakers who did or did not know English.

This chapter adds to these studies by approaching syntactic processing
through the Competition Model research paradigm concerning how
people assign the subject to the sentence (Bates & MacWhinney, 1981). The
question is whether the L2 users' processing of L1 syntax differs from that
of monolingual speakers in some respect. The litmus test is whether there
are differences in the first language of monolinguals and of L2 users who
know another language.

## The Competition Model Research Paradigm

In the Competition Model (Bates & MacWhinney, 1981), sentence
processing depends on the weight given to competing factors in a particular language. The standard example is deciding which noun is the subject
of the sentence. This depends on the varying balance between cues in

different languages. *Mr Bean* is the subject in *Mr Bean loves Teddy*, mainly because it comes before the verb *loves* and the object *Teddy*: word order is the main cue in English. But *Mr Bean* is not only first in the sentence but is also animate, nominative and in agreement with the verb, all of which in other languages are more vital cues than word order.

Hence the standard experimental task used in the Competition Model systematically varies the cues for the subject of the sentence. The subjects are presented with sentences with a range of possible cues, unnatural as some may seem in a particular language, so that the weighting for the cues can be established. An English person has, say, to choose between word order and agreement in deciding the subjects of *The Teddies loves Mr Bean* or *Mr Bean love the Teddies*.

Among the cues whose weighting varies between languages are:

*Word order:* The subject has to occur in a definite position in the sentence, say first in SVO (Subject-Verb-Object) languages such as English or second in VSO languages such as Arabic. Thus speakers of English identify *people* as the subject of *People like Jaffa-cakes* because it is the first N. (Though the subjects of test sentences are often phrases rather than words, in this research paradigm they are referred to as N rather than NP, the usage to be followed here.)

*Animacy:* The subject has to be animate rather than inanimate. So in a sentence such as *Jaffa-cakes like people*, speakers of languages with strong animacy cues (such as Japanese or Italian), prefer the animate second N *people* as the subject in their equivalent L1 sentences.

*Case:* The subject has to be in the subjective (nominative) case, as in *Amor vincit omnia* where *Amor* is in the Latin subjective case. In languages with strong case cues, speakers choose the second N *Jaffa-cakes* in a sentence such as *John likes Jaffa-cakes* (subjective), thus overriding the order and agreement cues. English uses case minimally for deciding the subject with regard to pronouns *I/me, they/them,* etc.

*Agreement:* The subject may agree with the Verb in number, whether plural or singular, *John likes Jaffa-cakes* versus *John and Mary like Jaffa-cakes*, or in gender. Languages where the agreement cue is very strong treat *Jaffa-cakes likes John* as having the subject *John*.

As the examples show, finding the subject of the sentence is not a matter of either/or but of the relative strength of particular cues. While English may be dominated by word order, there are still enough traces of agreement and of case to enable us to identify the subjects in *Where the bee sucks there suck I* or *In my beginning is my end*.

## The Competition Model and the L2 User

With few exceptions, L2 research in the Competition Model has looked at the extent to which the L2 weightings for the subject cues carry over those from the first language. Harrington (1987) established that Japanese L2 users of English had gone some way to adopting the English reliance on word order in Noun-Verb-Noun (NVN) English sentences, but not in VNN or NNV sentences, and, though prepared to allow inanimate subjects to some extent, they still preferred animate subjects as much in English as in Japanese. Hence their processing of the L2 English has moved some way towards the weightings of the language in question but is still heavily influenced by their L1 Japanese. Kilborn and Cooreman (1987) looked at the processing of L2 English by Dutch L1 speakers and found a lesser reliance on word order and a greater reliance on agreement than for native English speakers. Other research has shown the importance of animacy for English and Turkish learners of Dutch (Issidorides & Hulstjin, 1992) and of morphology for Dutch learners of English (McDonald, 1987).

Research with effects of the second language on the first language is less extensive. Liu, Bates and Li (1992) found some 'backward' transfer in Chinese speakers learning English in the United States, affected non-monotonically by age (effects for under-4s and 12–16 year olds but not for 6–10 year olds and late bilinguals) and by family use. Su (2001) found that advanced Chinese learners of English used the same strategies in both languages. Their Chinese processes were influenced by English, though this was not true of lower-level learners, nor of English speakers learning Chinese, summed up as 'There was little evidence indicating that the learners' knowledge of the second language was influencing their processing of the first language, except in the advanced subjects' (Su, 2001: 106).

The Competition Model technique thus provides a clear-cut way of measuring differences between L2 users and monolinguals across languages that is neutral about direction of transfer between first language and second language (Su, 2001) as it involves a unitary model of mind close to connectionism (MacWhinney, 1997). The research here was not conceived as a contribution to the Competition Model itself so much as a use of the technique as a tool to test for differences in the L1 between monolinguals and L2 users. The Competition Model paradigm is useful because it applies cross-linguistically, uses a relatively simple design with clear-cut data, and has been tried across several first and second languages.

## The Common Core to the Experiment

The aim was to run a version of the classic Competition Model experiment (Bates & MacWhinney, 1981) in a range of languages, using the same instructions and equivalent materials. Two groups of people would be tested in each language; one would have English as a second language, the other would not. The hypothesis is that the L2 users would be influenced by the cues of the second language in the processing of their first language. The languages to which easy access could be obtained were Japanese, Spanish, Greek and English, each spoken as first languages by one of the present writers.

English was kept as the sole second language to control one possible variable: it would be difficult to compare, say, the results of learning Spanish as a second language for Japanese speakers with learning Russian as a second language for French speakers. Because of the international nature of English, it was hard to find people with zero English. Furthermore, the differing goals and success of English teaching in different countries meant that it was hard to establish whether all the subjects had the same level of English proficiency. Hence the decision was made to standardise the 'minus L2 factor' as minimal rather than zero English and the 'plus L2 factor' as students of English at university level. Indeed, given the high proportion of people in the world who use more than one language, much research now finds it difficult to get 'pure' monolinguals and has to be content with 'minimal bilinguals'.

## Relevant Characteristics of the Four Languages

### Japanese

*Word order/sentence structure*

While Japanese word order is typically SOV, sentences are quite flexible; order depends more on the context than on the fixed structure itself (Nakajima, 1987).

*Animacy*

Animate subjects are preferred as 'action doers'. However Japanese tends to prefer a *static* description of a certain situation or fact, rather than using a *dynamic* structure of a subject as the action-doer followed by the action-verb as in English (Nakajima, 1987).

*Case*

Japanese nouns do not inflect for case. There is nevertheless a system of case particles that mark particular functions. Two main particles, *ga* and *wa*, which follow the subject N (as postpositions), mark 'subjective case'. While *ga* introduces new/unknown information:

> Neko-*ga* nezumi-*wo* oikakeru.
> 'It's cats (not other animals) who chase mice.'
> cats (new inf.) mice (obj) chase (V)

*wa* marks the topic of the sentence:

> Neko-*wa* nezumi-*wo* oikakeru.
> 'As for cats, (they) chase mice.'
> cats (topic) mice (obj) chase (V)

*Agreement*

Japanese nouns are not inflected for number, but have a complex system of classifiers. Verbs are marked with the inflection -*u* in all persons of the present tense. Hence there is no agreement system for number.

## Spanish

*Word order*

According to Comrie (1987: 253), Spanish has free or relatively free word order. In everyday language, object and complement always come after the verb in affirmative sentences:

> Pedro compró un regalo.
> 'Peter bought a present.'

but VO/SVC order is preferred when the subject is a single proper noun or a short phrase. In formal registers VSO order is used with very long phrases, which follow the verb:

> Ahora han llegado todos los pasajeros que viajaron con la Compañía X.
> 'All the passengers travelling with Company X have now arrived' (Comrie, 1987: 254).

VS order is adopted for most subordinate clauses:

> No presté atención a lo que estabas haciendo.
> 'I didn't pay attention to what you were doing.'

VS order also appears in existentials:

> Viven gitanos en las cuevas.
> 'There are gypsies living in the caves.'

and it is used in questions that start with an interrogative word:

¿Qué estaba haciendo? .
'What were you doing?'

### Animacy

Animacy is involved in the selection of prepositions to mark direct objects, as we see below.

### Case

According to Zamora (1999: 1), Spanish uses the preposition *a* ('to') to mark personal or affective direct objects, as in *querer a una persona* ('to love a person') and *querer a un gato* ('to love a cat'). It also uses *a* ('to') for direct object, as in *dar algo a alguien* ('to give something to somebody'). Full subject NPs are not themselves marked for case.

### Agreement

Spanish marks number and gender on all modifiers within the noun phrase, and has concord of number and person (and occasionally gender) between the subject and verb (Comrie, 1987: 255). The verbal inflections show agreement through person and number: *comemos* ('we ate') presupposes a first person plural subject. Only when this is ambiguous does the position of the NP before the verb determine this function. For instance,

Los poblamientos humanos destruyen los bosques.
'Human settlements destroy forests.'

would change subject from the reverse order:

Los bosques destruyen los poblamientos humanos.
'The forests destroy human settlements.'

## Greek

### Word order

While the typical Greek word order is SVO, other combinations are acceptable. For example as well as:

O Petros agorase ena doro
'Peter bought a present.'

one could also say:

Ena doro agorase o Petros.
'A present bought Peter.'

or:

Agorase ena doro o Petros.
'Bought a present Peter.'

or:

Agorase o Petros ena doro.
'Bought Peter a present.'

Greek word order is thus flexible, though the dominant word order is SVO.

*Animacy*

Both animate and inanimate subjects are acceptable, without restriction.

*Case*

Nouns are inflected for gender, number and case. The subject takes subjective case and the object takes accusative case. For example the ending -*os* in *Petros* shows that the word is masculine, singular and in the subjective case.

Number agreement: Greek verbs are inflected in all persons. The verb agrees with the subject in both number and person. For example the verb ending -ω (omega) presupposes a first person singular subject.

## English

*Word order*

English is an SVO language with the subject almost always coming first in the declarative sentence.

*Animacy*

Whether the Noun is animate or inanimate is not relevant in English to the choice of the subject.

*Case*

The only vestigial aspects of surface case in English that are relevant are the difference between the subjective and objective forms of pronouns, for example

They despise them.

*Number agreement.*

Only present tense verbs and auxiliaries have subject-agreement for number in English:

'He likes beer' vs. 'They like beer.'

Apart from English, all the languages involved in this experiment are pro-drop, that is to say they allow sentences with null subjects. So a sentence such as *Speaks* would be grammatical in all of them except English. This has implications for the research methodology, since test sentences with pronouns present would be marked in these languages.

If the second language has an effect on the first language, people with two languages should use different cues in deciding the subject from those used by people with one language. The prediction is therefore that the strength of cues in L2 users will be influenced by the strength in English. We might expect, then, the dominance of word order in English to affect the case, animacy and agreement cues utilised in the other languages, though other unanticipated differences may emerge.

## Common Design and Materials

### Factors and sample sentences

All the 81 sentences in the materials consisted of three elements, two Noun Phrases (Ns) and a Verb (V). The vocabulary was selected from the set in Harrington (1987) and consisted of nine Verbs (such as *greet*), six Inanimate Nouns (such as *spoon*) and ten Animate Nouns (such as *pig*). The sentences were translated into each language using translation equivalents for these items (problems to be noted below).

Because of the differing combinations, the number of sentences for each type varied slightly and will be indicated below. Using the English version of the test sentences as the starting point, the separate factors tested were:

*Word order*

Three word orders were tested:

(a) NVN: The dog pats the tree.
(b) VNN: Watches the monkey the pen.
(c) NNV: The horse the rock kisses.

The test sentences in the other languages are direct translations of these; in Japanese no singular inflection is required for the verb.

*Animacy*

Keeping to the NVN order for illustration, three possibilities for animacy were tested varying the combinations of animate and inanimate Ns:

(a) N1 (animate)/V/N2 (inanimate): The bears kiss the tree.
(b) N1 (inanimate)/V/N2 (animate): The pencil smells the giraffe.
(c) N1 (animate)/V/N2 (animate): The dog pats the donkey.

*Case*

Since English NPs do not have full surface case, the specification of Subjective case is indicated in brackets, keeping to the SVO and Animate/ Animate examples. Where possible only the Subjective case was marked, not the Objective, to avoid providing double cues to the subject.

(a) N1(Subj): The cow (Subj) pats the monkey.
(b) N2(Subj): The dog eats the donkey (Subj).

To get parallel sentences in Spanish it was necessary to include a prepositional particle as in *A la tortuga la yegua saluda*, as we see below. To avoid the issue of null subject pronouns and the marked nature of subject pronouns in some languages, full NPs rather than pronouns were necessary throughout.

*Number (agreement)*

Using SVO and Animate Noun examples for English, the types of sentence were:

(a) N1(singular)/V/N2(plural): The turtle smells the bears.
(b) N1(plural)/V/N2(singular): The dogs bites the monkey.

The verb in (a) therefore agreed with N1, the verb in (b) with N2.

*Language-specific factors*

The main differences from the classic Competition Model paradigm were necessitated by the cross-lingual application of the instrument. Rather than each set of sentences being uniquely generated for each subject, they were decided in advance, since random collocations of vocabulary that work in English were unlikely to be successful across languages. Certain adaptations had to be made to make the experiment work in each language. The starting point was to attempt direct translations of the English sentences and then to make the minimal adjustments necessitated by the language in question.

## Japanese

*Case*

Case particles are not included unless specified in the test condition, since information is retrievable from the context and NPs without particles are common in speech. When the subject case was called for, *wa* and *ga* were used as subject markers as appropriate.

*Agreement*

Plural nouns are indicated by adding *tachi*, but there is no inflectional agreement with the verb.

## Spanish

*Gender*

Since all NPs in Spanish are marked for gender, translating the sentences exactly into Spanish would give undesired gender cues. Nouns had to be substituted in several sentences so that the same gender was used in both Ns in the sentence. For example:

> Smells the pencil the giraffes.
> 'Huele la lapicera ('pen') las jirafas.'

As there is no masculine Spanish translation for *giraffes*, the word for *pencil* was changed to the similar word for *pen*, which has feminine gender

*Object marking with prepositions*

Spanish transitive verbs may be followed by more than one objective complement (Gili Gaya, 1961: 208). They are followed by a direct object when they have only one complement, for example:

> (a) Juan vio a María.
>     'John saw Mary.'

and

> (b) Juan compró una rosa.
>     'John bought a rose.'

In (a) the direct object is preceded by the preposition *a* ('to') because direct objects in Spanish are preceded by the preposition *a* when animate, but not when inanimate as in (b). Conversely, we may speak about 'indirect objects' when transitive verbs are followed by two objective complements, for example:

> El mozo trajo la cuenta a su cliente.
> 'The waiter brought the bill to his customer.'

In this instance, the same rules apply to the indirect object.

If the prepositions were omitted from the Spanish sentences, the problems would be:

(1)   subjects might be reversed thus altering the original order in the English master sentences;
(2)   sentence ungrammaticality would lead to ambiguity;

thus drastically altering the original experimental design. Prepositions were therefore added before Objects, as in the following Spanish sentences, prepositions underlined.

<u>A</u> las jirafas muerde la osa.
'The giraffes bites the bear.'

Saludan los perros <u>al</u> caballo.
'Greet the dogs the horse.'

Mira <u>a</u> los tortugos el cigarrillo.
'Watches the turtle the cigarette.'

Additionally the Spanish verb *tirar* ('pull') must be followed by the preposition *de* ('de'), for example:

Tira de la cerda la vaca.
'Pulls the pig the cow.'

## Greek

### Gender

Neuter nouns were used where possible to avoid any obviously inflected words, since in neuter nouns the subjective and accusative endings are the same. In many cases a word with a gender different from the direct translation equivalent was used to preserve the same gender and number in both Ns. For example in the sentence:

Smells the pencil the giraffes.

since the Greek word for *giraffe* is feminine, *pencil* (neutral) was changed to a similar feminine word *pena* (pen). In other cases we adopted a free translation for one of the two nouns in the sentence. For example the sentence:

The ball the donkeys watches.

became:

To topi ta gaidouria parakolouthi.

because the neuter word *to topi* ('the ball') keeps the gender constant.

## Subjects

The subjects were adults over 18 years old belonging either to a 'monolingual' non-university group with little English or to a 'bilingual' university group studying English in the respective countries (Japan, Greece and

Argentina) numbering 24 Japanese bilinguals, 21 Japanese monolinguals, 20 Spanish bilinguals, 20 Spanish monolinguals, 26 Greek monolinguals and 51 Greek bilinguals.

## Prediction

The overall prediction is then that in their first language bilinguals will use cues differently from monolinguals. While this may mean simply adopting a weighting that is closer to the second language (English), the difference may manifest itself in other ways. The differences between languages are interesting in themselves, but are not the point of the present experiment, which is concerned only with monolinguals versus bilinguals.

## Method

Subjects in each group were instructed to read the sentences to indicate which of the two Ns was the subject, i.e. the doer of the action:

> You have to say which one of the two nouns in each sentence is the subject, that is to say which one does the action. The subject must be one of the two nouns that are actually in the sentence.

This was translated into the three other languages. The latter part of the instruction was necessitated by the pro-drop nature of the first languages; both nouns in the sentence could otherwise be treated as objects with an unexpressed subject. The subjects were told not to worry if the sentences seemed odd. They were also told to concentrate on the task and not to talk to their companions. The subjects were tested in groups in a quiet classroom environment.

## Results

Throughout, the results compare the performance of the 'monolingual' and 'bilingual' groups of subjects for each language in terms of the percentage of responses choosing the first N rather than the second N as subject, as is standard in the Competition Model paradigm. That is to say, a score of 75% means that the N1 was chosen rather than the N2 for 75% of the relevant sentences. Whether the response is appropriate depends on the specific language involved and on the cue being tested. The results are also presented in all the graphs in terms of the three word orders from left to right (NVN, VNN, NNV) again as standard in this paradigm. The groups will be referred to as bilinguals and monolinguals for convenience, though as defined above they were strictly speaking maximal and minimal bilinguals. For reasons of space only a selection of the results will be presented here.

## Word order

The sentence types testing the three word-order variants were illustrated by the English master sentences:

(a) NVN: The dog pats the tree.
(b) VNN: Watches the monkey the pen.
(c) NNV: The horse the rock kisses.

Three sentences were tested for each word order, all with singular N1 and N2. Agreement provided no cue, since both Ns were singular; animacy and inanimacy were systematically varied. Figure 10.1 shows the results for the monolingual and bilingual groups for each language.

Looking at monolinguals, the importance of word order to Spanish is shown by the 67% score for N1 in the NVN word-order compared with 11% in the NNV order (i.e. 89% preferring N2). Greeks also score 62% for N1 in the NVN sentences but differ from Spanish speakers in having no real preference in VNN and NNV. Japanese monolinguals have a low score for N1 in all orders (32%, 36%, 32%), thus showing a preference for the second N. In none of these languages, however, is there a significant difference between the bilingual and monolingual groups (*t*-tests, two-tailed).

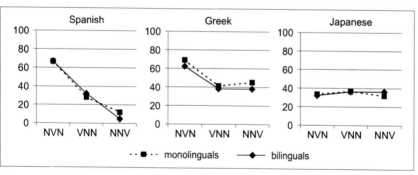

**Figure 10.1** Word order

## Animacy

The results for animacy need to be divided into three categories, depending whether the N1 and the N2 have different animacy or both N1 and N2 are animate, all with singular Ns and singular Verb.

*(1) N1(animate)/N2(inanimate): The cat pats the pen*

Three sentences were tested for each word order. (Figure 10.2).

When N1 is animate and N2 inanimate, animacy is of minor importance in Spanish and Greek monolinguals, Greeks having a slight overall preference for animate N1 in all word orders. Japanese monolinguals have a strong preference for animate N1 across word orders (70%, 83%, 81%). Japanese bilinguals have higher scores than monolinguals for animate N1s in all three word orders, significantly so for NVN (94% versus 70%) (*t* test, d.f. 43, *p* < 0.002). In other words, bilinguals show greater preference for a cue than monolinguals do.

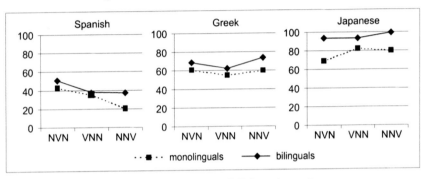

**Figure 10.2**  Animacy (1): N1(animate)/N2(inanimate)

*(2) N1(inanimate)/N2(animate): The pencil smells the giraffe.*

Four sentences were tested for each word order (Figure 10.3).

When N1 is inanimate and N2 is animate, Spanish monolinguals score high for N1 in NVN (75%) but not in other orders. Greek monolinguals

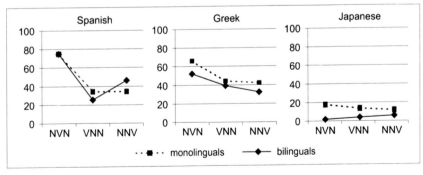

**Figure 10.3**  Animacy (2) N1(inanimate)/N2(animate)

score high in NVN (67%) and low in NNV (32%). Japanese monolinguals have low scores for N1 in all orders (18%, 13%, 11%), again showing their preference for the animate Noun. However Japanese bilinguals choose the inanimate N1 significantly *less* than the monolinguals on NVN (1% versus 18%) (*t*-test, d.f. 43, $p < 0.006$), thus showing an increased preference for animacy.

*(3) N1(animate)/N2(animate): The dog eats the donkey.*
    Four sentences were tested for each word order (Figure 10.4).
    When both Ns are animate, Spanish and Greek monolinguals score high for N1 in NVN order (74% and 77% respectively); Japanese are neutral. There are significant differences between monolinguals and bilinguals. Spanish bilinguals score N1 less than monolinguals in NNV (43% versus 49%) (*t*-test, d.f. 38, $p < 0.04$). Greek bilinguals score N1 less in NVN (70% versus 77%) (*t*-test, d.f. 75, $p < 0.04$) but more in NNV (58% versus 50%) (*t*–test, d.f. 75, $p < 0.04$). Japanese bilinguals score N1 less than the monolinguals in NVN (34% versus 55%) (*t*-test, d.f. 43, $p < 0.02$). The preference of bilinguals for animacy has then changed in all three languages, most markedly in Japanese.

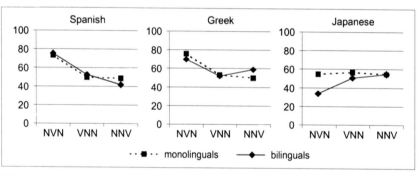

**Figure 10.4** Animacy (3): Both Ns animate

*Case*
    The results for case are divided into two categories depending on whether N1 or N2 was marked as Subject. In Japanese this therefore means marking with the particles *ga* and *wa* rather than with inflections.

*(1) The rock (Subj) licks the turtle*
    Three sentences were tested for each word order (Figure 10.5)
    The N1 marked as Subjective is preferred strongly by the Spanish monolinguals in NVN (98%) but not in VNN (5%); N1 is preferred by Greeks across

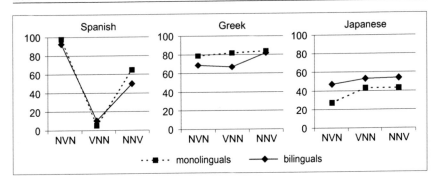

**Figure 10.5** Case (1): N1 (Subjective)

orders (79%, 82%, 84%). Japanese monolinguals are little affected by case across orders. Spanish bilinguals have significantly less preference than bilinguals for N1 in NNV (50% versus 65%) (*t*-test, d.f. 38, $p < 0.05$), Greek bilinguals show significantly less preference for N1 in VNN (67% versus 82%) (*t*-test, d.f. 43, $p < 0.03$), Japanese bilinguals have significantly more preference for N1 in NVN (47% versus 27%) (*t*-test, d.f. 43, $p < 0.05$). In all three languages, the cue of Subjective case has then changed for bilinguals

*(2) N2 (Subj): The dog eats the donkey (Subj).*
Five sentences were tested for each word order (Figure 10.6)

When the second N is marked as Subjective, the N1 scores low in all orders for Greek and Spanish monolinguals, in other words, they go with the Subjective N2, but the equivalent distinction in Japanese has little effect. Greek bilinguals are significantly different from monolinguals for VNN, preferring N1 more (29% versus 19%) (*t*-test, d.f. 75, $p < 0.03$). Japanese

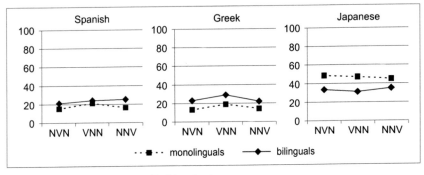

**Figure 10.6** Case (2): N2 (Subjective)

bilinguals prefer the N1 less than the monolinguals, significantly so for VNN (32% versus 47%) (*t*-test, d.f. 43, $p < 0.05$). Again for two of the languages there are differences for bilinguals for the case cue.

## Number

Number is a composite factor of the number of the N and the agreement of the verb with singular or plural N, except in Japanese where it applies only to the Noun. Sentences testing Number are divided into those with N1 plural + N2 singular + singular verb and those with N1 singular + N2 plural + plural verb.

*(1) all animate: N1(plural)/V(singular)/N2(singular): The dogs bites the monkey.*
Four sentences were tested for each word order (Figure 10.7).

Given a choice between plural N1 and singular N2 with singular Verb agreement, Spanish and Greek monolinguals score low for N1 in all word orders: Japanese monolinguals show a slight consistent preference for plural N1s overall. Japanese bilinguals score higher than monolinguals for plural N1 in all three orders: NVN (94% versus 64%) (*t*-test, d.f. 43, $p < 0.001$), VNN (83% versus 65%) (*t*-test, d.f. 43, $p < 0.005$) and NNV (90% versus 67%) (*t*-test, d.f. 43, $p < 0.05$). Since the Verb is not marked for agreement in Japanese, this effectively means that Japanese bilinguals prefer plural Ns as subjects over singular nouns.

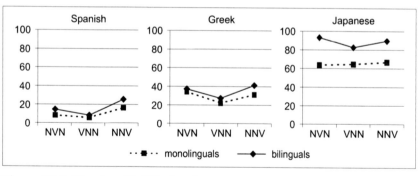

**Figure 10.7** Number (1): N1 plural

*(2) N1(singular)/V(plural)/N2(plural) The bear lick the dogs.*
Three sentences were tested for each word order (Figure 10.8).
When N1 is singular and N2 plural in agreement with a plural verb,

Spanish and Greek monolinguals score less than 10% for the N1, but higher for NVN order (35% and 42% respectively). The Japanese have a similar pattern with slightly higher N1 scores. Japanese bilinguals have lower scores for the singular N1 in all orders than monolinguals, significantly so for NVN (21% versus 48%) (*t*-test, d.f. 43, $p < 0.005$). Again Japanese bilinguals have a stronger preference for plural nouns than monolinguals.

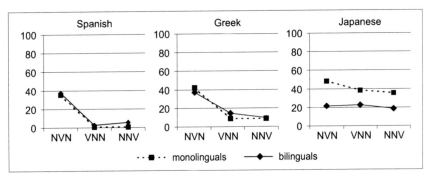

**Figure 10.8** Number (2): N2 plural

## Discussion and conclusions

Let us sum up the significant results and issues language by language.

### Spanish bilinguals

When there is no difference in animacy, Spanish bilinguals tend to prefer the N1 less in NNV sentences than monolinguals do. When the N1 is marked for subjective case, they tend to rely less on subjective case in VNN sentences. This does not resemble adaptation to English since there are no particular reasons for distrusting English word order when both nouns are animate or the first is marked as subjective; it is more like a weakening of the case cue.

### Greek bilinguals

When both nouns are animate, Greek bilinguals prefer N1 less in NVN, more in NNV. When the N1 is subjective, they prefer it less in VNN, when the N2 is subjective they prefer N1 more in VNN, in other words they tend to score lower on nouns marked by case whether in first or second position. The cue of case has lost strength.

## Japanese bilinguals

For animacy the Japanese bilinguals scored significantly differently on all three types: animate N1s and animate N2s are preferred more; when there is no difference between the two Ns, the first is preferred more than by monolinguals. The animacy cue in Japanese seems to have become hyper-animacy – above the monolingual state rather than towards English. In view of Harrington's findings for Japanese (Harrington, 1987), the reliance on animacy is not surprising but the extra reliance on it in the first language is remarkable. In terms of case, the Japanese bilinguals showed more preference for N1 subjective in NVN and for N2 subjective in VNN than did the monolinguals. That is to say, the Japanese bilinguals rely less on the subjective case, marked by the particles *ga* and *wa*, than the monolinguals. This does not seem ascribable particularly to English, which would have predicted a word order effect. In terms of Number, Japanese bilinguals scored plural Ns higher than monolinguals for all three orders when N1 was plural, and for the NVN order when the N2 is plural. There is no obvious reason in either English or Japanese why plural nouns should be more attractive to bilinguals than to monolinguals.

All three groups of bilinguals, then, exhibit some differences from monolinguals. It would be convenient if these could simply be ascribed to English as the second language. However the shift does not seem solely in the direction of English. For example it might have been expected that English SVO would have affected primarily Japanese SOV word order; but there were no significant effects for word order alone; while other significant effects such as animacy may have shown up primarily in NVN sentences, they were nevertheless present in the other two orders. The Number effect clearly applies more or less across the board for the three word orders.

The Japanese bilinguals became in a sense more Japanese rather than more English in that they used animacy even more as a cue than did the monolinguals; the Spanish and Greek bilinguals relied less on subjective case, which is only in a vague sense a prediction from English. The Japanese results show highly unexpected reliance on plurality, true of neither English nor Japanese, and not a recorded strategy. Why should plural nouns be more attractive to bilinguals when agreement is not relevant to Japanese, and plurality is irrelevant in English to choice of subject? Japanese speakers have suggested to us that it might be related to the topic issue in Japanese syntax, or to the fact that plurality is a concept only to those Japanese who have studied a second language and hence has a peculiar salience. In other words, the Competition Model paradigm of subject assignment needs adaptation for Japanese, particularly as of course the cue of agreement to which Number relates in many languages does not exist in Japanese.

There thus seem to be two separate tendencies, neither of which is a movement towards processing strategies in the second language, English:

(1) *Weakening of cues.* The bilinguals do not trust familiar cues such as animacy or case as much as the monolinguals do.

(2) *Adoption of novel cues.* Japanese bilinguals in particular, by using animacy and plural cues more than monolingual do, are behaving in unexpected ways.

Both tendencies can be considered to be general effects of acquiring a second language on the person's concept of language, partly by reducing their trust in their existing way of processing less, partly by making them aware of categories that they had not encountered in their first language – this is an aspect of the bilinguals' enhanced metalinguistic awareness that Bialystok (1993) and others have argued for. Japanese bilinguals are susceptible to animacy or plurality because in some way acquiring English has opened their eyes to universal grammatical categories. Certainly this genre of research into L2 effects on the L1 must be prepared to find differences between monolinguals and bilinguals that are due to the overall changed state of the L2 user (ie, their multi-competence) rather than to the specific effects of learning a particular second language. But, whatever the explanations that future research may come up with, this experiment has clearly shown that L2 users do not process the sentences of their first language in the same way as monolingual native speakers do.

## Acknowledgements

We would like to thank Jean-Marc Dewaele for carrying out the statistical analysis, Gloria Chwo for contributing to the early stages of the experiment, and various people for comments after presentations of parts of the material at EUROSLA and AAAL conferences.

## References

Balcom, P. (1995) Argument structure and multi-competence. *Linguistica Atlantica* 17, 1–17.

Bates, E. and MacWhinney, B. (1981) Second language acquisition from a functionalist perspective. In H. Winitz. (ed.) *Native Language and Foreign Language Acquisition* (pp. 190–214). Annals of the NY Academy of Sciences (Vol. 379). New York: New York Academy of Science.

Bialystok, E. (1993) Metalinguistic dimensions of bilingual language proficiency. In E. Bialystok (ed.), *Language Processing in Bilingual Children* (pp. 113–140). Cambridge: Cambridge University Press,.

Cook, V.J. (2002) Background to the second language user. In V.J. Cook (ed.) *Portraits of the L2 User* (pp. 1–28). Clevedon: Multilingual Matters.

Comrie, B. (1987) *The World's Major Languages*. London: Croom Helm.

Gili Gaya, S. (1961) *VOX. Curso Superior de Sintaxis Española*. Barcelona: Bibliograf S.A.

Harrington, M. (1987) Processing transfer: Language specific processing strategies as a source of interlanguage variation. *Applied Psycholinguistics* 8, 351–377.

Issidorides, D.C. and Hulstijn, J. (1992) Comprehension of grammatically modified and non-modified sentences by second language learners. *Applied Psycholinguistics* 13 (2), 147–161.

Kecskes, I. (1998) The state of L1 knowledge in foreign language learners. *Word* 49 (3), 321–340.

Kilborn, K. and Cooreman, A. (1987) Sentence interpretation strategies in adult Dutch-English bilinguals. *Applied Psycholinguistics* 8, 415–431.

Liu, H., Bates, E. and Li, P. (1992) Sentence interpretation in bilingual speakers of English and Chinese. *Applied Psycholinguistics* 13, 451–84.

MacWhinney, B. (1997) Second language acquisition and the Competition Model (pp. 113–144). In A.M.B. de Groot and J.F. Kroll. (eds) *Tutorials in Bilingualism*. Mahwah, NJ: Lawrence Erlbaum Associates.

McDonald, J. (1987) Sentence interpretation in bilingual speakers of English and Dutch. *Applied Psycholinguistics* 8, 379–413.

Nakajima, Fumio (1987) *'Nihongo no Kouzou' Japanese Language Structure*. Iwanami Shinsho

Su, I-Ru (2001) Transfer of sentence processing strategies: A comparison of L2 learners of Chinese and English. *Applied Psycholinguistics* 22, 83–112.

Zamora, S. (1999) ¿Cómo es el español gramaticalmente? *La Lengua Española* (on the web at http://www.sergiozamora.com). Guadalajara, Jalisco, México.

## Chapter 11

# Economy of Interpretation: Patterns of Pronoun Selection in Transitional Bilinguals

TERESA SATTERFIELD

A productive area of syntactic research in generative grammar and second language acquisition (SLA) research for 20 years has been the pro-drop parameter (White, 1985, 1989; Phinney, 1987; Liceras, 1988, among others). The basic syntactic description is that non-pro-drop languages such as English require a surface subject to appear in a tensed clause. Thus, we have to say *He loves* and not just Ø *loves*. Pro-drop languages (the vast majority of the world's languages), however, do not require a surface subject; so in Spanish *El ama* is possible, as well as Ø *ama*. In other words Spanish can have null subjects, symbolised in underlying structure by *pro* (e.g. *pro ama*) but not corresponding to phonetic information in the surface sentence. One aspect of the null subject discussion that receives little treatment concerns the surface distribution of overt and empty pronominal elements within bilingual speech patterns; that is to say whether or not bilingual speakers maintain a pro-drop setting in their L1 when it differs from their L2. This chapter formulates an analysis of a class of pronominal phenomena, represented by bilingual speakers whose English competence has come to dominate their near-native proficiency in Spanish. It works within the Minimalist Program – the current version of Chomsky's theory (Chomsky, 1995, 1998, 2000), which attempts to reduce language to a few powerful principles such as Economy.

## Introduction

The current work offers a syntactic-semantic characterisation of pronouns, drawing largely from Lipski (1996) and a multi-phase investigation of a specific population of Spanish/English bilinguals. Based on findings from Lipski's pilot study, one can tentatively conclude that there are two predictable differences between monolingual Spanish speakers and these individuals who exhibit greater competence in English, yet who are not L2 learners of Spanish, as they acquired the language natively.

- The bilinguals do not maintain the same distribution of non-overt and lexical subjects in their speech.
- They do not exhibit the same rigid focus/contrastive distinctions with regard to pronominal interpretation as do the Spanish monolinguals.

Consider the examples in (1):

(1)(a) Ella$_i$ hablaba el inglés que *ella$_i$ / pro$_i$ sabía.

    She speak (3 sg/imprf) the English that *she/Ø know (3 sg/imprf)
    'She spoke the English that she knew.'
    (monolingual Spanish)

  (b) Ella$_i$ hablaba el inglés que ella$_i$ sabía.

    She speak (3 sg/imprf) the English that *she/Ø know (3 sg/imprf)
    'She spoke the English that she knew.'
    (bilingual Spanish) (Lipski 1996)

When the null subject *pro* and *ella* are equally acceptable within the subordinate clause in syntactic terms, monolingual Spanish speakers intuit the occurrence of the overt pronominal as signaling a contrastive, or disjoint, reference between the antecedent subject in the matrix clause and the embedded pronoun. As shown in (1a), *pro* is uniformly perceived by these speakers as the neutral or unmarked reading that must co-refer with the overt subject. The datum in (1b) suggests that unlike the 'standard' Null Subject Language (NSL) distribution of pronominals, these bilingual speakers permit the overt pronoun to appear in areas typically reserved for *pro*, where it takes on the null subject's unmarked and non-contrastive interpretation as well.

The investigation of bilingualism is important, since the standard L2 acquisition explanation cannot be called upon to capture all the grammatical facts. The data do not indicate that these bilingual speakers merely experience interference or transfer effects from a dominant English to a recessive Spanish. Nor does it appear to be a case of Spanish attrition, as the speakers do not seem to completely adopt non-NSL tendencies into their Spanish grammar. Instead, we argue that a unique status for lexical pronouns seems to be emerging in the bilingual grammar, one that reflects an optimal interplay between universal properties of language and syntactic operations. Moreover, the existence of this new class of subject may not be confined solely to contexts of bilingualism or language contact, as stabilised patterns in monolingual Brazilian Portuguese (Kempchinsky, 1984; Negrão & Müller, 1996; Tarallo, 1983) and Italian dialects such as Neapolitan (Ledgeway, 2000) can be shown to parallel certain features of Lipski's bilingual corpus.

To the extent that the syntactic and referential lines designating overt subjects and their null counterparts are erased for particular groups of speakers, the occurrence of such intralinguistic variation represents fertile grounds for rigorously testing claims put forth in current linguistic theory. One particularly intriguing question concerns assumptions of general principles of Economy (Chomsky, 1991, 1995, 1998, 2000), and how to reconcile types of redundant or optional linguistic rules with the notion of costliness of derivation. The main purpose of this work is to offer a principled explanation, framed largely within Minimalism, for the pronominal distributions uncovered. Within a wider scope, we wish to account for why convergence based on multiple solutions (*modulo* syntactic-semantic structures) within the same grammar may actually be the most optimal choice for speakers. The claims advanced here serve to demonstrate how the need to preserve grammatical resources may drive speakers to minimise even those operations considered central to the computational system, such as Merge or Agree, whenever possible. We attempt to go beyond the conventional wisdom that null subjects are preferable, since they are inherently less costly to the system than overt elements. Instead, we argue that the conditions of economy are not absolute: they allow for a range of behaviours that encompasses both zero and lexical pronouns, adapting to conditions present in the grammar in order to attain the most referentiality for the least computational effort.

The organisation for the rest of the chapter is as follows: the next section briefly sketches the structural and interpretive functions of NSL pronouns, with emphasis on the behaviour of focus subjects. We then profile bilingual patterns, relying primarily on data from the Lipski (1996) corpus. Next, we propose an economy-based analysis that accommodates a large pool of speakers and may provide new insights into the conceptual underpinnings of Economy, as well as supplying a more articulated characterisation of Spanish/English bilingual speakers. The final section offers some additional implications and ends with concluding remarks.

## Background

As is well known, a sentence such as (2a) below is inadmissible in English or French, while its counterpart (2b) is the norm in standard NSLs, such as Spanish:

(2)(a) *Were injured (some men).

(b) Fueron heridos (unos hombres).

In terms of learnability, Rizzi (1982, 1986) and Jaeggli and Safir (1989) provide seminal explanations for this state by invoking the Null Subject Parameter. Within the [+ null subject] option, it would initially appear that the sentence pairs in (3) present themselves as freely interchangeable:

(3)(a) *Pro* hablan español e inglés.

(b) Ellos hablan español e inglés.

'(They) speak Spanish and English.'

Despite the L2 pedagogical claim that lexical subject pronouns are always 'optional' in Spanish, the fact is that in particular environments, the null subject must generally be present instead of an overt form of the subject, such as in impersonal and quasi-argument constructions, as well as for expletives (i.e. 'dummy subject' pronouns such as English *it* and *there*). See Silva-Villar (1997) for an analysis of expletives attested in a small group of historically null subject languages.

(4)(a) *Ello/ *El/*Pro*$_{arb}$ me han vendido un libro viejo en ese negocio.

It/he/Ø to me + have-pres(3pl) + sold a book old in that store

(b) They$_{impersonal}$ have sold an old book to me in that store.

(5)(a) Antes *él/*ello/*pro* hacía más calor.

Before he/it /Ø make-past (3-sg) more hot

(b) 'It was hotter before.'

(6)(a) *El/*Ello/ *Pro* é cierto que (él/ella/*pro*) baila bien.

He/It/Ø be-pres(3-sg) certain that he/she/Ø dance-pres (3-sg) well

(b) 'It is true that s/he dances well.'

Because of numerous conditions imposed by binding relationships and structural restrictions, there are also cases that require the presence of an overt subject; for example, when the head of the relative clause subject is [+animate]:

(7)     La mujer$_i$ que él/*pro* ama (*pro*$_i$) odia a Juan.

The woman that he/Ø love-pres (3-sg) Ø hate-pres(3-sg) part + Juan
'The woman that he loves hates Juan.'

In addition to the above syntactic contexts that are distinguished with respect to null versus non-null arguments, the property most germane for what follows is the case of seemingly unrestricted alternation between a null and an overt subject. Below, when *pro* and *él* are equally acceptable in syntactic terms, native speaker intuitions suggest a disjoint reference between the full DP subject *Juan* and the overt pronoun, such that *él* is understood as a focused element, instead of binding with *Juan*:

(8)(a) Cuando *pro*$_i$ / *él$_i$ trabaja, Juan$_i$ no bebe.

       when Ø/he work-pres (3-sg) Juan neg drink pres(3-sg)
       'When (he) works, Juan does not drink.'

  (b) Cuando Juan$_i$ trabaja, *pro*$_i$ / *él$_i$ no bebe.

      'When Juan works, Ø/he doesn't drink.'

Moreover, (8b) illustrates that, regardless of their relative placement in either the main or the embedded clause, the unbound reading obtains between the lexical subject and the overt pronoun. Similarly, in sentences such as the Spanish equivalent to 'When Juan$_i$ is working, (él)/HE$_i$ doesn't get anxious, though HIS$_i$ WIFE does,' the presence of lexical *he* (*él*) would still trigger a non-coreferential reading with *Juan*, even when contrastive with another referent, such as *his wife*. Native speaker intuitions suggest that, in the default interpretation, both *pro* and *HIS* are bound to the antecedent *Juan* for reference, whereas an intermediate *él* signals a disjoint reading with *Juan*, while establishing coreference with the following pronoun *his*.

In these instances, Chomsky (1981) presumes the operation of a simple pragmatic metric known as the Avoid (Lexical) Pronoun Principle (APP), which confines the choice to the topic null-subject preference rather than to the focus overt pronoun, in the context where both classes of pronominals may potentially appear. Since this contrastive distinction does not derive from intonationally-based cueing in NSLs, it would be possible to use the overt pronoun co-referentially in a hyper-emphatic manner, given phonological stress.

It must also be noted that overt Spanish pronouns do not possess implicit contrastive status, nor are they uniformly stressed, independent of their syntactic context. When the lexical subject is part of a conjunct or when the pronominal appears as the object of a preposition, the null option is not available. The realised pronouns are then perceived as non-contrastive or non-emphatic, with their anaphoric possibilities converging to neutral forms rather than to stressed ones:

(9)(a) Cuando *pro_i/él_i y su mujer trabajan, Juan_i no bebe.

  When Ø/he and his woman work-pres (3pl) Juan neg drink-pres (3sg)
  'When he and his wife work, Juan does not drink.'

 (b) Cuando pro hablan de *pro_i/él_i, Juan_i se irrita.

  When Ø speak-pres (3pl) about Ø/him Juan SE + irritate-pres (3sg)
  'When they talk about him, Juan gets upset.'

In the relevant cases however, the semantic effect of the syntactic selection is such that the occurrence of a non-stressed lexical pronoun provides contrast, whereas only pro is judged as bound when present with the overt subject DP; hence, the early appeal of the APP.

The APP proves to be a heavy-handed reflex, in the light of noteworthy data that further distinguish the distribution of overt lexical pronouns and zero elements in terms of their distinct interpretive behaviours. Insights behind the Spanish overt-null alternation facts are found early on in accounts by Zubizarreta (1982), Luján (1986), Soriano (1989), and subsequently Larson and Luján (1992). Larson and Luján, by essentially positing a quantification analysis of focus, provide a principled explanation for the perception of overt pronouns as focused in contexts where both null and lexical pronouns can occur. By analogy with focus phrases with *only* (*sólo* in Spanish) in (10a) below, Larson and Luján (1992) suggest that an expanded quantifier phrasal construction houses the non-null subject in (10b), such that the lexical pronoun behaves like the focused element in (10a). The exception is in the latter example, where the head of QP is equivalent to a phonologically unrealised quantifier expression. (10c) illustrates that, while the surface configuration of the overt pronominal and pro appear to coincide, the two classes of pronouns actually occupy different phrasal positions in the syntactic structure, and also require distinct licensing and identification mechanisms in order to be licit in the syntax. To wit, the contrastive reading implies a sort of syntactic complementary distribution according to Larson and Luján (Note that capitals denote emphatic, contrastive):

(10)(a) [_QP Only HE_i]_j [nobody] [t_i believes] [t_i is completely happy]]]

 (b) ...[_QP { Ø } [_NP El_i ]_j trabaja

  he work-pres(3-sg)
  'HE works.'

 (c) ...[_NP Pro ] trabaja

  '(He) works.'

Furthermore, the specialised focal structure available for lexicalised pronouns lends itself to the inherent differences between null and overt pronominals given licensing and identification requirements imposed on null subjects (à la Rizzi, 1986).

Notably, Montalbetti (1984) attributes another environment for avoidance of lexical pronominals in Romance languages to the Overt Pronoun Constraint (OPC).[1] The OPC is constructed in terms of Linking Theory. (See Higginbotham (1983) for a detailed account.) This series of structural restrictions is imposed on phonetically-overt pronouns, making it illegal for them to be linked to the formal variable (i.e. empty category in an A-position) of a raised quantifier or moved interrogative expression when the overt empty alternation holds, as shown in (11a) and (11b), respectively:

(11)(a) [Todos los estudiantes]$_i$ [t]$_i$ piensan que [$pro_{i/j}$ /*ellos$_i$] son inteligentes.

'All students$_i$ think that (*they$_i$) are intelligent.'

(b) ¿[Quién]$_i$ [t]$_i$ piensa que [$pro_{i/j}$ /*él$_i$] es inteligente?

'Who$_i$ thinks that (*he$_i$) is intelligent?

(c) [Muchos estudiantes]$_i$ dijeron que [$pro$]$_i$ piensan que [ellos]$_i$ son inteligentes.

'Many students$_i$ said that Ø$_i$ think that they$_i$ are intelligent.'

The claim is that only *pro* can receive both the free and the bound variable interpretation with a c-commanding *wh*-phrase or quantifier as its antecedent, since the null subject contains no phonological content. However, in (11c) the overt pronoun *ellos* in the final embedded clause may licitly link to the intermediate *pro*, which is construed as a bound variable, and imparts a bound reading on the lexical pronoun in the lower clause.

Both aspects of pronominal distribution (i.e. focus contexts and OPC effects) have related manifestations with respect to non-NSL pronouns. In English, the phonologically-emphatic subject corresponds to the Spanish contrasting overt pronoun, whereas the English neutral or unstressed pronoun parallels *pro*. As concerns bound variable contexts, Luján (1986) claims that English and Spanish share the same restrictions, given the stressed–unstressed characterisation of subject elements cross-linguistically. More recently, Pérez-Leroux and Glass (1997) have argued that, unlike Spanish, this interpretive component does not constrain English to any great extent. Interestingly, the apparent lack of OPC-like restrictions in English does not affect L2 structures. Their study of L2 Spanish learners whose L1 was English concludes that advanced students attained native-like Spanish OPC effects with little effort.

While these previous analyses make sound empirical predictions for the non-occurrence of overt pronouns in null subject grammars such as standard monolingual Spanish, they do not make predictions in a unified manner for all so-called NSLs. (We note that Montalbetti (1984) addresses this shortcoming by postulating a second version of the OPC, which applies to Japanese, BP, and Catalan.) This distinction relies on the notion that antecedence involves a transitive relation, whereas linking (OPC1) incorporates non-transitive relations. Given the contradictory data discussed as well as the data to be examined in the next section, it is difficult to make a purely structural claim for the contrast in subject elements in the case of bilingual Spanish/English speech. Moreover, if the OPC holds across grammars, it appears to be necessary to go beyond a distinction based on phonological content in order to capture the subtle linking alternations between lexical and null pronouns. We do not take up these issues here, but the reader is directed to the references listed at the end of the chapter for detailed theoretical and technical argumentation.

## The Nature of the Bilingual Problem

Lipski (1996) represents a notable minority in the attempt to situate bilingual data empirically and theoretically within current treatments of formal syntax. In order to examine bilingual patterns for the distribution of pronominal subjects, a pilot study was carried out, targeting groups of Spanish-speakers from Mexican, Puerto Rican and Cuban ethnic backgrounds living in the United States. The participants were later classified under three experimental categories: monolingual controls, 'balanced' bilinguals and transitional bilinguals. The third group (henceforth 'transitionals') comprised individuals identified as English-dominant speakers of Spanish, given their backgrounds and high near-native competence in Spanish. The control subjects were mainly Cubans who were recent arrivals to the United States, learning L2 English.

While the transitionals' data are the main area of enquiry for the current work, preliminary results with regard to grammaticality judgement tasks and spontaneous production data across all experimental groups suggest that the status of overt pronouns in the community is in a genuine state of flux. This said, Lipski (1996: 179) cautions that the pilot study's conclusions are tentative at best owing to the high level of linguistic variability among individual speakers and the dialectal uses of pronominals in Spanish. Spanish/English bilinguals, especially the transitionals, have loosened the boundaries between overt and null pronoun usage in their Spanish grammar, treating phonetically realised pronominals consistently as non-contrastive elements, equivalent in interpretation to *pro*. The transitionals' preference for non-focused lexical subjects, especially in the subordinate clause, deviates from the monolingual election of co-referential *pro*, as noted in the previous section. Consider examples taken from transitionals in the Lipski data:

(12)(a) *Yo* decidí ser maestra porque *yo* estuve trabajando con niños y *yo* pensé que *yo* podía hacer lo mismo. (Transitional bilingual utterance)

'I decided to be a teacher because I was working with children and I thought that I could do the same thing.'

(b) Cuando *ellos*$_i$ vienen aquí, *ellos*$_i$ lo pierden. (Transitional bilingual utterance)

'When they come here, they lose it [their language].'

In contradiction to the monolingual counterparts, the transitional corpus *likewise indicates a tendency* for non-contrastive overt subjects to be linked to formal variables, at odds with versions of the OPC:

(13)(a) [*Todos los cubanos*]$_i$ [t]$_i$ piensan que [*ellos*]$_i$ van a volver para Cuba.

'All Cubans$_i$ think that they$_i$ are going to return to Cuba.' (Transitional bilingual utterance)

(b) ¿[*Quién*]$_i$ [t]$_i$ piensa que [*él*]$_i$ sabe más que los demás?

'Who$_i$ thinks that he$_i$ knows more than the others?' (Transitional bilingual utterance)

## Possible Explanations and Solutions

### Language transfer and change

How can these data be accounted for? At first inspection, it would seem that the contradictions illustrated might be most simply attributed to historical patterns stemming from language contact or transfer, or other such L2-learning scenarios which can bring about changes in L1 verb paradigms and verbal morphology. In cases where verbal inflections have become modified, reduced or in some manner less 'transparent' to the speakers, the grammars subsequently reflect potential inconsistencies that can eventually lead to a loss of null subjects. This process may possibly have occurred on a large scale with Old French as it evolved from a [+ null] to a [− null] subject language (Adams, 1987), where instances of *pro* were converted first to non-emphatic lexical subjects, and ultimately to the subject clitics found today in Modern French. Speculations of similar non-NSL leanings in the transitionals' speech patterns are fueled by tokens of morphological instabilities as shown in (14):

(14)(a)*Pro*ᵢ no pude creer que *yo*ᵢ **ha** hecho esos errores.

Ø neg can-pret (1sg) believe(inf) that I **have-pres-indic (3sg)** + make (past partic.) those mistakes.
'(I) couldn't believe that I had made those mistakes.'

(b) Cuando *ello*ᵢ **hablo,** *ello*ᵢ comprenden.

When they speak-pres **(1sg)**, they understand-pres (3pl).
'When theyᵢ speak, theyᵢ understand.'

It is argued that there is no strict correspondence between the availability of nominative Case and subject–verb agreement (Vincent, 1998; Ledgeway, 2000). On the strength of empirical evidence, we also assume that the subject in these instances is nominative in spite of agreement failure. Such examples chiefly demonstrate the syntactic effects that produce a mixture of compatible and incompatible verb forms accompanying the transitionals' pronominal subjects. In (14a), the transitional bilingual speaker shows an awareness of the 'standard' configurations and employs the null subject with the corresponding 1st-person singular form of the verb (e.g. *can/able: pude* = root: *pud* + first_person singular, past-tense inflection: *-e*) in the matrix clause. In the subordinate clause however, s/he selects the non-contrastive lexical pronoun in 1st-person (e.g. *yo*), and deploys a 3rd-person singular verb inflection in the present tense (e.g. *ha*), instead of the expected 1st-person past subjunctive form (e.g. *hubiera*). Sentence (14b) shows a related occurrence with the 3rd-person plural overt subject in the main clause (e.g. *ello(s)*) that does not agree with the 1st-person singular verb inflection implemented (e.g. speak: *hablar* = root: *habl*+ first person singular inflection *-o*, instead of third person plural inflection *-an*).

The primary difficulty in embracing this particular account of language change is that it is rather heavy-handed, and does not offer fine-grained explanations for the evolving *transitional* grammars. There are many reasons to suspect that the transitionals' samples cannot be exclusively attributed to the effects of convergence or parameter-shift in Spanish-recessive speakers. First, it is clear that the bilingual participants do not categorically comply with non-NSL subject patterns. If this were strictly a case of language change, we would expect to find *transitional* speakers randomly violating the more restricted environments of *pro*. However, findings indicate that the bilinguals show a preference that does not deviate from monolingual Spanish speakers in contexts where null subjects are considered obligatory, as in the examples with expletives in (4)–(6) above. This said, it is important to recall that the monolingual and bilingual distinctions primarily fall out of environments where the null-overt alternation is syntactically, yet not semantically, licit. Thus, there appears to be the possibility of truly exercising free variation of non-contrastive elements with no distinction on interpretive grounds in the transitionals' elicitations shown below, whereas this type of optionality is not attested in typical Spanish monolingual patterns:

(15)(a) Siempre cuando *pro*$_i$ estaba en Cuba *él*$_i$ dijo que si *él*$_i$ va para atrás a Cuba que no *pro*$_i$ va poder salir más.

'Always when (he) was in Cuba he said that if he goes back to Cuba that (he) will not be able to leave again.'

(b) *Ellos*$_i$ tienden a ir a tiendas donde *ellos*$_i$ saben que *pro*$_i$ se van a entender con los empleados que la mayoría son latinos.

'They tend to go to stores where they know that they are going to deal with employees the majority of whom are Latins.'

As well as illustrating the similar status of non-stressed lexical pronouns and *pro* for transitional bilingualism, this type of evidence also calls into question the claim that the bilinguals are experiencing unilateral transfer from the dominant grammar. The critical observation is that there is a gradual transition towards a wider usage of lexical pronominals, but only in specific contexts. The current study departs from previous hypotheses by claiming that, regardless of morphological transparency or its absence, transitional speakers have actually broadened Spanish binding constraints on overt subjects in ways beneficial to the syntax. What remains to be explained is why speakers would amass an interchangeable class of pronouns that can be considered syntactically and semantically equivalent, but also derivationally redundant. Logically, such a state should lead to extreme instability in the grammar. In the light of these questions, we explore how the transitional facts might actually inform us about economy-driven operations internal to the computational system.

## A working hypothesis of economy-driven subjects

Working within a Minimalist framework, we propose that the crucial difference between transitional bilingual Spanish and its Romance NSL counterparts, as well as bilingual Spanish and English, emerges at a level in the computational system ($C_{HL}$ i.e. Computational system for Human Language) where 'universal' syntactic operations are performed, rather than at the micro-level of instantiating parameterised values and strong/ weak categorical features. Very few theoretical linguists have contemplated the nature of these inner-workings with any real scrutiny, thus we take the position that central to $C_{HL}$ are transformational components such as Merge, Agree and Move. For instance, the agree operation establishes a matching relation, agreement or Case-checking, between a lexical item and a feature in some restricted space or domain. Matching can also be said to underlie the mechanisms of licensing and identification; the former to 'certify' in Lasnik's terms (Lasnik, 2000: 182), given elements in the derivations and the latter to ensure retrieval of information for expression and reference. It is often presumed that properties of $C_{HL}$ function invariantly. However, we argue that the economy conditions stipulated in syntactic theory (e.g. Procrastinate and Minimal Link Condition), much like constraints on processes in many biological systems, are in place solely to preserve and protect the limited capacities of the system. It is reasonable, then, that principles of economy carry out this role of 'regulator' based on the grammatical resources available or given direct evidence in the language. In response, particular $C_{HL}$ mechanisms can come to have more of an effect in one grammar than another. Stated another way, optimal representations emerge in grammars that are not due to a uniform functioning of all the syntactic components, so much as to a specialised balancing of operations adapting the necessary mechanisms (i.e. Merge or Move) to recover information in the most efficient way for the language at hand. Chomsky (2000) supposes this to be the case in the computation of PF, such that features are implemented in the course of computation in different ways for different languages. The question is whether the narrow syntax (LF interface) should exhibit this adaptive characteristic to any degree. Given the bilingual evidence, we claim that it may indeed be possible.

Consequently, in the transitional Spanish grammar it is equally 'costly' in terms of syntactic operations to express reference via the null or overt subject. We will assume that referential subjects are licensed through morphological or abstract Case-marking at the level of syntax. (See also Satterfield (1999) for arguments related to the costliness of nominative Case-checking and null subjects.) Nevertheless, we reject Rizzi's (1997) claims that the null subject element, as an endowment of Universal Grammar, is invariant across languages (i.e. *pro* Catalan equals *pro* Italian equals *pro*). In further contradiction to Rizzi, we also do not accept that *pro* patently 'comes for free' as compared to overt subjects. Instead, we argue that there are compelling reasons to support the view that the morphological 'richness' previously associated with AGR in NSL grammars is not relevant for the syntactic presence of *pro*. However, in opposition to Chomsky (1995), we show that the AgrS projection is still necessary in NSLs for the *interpretation* of the subject argument selected. Rizzi (1997) offers examples of two null subject environments in Italian: only in the first does the verb display overt agreement and permit a [+referential reading]. In the subsequent two examples the non-referential interpretation stands:

(16)(a)Gianni ritiene [che ___ sia simpatica]

　　　　'Gianni believes that ___ is nice (fem/sg)'

(17)(a)Gianni ritiene [che ___ sia probabile que...]

　　　　'Gianni believes that ___ is likely that...'

　　(b)Gianni ritiene [esser ___ probabile che...]

　　　　'Gianni believes ___to be likely that....'

On the basis of the same theory-driven constraints, the point can further be argued that only *pro* in non-referential contexts actually economises the derivation to any extent. When *pro* is used within a [+referential] context, the null element consequently must undergo movement operations that formally identify and recover the referential features that are specified through Agreement with respect to *phi*-features, as in (18):

(18)(a)*Pro*/Ella va a regresar a la oficina.

　　　　∅ / She go (1 sg-pres prog) to + return to the office

　　　　'She is going to return to the office.'

Along the lines of Picallo (1994) and Larson and Luján (1992), we posit that overt subjects inherently possess minimal referential (*phi-*) features in the lexicon and need not completely rely on identification and recovery mechanisms to regain this information, while [+referential ] *pro* must recover these features entirely in the syntax. It thus seems logical that, while a null subject with referential material may be more efficient at the interface level of PF, a non-focused overt subject may actually be less costly in terms of the number of computational operations that it requires to be fully visible in the syntax. Point-by-point, the benefits of null versus overt subjects can be determined as equivalent in overall derivational cost.

The most economic choice may very well be when no specific reference in terms of *phi*-features is expressed in the subject position of the sentence. Here, [+null subject] languages might then be said to gain an edge with the occurrence of [−referential] *pro*, which need not be identified and analysed for the referential content to be fully licit in the grammar, but instead can be purely merged into the derivation. (See Alexiadou & Anagnostopoulou (1998) for similar conclusions derived from an independent analysis.) Perhaps expletive *pro* enjoys such wide usage across languages precisely because it is more efficient than invoking an overt pleonastic counterpart. It is independently clear that in Icelandic, German or Yiddish (Prince, 1998), where [+referential *pro*] is not permitted, these V-2 grammars implement [−referential *pro*] in impersonal contexts and certain *wh*-constructions.

The crux of these examples is that speakers do not appear to merely 'avoid (lexical) pronouns', as many have previously claimed.[2] Instead, we propose that speakers ultimately seek to avoid costliness (in this case, the cost of identification and recovery operations in the syntax) to whatever degree possible. To the extent that such a reflex is on the right track, it is important to note that in language, as in many biological spheres, avoidance of one operation is often merely an exercise in displacement, and not one of overall simplification or reduction. For reasons of survival, valuable traits are jealously retained by the organism. Likewise for a grammar, what is of optimal use cannot be phased out, but must surface elsewhere in the derivation, even at the risk of compromising, or settling for less economical adaptations at secondary or minor junctures in the structure.

In the light of our working hypothesis, if both lexical pronouns and [+referential] *pro* within the same interpretive context incur about the same cost, then why is the overt option not characteristic for other NSLs besides transitional Spanish?[3] One reason may be that the 'savings' gained with low-cost non-contrastive lexical subjects cannot be reconciled with the necessary expression of focus features in typical NSLs. From the previous monolingual examples, recall that an overt pronoun attains contrastive interpretation based on the nature of its antecedent and its subject status in the syntax. The same possibility does not hold for phonetically unrealised *pro*, which cannot acquire a focused reading. Suppose that, in order to recover their full subject status beyond agreement features and thematic content, all pronominal subjects must be *identified* as well as licensed. Identification of overt pronouns would not entail matching *phi*-features, but instead identifying a [focus] feature on the DP that must be matched for [+focus] in [Spec, T].

It is widely held that bilingual speakers must organise and manipulate multiple syntactic systems, on some level(s) of the language module. Then in the interest of reducing computational complexity, it stands to reason that the bilingual would seek to minimise the cognitive burden in ways that the unilingual counterpart may not need to resort to. Thus, suppose that what has occurred for the transitional Spanish is an increased avoidance of syntactic identification operations. This circumstance could account for the attested lower incidence of [+referential] *pro*. Moreover, less reliance on identification mechanisms could also explain the presence of unfocused lexical pronouns. By relaxing identification, the overt subject pronoun, by default, now becomes unspecified for focus, and it will not automatically obtain a [+focus] contrastive reading, as will become apparent from its more compact syntactic configuration. Representationally, we envisage a subject architecture as shown in (19) below:

(19)

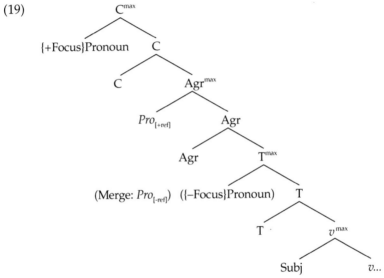

Given this simplified diagram, we claim that subject elements come to be situated in specialised areas in the specifiers of C, Agr, and T as determined on the basis of cost. Owing to the flexibility of the economy principles to regulate a given grammar, the minimum amount of structure is utilised for the derivation in question. Unlike similar analyses offered by Cardinaletti and Starke (1994), Cardinaletti (1997) and Alexiadou and Anagnostopoulou (1998), this representation is distinguished, not according to a strong–weak typology of pronominals, but rather by the accumulation of operations that supply the appropriate quantity of referentiality. The subjects found lower in the tree are by default less costly because they do not require as much identification of agreement features to be visible in the syntax. Hence, the most economical structure is [-referential] *pro*, since it can be merged and must only undergo licensing (minimally, this would entail pure merge for EPP-features in T and maximally, the checking of D-features and Nominative Case.), and would not require PF operations. The next economical choice is also found in [Spec, T]. Unlike the non-referential element however, the non-contrastive lexical pronoun is endowed with its referential material intact and certified in the lexicon, and must undergo a costlier move operation by raising to [Spec, T]. In essence, Agr contains the identification component that would be found in NSLs, and is structurally more costly, but has no PF cost. [Spec, Agr] is for [+referential] *pro*, where the null subject must undergo its series of checking operations by raising to its target in Agr where identification takes place. Finally, an overt pronoun destined to be the subject does not identify agreement features in Agr, but must be identified for [focus] to recover its full subject reference. Following Chomsky (2000), we posit that no additional information can be supplied in the derivation; that is to say, the [focus] feature would come as part of the set of lexical information, according to the Inclusiveness Principle. Furthermore, it seems logical to adhere to Chomsky (2000: 113) in terms of the notion that outside of TP are systems deemed peripheral to the 'narrow syntax,' but which provide richer systems. In the context of this particular analysis, we find that *pro* undergoes A'-movement, as one would predict for richer systems targeting the edge of the phrase. Likewise, if this subject must recover more emphatic content such as to express intonationally-marked focus, then the structure would extend to accommodate the further raising of the overt pronominal to a higher C projection, thus exacting even greater derivational cost. In the light of the possible options, Table 11.1 summarises the costs expended across the range of observed transitional bilingual Spanish pronominals:

**Table 11.1** Feature Checking operations and 'Economy of Derivation' in *transitional* Spanish

|  | Contrastive Pronoun | Pro [+referential] | Overt Pronoun | Pro [-referential] |
|---|---|---|---|---|
|  | D-feature | D-feature | D-feature | D-feature |
|  | Nom. Case | Nom. Case | Nom. Case | (Nom. Case) |
|  | X | Agreement | X | X |
|  | +Focus | X | X | X |
|  | PF | X | PF | X |
| **Cost:** | ++++ | +++ | +++ | +(+) |

For transitional bilingual Spanish, the emphatic lexical pronoun comes at the absolute highest cost, based on the number of checking operations involved. Non-contrastive overt pronominals and null subjects generate lower costs in the final analysis, with expletive *pro* as the most efficient subject element. Including interface operations outside of the syntax, non-focus overt subjects require less computations then either [+referential] *pro* or a contrastive subject. In typical monolingual pro-drop languages by comparison, the overt subject inevitably emerges as much more costly than [+referential] *pro*, since in these grammars further identification of the phonologically realised subject is integral when both elements are equally acceptable in the syntax. Thus, lexical pronouns implicitly carry an identifiable [+focus] component to elicit the disjoint reference reading, whereas *pro* is implicitly unable to check for focus.

## Concluding Remarks

In sum, Lipski (1996) succeeds in providing a theoretically relevant and documented account of bilingual null subject patterns. Given the tentative conclusions of his pilot study, a more in-depth analysis reveals that, in order to reduce their cognitive 'load,' transitional bilinguals have relaxed those operations in their Spanish grammar that drive identification and recovery of null subject information, and also those that signal syntactically-marked focus. The current analysis is advantageous, since standard 'L1–L2 effects' explanations cannot be called upon to capture all the pronominal subtleties or distributional facts illustrated by the transitionals, and monolingual accounts are not unified cross-linguistically.

On the basis of our hypothesis, further issues can now be addressed with respect to subject distribution. We now see why facts in transitional Spanish appear on the surface to line up with the configurations of English, consequently attracting pronouncements of interference or transfer. The absence of *pro* in English causes an overt subject pronominal to be judged as non-stressed when it co-refers to its antecedent, while the phonologically stressed, emphatic pronoun is deemed contrastive:

(20)   When he$_i$/*HE$_i$ works, John$_i$ doesn't drink.
       (Akmajian & Jackendoff, 1970)

The key difference is that English achieves these interpretations through costlier identification operations that are consistently avoided in transitional bilingual Spanish. Without access to the null subject, it seems logical that English-type languages displace the cost of licensing and identifying *pro* in Agr. Instead, contrastive subjects must undergo even greater identification (i.e. raising to a higher projection) in order to obtain the fully stressed, intonationally-marked reading. Transitional Spanish, in keeping with the proposed analysis, may not necessarily exhibit this less economic English focus strategy:

(21)   *Ellos*$_i$ venden y *ellos*$_j$ van.

     'They$_i$ sell and they$_j$ go.'

The datum in (21) contrast with (20) in that the transitional speaker produces no phonetically-based contrast between the overt non-coreferential pronouns, thus demonstrating the expected avoidance of identification for focus features. Predictions for transitionals' Spanish can perhaps now be confirmed empirically in future studies: when syntactically acceptable, non-emphatic lexical subjects and [-referential] *pro* should be most frequently selected as the optimal subject elements in transitional bilingual syntactic structures, allowing for the bilingual speaker to most efficiently utilise the computational system.

Lastly, while it is difficult to predict in its current state if transitional bilingual Spanish pronouns will follow the route of Old French, conditions for maintaining this expanded pronominal inventory at present appear relatively stable. Transitionals are not forsaking Romance language options offered by use of *pro*, nor are they adopting a complete non-NSL structure that may ultimately resemble English. Instead a unique status of non-contrastive lexical pronouns that reflect an optimal interplay between universal properties of syntax-semantics and morphology seems to be emerging, based on the bilingual grammatical resources of these particular speakers.

## Notes

1. As Pérez-Leroux and Glass note:

    Speakers' intuitions on OPC effects are subtle. Some speakers do not have clear intuitions, and the strength of the overt/null contrast may vary with different types of operators involved...Variation in judgements aside, the effects of the OPC are consistently present in [Spanish] grammar. (Pérez-Leroux and Glass, 1997: 153)

2. Along these lines, a reviewer suggests that speakers generally attempt to *avoid phonetics*; that is, they minimise phonetic content, such as dropping initial consonantal segments in (British) English: (h)e, (h)is, etc. To the extent that this notion is distinct from Procrastinate, a syntactic operation that seeks to limit the effects on PF, we find such a stipulation a bit extreme, in that its consequences seem difficult to generalise and may be more conducive to a 'one-fell-swoop' approach.

3. It is true that monolingual Italian also appears to possess this capacity with *pro* and *egli*, but in limited contexts:

Gianni$_i$ partirà quando *pro*$_i$/*lui$_i$/egli$_i$ avrà finito il lavoro (Cardinaletti & Starke, 1994).
'Gianni will leave when pro/*he/he will have finished the work.'

The distribution of overt and null pronouns in monolingual Brazilian Portuguese strikingly parallels that of transitional bilingual Spanish:

Alguns convidados$_i$ disseram que eles$_i$/*pro*$_i$ vão trazer uma garafa de vinho.
Some invitees say-past(3-pl) that they/0 go-pres(3-pl) bring(inf) a bottle of wine
'Some guests said that they are going to bring a bottle of wine' (Negrão, 1997).

## References

Adams, M. (1987) From Old French to pro-drop. *Natural Language and Linguistic Theory* 5, 1–32.

Akmajian, A. and Jackendoff, R. (1970) Coreferentiality and stress. *Linguistic Inquiry* 1, 124–126.

Alexiadou, A. and Anagnostopoulou, A. (1998) Parameterising AGR: Word order, V-movement and EPP-checking. *Natural Language and Linguistic Theory* 16, 491–539.

Cardinaletti, A. (1997) Subjects and clause structure. In L. Haegeman (ed.) *The New Comparative Syntax* (pp. 33–63). London: Longman.

Cardinaletti, A. and Starke, M. (1994) The typology of structural deficiency. On the three grammatical classes. In H. van Riemsdijk (ed.) *Clitics in the Languages of Europe, Vol. 8*. Berlin: Mouton.

Chomsky, N. (1981) *Lectures on Government and Binding*. Dordrecht: Foris.

Chomsky, N. (1991) Some notes on economy of derivation and representation. In R. Freiden (ed.) *Principles and Parameters in Comparative Grammar* (pp. 417–454). Cambridge, MA: MIT Press.

Chomsky, N. (1995) *The Minimalist Program*. Cambridge, MA: MIT Press.

Chomsky, N. (1998) Some observations on economy in generative grammar. In P. Barbosa, D. Fox, P. Hagstrom, M. McGinnis and D. Pesetsky (eds) *Is the Best Good Enough?* (pp.115–128). Cambridge, MA: MIT Press.

Chomsky, N. (2000) Minimalist inquiries: The framework. In R. Martin, D. Michaels and J. Uriagereka (eds) *Step by Step* (pp. 89–155). Cambridge, MA: MIT Press.

Higginbotham, J. (1983) Logical form, binding, and nominals. *Linguistic Inquiry* 14, 395–420.

Jaeggli, O. and Safir, K (eds) (1989) *The Null Subject Parameter*. Dordrecht: Kluwer.

Kempchinsky, P. (1984) Brazilian Portuguese and the null subject parameter. *Mester* 13, 3–16.

Larson, R. and Luján, M. (1992) Focused pronouns. Unpublished manuscript.

Lasnik, H. (2000) *Syntactic Structures Revisited*. Cambridge, MA: MIT Press.

Ledgeway, A. (2000) *A Comparative Syntax of the Dialects of Southern Italy: A Minimalist Approach*. Oxford: Blackwell.

Liceras, J. (1988) Syntax and stylistics: More on the pro-drop parameter. In J. Pankhurst, M. Sharwood Smith and P. Van Buren (eds) *Learnability and Second Languages: A Book of Readings* (pp. 71–93). Dordrecht: Foris.

Lipski, J. (1996) Patterns of pronominal evolution in Cuban-American bilinguals. In A. Roca and J. Jensen (eds) *Spanish in Contact* (pp.159–186). Somerville, MA: Cascadilla Press.

Luján, M. (1986) *Stress and Binding of Pronouns.* Chicago Linguistic Society 21, 424–438.

Montalbetti, M. (1984) After binding: On the interpretation of pronouns. PhD thesis, MIT.

Negrão, E. (1997) Asymmetries in the distribution of overt pronouns and empty categories in Brazilian Portuguese. In J. Black and V. Motapanyane (eds) *Current Issues in Linguistic Theory #140: Clitics, Pronouns and Movement* (pp. 217–236). Amsterdam: Benjamins.

Negrão, E. and Müller, A. (1996) As mudanças no sistema pronominal do Português Brasileiro: substituição ou especialização de formas? *DELTA* 12 (1), 125–152.

Pérez-Leroux, A. and Glass, W. (1997) OPC effects on the L2 acquisition of Spanish. In A. Pérez-Leroux and W. Glass (eds) *Contemporary Perspectives in the Acquisition of Spanish* (pp.149–165). Somerville, MA: Cascadilla Press.

Picallo, M. (1994) Catalan possessive pronouns: The Avoid Pronoun Principle revisited. *Natural Language and Linguistic Theory* 12, 259–299.

Phinney, M. (1987) The pro-drop parameter in second language acquisition. In T. Roeper and E. Williams (eds) *Parameter Setting* (pp. 221–238). Dordrecht: Kluwer.

Prince, E. (1998) Subject pro-drop in Yiddish. In P. Bosch and R. van der Sandt (eds) *Focus: Linguistic, Cognitive and Computational Perspectives* (pp. 82–101). Cambridge: Cambridge University Press.

Rizzi, L. (1982) *Issues in Italian Syntax.* Dordrecht: Foris.

Rizzi, L. (1986) Null objects in Italian and the theory of *pro. Linguistic Inquiry* 17, 501–557.

Rizzi, L. (1997) A parametric approach to comparative syntax: Properties of the pronominal system. In L. Haegeman (ed.) *The New Comparative Syntax* (pp. 268–285). Harlow: Longman.

Satterfield, T. (1999) *Bilingual Selection of Syntactic Knowledge.* Amsterdam: Kluwer.

Silva-Villar, L. (1997) Subject positions and the roles of CP. In A. Schwegler, B. Tramel and M. Uribe-Etxebarria (eds) *Romance Linguistics: Theoretical Perspectives* (pp. 247–270). Amsterdam: Benjamins.

Soriano, O. (1989) Strong pronouns in null-subject languages and the Avoid Pronoun Principle. *MIT Working Papers in Linguistics* (Vol. 21), MIT.

Tarallo, F. (1983). Relativisation on strategies in Brazilian Portuguese. PhD thesis, University of Pennsylvania.

Vincent, N. (1998) On the grammar of inflected non-finite forms. In I. Korzen and M. Herslund (eds) *Clause Combining and Text Structure. Copenhagen Studies in Language, 22,* (pp.135–158). Freriksberg: Samfundslitteratur.

White, L. (1985) The pro-drop parameter in adult second language acquisition. *Language Learning,* 35, 47–62.

White, L. (1989) *Universal Grammar and Second Language Acquisition.* Amsterdam: John Benjamins.

Zubizarreta, M. (1982) On the relationship of the lexicon to syntax. PhD thesis, MIT.

## Chapter 12

# A Dynamic Approach to Language Attrition in Multilingual Systems

ULRIKE JESSNER

## Introductory Remarks

An important aspect of language learning that tended to be ignored in dominant language acquisition theory for a long time is language attrition or loss. During the last few decades, however, this kind of influence of L2 on L1 has not only been touched upon in several publications on second language acquisition (SLA) and bilingualism (Seliger & Vago, 1991; De Bot, 1996) but it has also been acknowledged as playing a crucial role in the interplay between two languages in contact, as described by Kellerman and Sharwood Smith (1986) in their definition of cross-linguistic influence. In the meantime it has become clear that the influence between two languages is a much more diversified issue (Cummins, 1991; Grosjean & Py, 1991; Kecskes & Papp, 2000, this volume) than what was discussed under the label of the contrastive analysis hypothesis when the discussion of transfer primarily focused on the negative influence of the L1 on the L2.

In contrast to second language learning, cross-linguistic influence in multilingual acquisition is a much more multifaceted phenomenon, as shown in recent research on third language acquisition and trilingualism (Cenoz et al., 2001). Typology of languages, level of proficiency and recency of use are known to play important roles in the influence between the languages in contact in multilingual learners (Hammarberg, 2001), but there are other aspects involved in the contact between the language systems that should be taken into consideration. This chapter offers new perspectives on modelling language attrition in multilingual systems, which by definition involve more than two languages, by focusing on individual variability in multilingual proficiency.

## The Dynamics of Multilingual Proficiency

Traditional language acquisition research focusing on the first and second language learner has mainly worked with linear language growth models that have presented language learning as an ordered sequence of individual steps (Elman *et. al*, 1996: 42; Herdina & Jessner, 2000: 85).

In such a reductionist model, diachronic language change or variation on an individual level presents an issue to be ignored. Therefore language attrition or loss in language learning has not been addressed either.

This view of linear and continuous language growth, however, stands in clear contrast to biological growth, which has to be seen as a dynamic process characterised by the interplay of the systems involved. According to a dynamic systems approach, which has been known in other scientific disciplines (such as biology, physics, meteorology, ecology and mathematics to name but a few) for several decades (Gleick, 1987; Briggs & Peat, 1989), the development of a system in time is subject to investigation. And for some years now this promising approach has also begun to show its attraction for psycho-linguistics, for example Meara (1999) and MacWhinney (1999).

The understanding of the behaviour and the organisation of living organisms as dynamic systems represents the core of the theory. As defined by Van Geert (1994: 50) a dynamic system is '... a set of variables that mutually affect each other's changes over time'. Each variable of the system affects all the other variables in the system and thus affects itself. A system is thus by definition a dynamic system. The promise of dynamic systems theory as a theory of development can be found in the way that it connects real-time processes to change over developmental time. It offers new ways of thinking by providing the researcher with metaphors in the study of complex systems. Non-linearity and variability as well as self-organisation have been identified as key characteristics of chaotic systems. Autopoeitic structures (self-renewing autonomous structures with a separate identity), also form part of complex systems that can best be studied with the help of holistic concepts.

In a dynamic model of multilingualism (DMM) (Herdina & Jessner, 2002), dynamic systems theory has been applied to multilingual systems. This psycholinguistic model studies the complex relationships in multilingualism by focusing on the description of time-dependent changes in the psycholinguistic system, such as the change of dominance in a bilingual system with one language system deteriorating – as is the case in transitional bilingualism or in other words, the loss of L1 in an L2 environment (Seliger, 1996).

Our discussion is therefore not based on languages, but on the development of individual language systems that form part of the psycholinguistic system of the multilingual speaker.

According to a dynamic perspective, the relationship between socio- and psycholinguistic variation has to be considered in modelling to be able to present a holistic understanding of the behaviour and organisation of multilingual systems. Changes at the societal level have been discussed in a great many studies on language shift and reversing language shift (see, for example, Fishman, 2001) in bilingual and multilingual communities. However, variation on an individual level (i.e. changes in intralanguage and interlanguage), has not been considered so important in the history of L2 learning research (Ellis, 1994). In DMM it is the interaction between the two levels that is taken into consideration in arriving at a holistic view.

The nature of interaction between the systems involved in a complex system presents an important issue in a dynamic systems approach, since the development of one system influences the development of the others in ways that are not additive. Recent research on bilingualism has been influenced by Grosjean's bilingual view of bilingualism (Grosjean, 1982, 1992, 2001) followed by Cook's notion of multi-competence (Cook, 1991, 1993, 1996). Both stress the bilingual speaker as a competent speaker-hearer with a special or multi-competence that is nevertheless not comparable to mono-lingual competence in either language. In DMM we adopt this view, but add a dynamic component which, though a necessary part of a holistic view (Phillips, 1992), has not previously been integrated in the discussion. So we not only observe the phenomenon of multilingualism as a whole – and not just its parts – but also stress changes over time. A dynamic multi-lingual system will thus have properties that its parts do not. Or, in other words, the acquisition of a further language leads to the development of new qualities in the multilingual system.

Time-dependent variation plays an important role in language acquisition as known from numerous studies on first and second language acquisition, such as Gass *et al.* (1989), Hyltenstam and Obler (1989), and Hyltenstam and Viberg (1993). In multilingual learning this issue is of even greater importance; that is, within a growing number of language systems in contact, changes in multilingual proficiency exist in an enhanced way that is dependent on changes in (perceived) communicative needs. This has been described in various studies that focus on subjective theories of language learning (Kallenbach, 1996; Hufeisen, 2000a) and in multiliterate biographies (Hoffman, 1989; Belcher & Connor, 2001), but only to a limited degree in studies on language attrition.

In this chapter the process of language attrition will be discussed as one of the key features in the development of a multilingual system. Studies of bilingualism where transitional bilingualism (the change of dominance in the language systems of a bilingual speaker) has been found to present a common phenomenon (Seliger & Vago, 1996: 3) have made clear that language acquisition theory has to take language attrition into consideration. It also has to be taken into account in monolinguals since it is a fact that monolingual speakers show signs of language attrition, not just through dementia. If they do not use them regularly, they can lose certain of their skills (such as how to write an essay) or lose vocabulary for specific purposes. The theoretical perspectives on language learning as specified in DMM can serve as a bridge between SLA and bilingualism research because this model integrates both fully developed and developing language systems. The interaction of dynamic systems-related features (such as non-linearity, reversibility and stability) will be addressed in the following discussion of language attrition.

## Language Attrition and Loss

Multilingual learners often find themselves confronted with the phenomenon of language loss or deterioration and/or attrition in one of their languages. From a dynamic systems perspective, it can be said that incomplete or insufficent language proficiency resulting from language attrition, which is seen as a gradual process of decay, is to be observed in all forms of language learning. In language learning theory, psycholinguistic perspectives of language attrition are mostly linked with partial acquisition and/or non-pathological language loss. In other words, either a language system is acquired only incompletely because of cross-linguistic contact, or some of the linguistic knowledge of a sufficiently acquired language system has been forgotten (Sharwood Smith & van Buren, 1991: 22; De Bot, 1996).

It is a well-known fact that most language learners never achieve the expected level of proficiency (i.e. native speaker level), as shown in most studies on SLA (Ellis, 1994). According to DMM, this process of retardation, which can lead to fossilisation as defined by Selinker (1972), can be found in both native and non-native speakers and this criticism of (monolingual) native speaker competence as the norm in language learning (see also Cook, 1999) entails that the goal to be approached in language learning should rather be interpreted as an approximative system, as discussed by Nemser (1971). The issue of partial achievement has also been addressed in studies of bilingualism when the negative effects of the contact with two languages were discussed in early research on semilingualism, as in for example Hakuta (1986). Thus the so-called negative effects of the contact between two or more languages have been addressed in the literature with regard to issues of transfer, that is code-switching phenomena in bilinguals as well as interference and transfer in second language learners. The negative attitude towards interferences as originally defined by contrastive analysis studies has thus been confirmed in studies on bilingualism (Jessner & Herdina, 1996).

As is evident from various discussions on language attrition, the question of what exactly is lost and when attrition starts is difficult to answer. One of the obvious reasons is that attrition is traceable only through performance. Lambert and Moore (1986: 180) operate with units of competency and present a scale of loss that includes factors such as recency, frequency of reinforcement, complexity, contrast, linguistic distinctiveness, functional load, irregularity, centrality and pragmatic load.

Of the several hypotheses that have been formulated (Schmid, 2001) probably the best known is the regression hypothesis that dates back to Jakobson (1941). This claims that you forget items in the same order that you learned them (De Bot & Weltens, 1991). Whether parts of a language system can be forgotten or whether they are simply not accessible for some reason still remains an issue to be explored in psycholinguistic research. There are several methodological problems that language-related research on forgetting has to face; one of them is the applicability of research results from studies on general cognition (e.g. Morris & Gruneberg, 1994), which is linked with the tendency in experimental research to focus on items rather than on systems as expressed by Weltens & Grendel (1993: 137). Other doubts concern the accessibility of information. In recent literature on forgetting, there is no loss of memory but only inaccessability of information if the right cues are not used (De Bot, 1996: 583). Olshtain (1986: 197-8) adds the component of proficiency level when she points out that 'last learned forms which have not as yet been fully mastered, are early candidates for attrition.' And De Bot (1998: 351) points out several studies confirming that knowledge that has reached a certain threshold can become immune to loss.

For our purposes here we would like to discuss forgetting as a gradual process of information decay that is dependent on time. This way recall of information becomes more difficult and unlikely the longer the phase between learning and recall is.

It can be said that in many cases the speaker will try to counteract the effects of language attrition by using compensatory strategies (cf. Olshtain, 1986; Cohen, 1986), although there are cases where maintenance is not an issue, as can be observed in certain language communities where the attriting language has lost its prestige, as known from various minority language settings (Gal, 1978). In sociolinguistic studies L1 loss or death has been an issue worth investigating in cases of language change or language shift in immigrants where the majority language of the new speech community also becomes the dominant language, and L2 turns into L1 (Fishman, 1991; Paulston, 1994). This process can also affect L2 in an L1 environment, as is known from typical L2 learning situations or the loss of dialect forms in an otherwise monolingual environment (for an overview see also Weltens, 1988).

Whereas for about twenty years now most linguistic studies have mainly concentrated on language attrition in individuals who operate with two language systems (Weltens *et al.*, 1986; Seliger & Vago, 1991; De Bot, 1996), only a few studies focus on this aspect of language learning in multi-linguals. In his paper on language attrition in the lexicon of his two tri-lingual children aged 9 and 13, Cohen (1989) describes how lexical loss in Portuguese showed in the English/Hebrew bilingual children after three periods of discontinued contact with the third language. Cohen's paper gives examples of lexical production strategies used to compensate for forgotten vocabulary and lexical retrieval processes. Greater attrition was found in the younger of the two children. The dynamics of language learning also become evident when a language is first forgotten and then re-acquired. Faingold (1999) reports on the re-emergence of his son's first languages, Spanish and Hebrew, after six years in an English-speaking environment.

According to a systems-theoretic approach, in a multilingual system each language acquisition process reveals its effects on prior language systems and thus language attrition can be observed in all languages in contact, not exclusively in L1. If we allow for a dynamic perspective in the development of a multilingual system, we have to take into consideration that the dominance within the language systems involved might change (as known from studies with two languages), which puts common termi-nology into question.

## Order of acquisition

This issue is of great importance in a discussion of multilingual studies where the chronological order of language acquisition does not necessarily correspond to the levels of proficiency of the individual languages (Hufeisen, 2000b). For example, a multilingual person in my neighbour-hood grew up in a bilingual environment with German and French in Belgium (where she also came into contact with Flemish very early), then moved to Germany and is married to an Englishman. She mostly uses German with her children and outside the house, but also uses English with her husband; her level of proficiency in French has changed since she uses it only on the phone occasionally when speaking to her relatives in Belgium. So one part of her bilingual system has become dominant while French (also her L1) is deteriorating. She definitely uses more English than French nowadays. To refer to French as her L1 obviously does not seem useful in the discussion of her multilingual proficiency. The DMM therefore makes use of the terms 'primary', 'secondary' and 'tertiary' language systems in a discussion of the development of the multilingual system in order to distinguish them from L1, L2 and L3. This is not a totally new issue in second language acquisition research, since other researchers have used 'primary' instead of 'first' language but it certainly becomes a more relevant issue in studies going beyond learning a second language.

## Language Attrition and Language Maintenance in DMM

In our opinion the phenomenon of language attrition can best be approached with the help of a systems-theoretic or ecological view of the declining language system (Herdina & Jessner, 2000). Since language attrition is not initially observable in DMM, we assume that it takes the form of an increased scatter that indicates the erosion of proficiency prior to negative growth of the language system concerned. Figure 12.1 shows performance scatter in the course of attrition of the language system concerned. It is specified as negative as it is only observed as deviation from language norms. As soon as the language system attains a new level of stability, scatter is reduced.

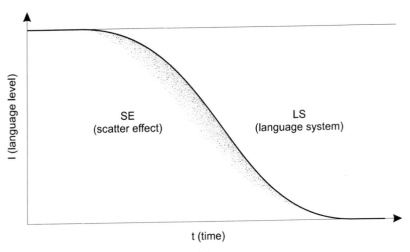

**Figure 12.1** Scatter of language attrition

(Based on Herdina & Jessner, 2002: 96)

Thus the balance between systems plays an important role in DMM and, as already suggested in Herdina and Jessner (2000: 137), the development of the multilingual system depends on a dynamic balance between the individual psycholinguistic system and its environment. In other words, the developing multilingual system is seen in a continuous process of adaptation to constantly changing (perceived) communicative requirements of the environment. At the same time, for modelling purposes, it is interpreted as a dynamic and complex process of competition between existing and/or developing psycholinguistic systems for limited resources in terms of language effort over time. Thus, while one of the language systems will be maintained or stabilised, the other will gradually erode. And this development will lead, as discussed above, to systems displacement due to the change of dominance.

Language maintenance work (such as the consulting of a dictionary on the spelling of a word or the regular use of the L2 or L3 lexicon) is well known and therefore considered natural to most (educated) speakers. However, apart from Harley (1994), it is rather under-represented in psycholinguistic research (Hyltenstam & Stroud, 1996). In DMM we consider it a key factor in multilingual acquisition because its lack presents one of the possible causes of language attrition. From a systems-theoretic point of view, it is suggested that the two gradual processes of language attrition and replacement go on simultaneously in the brain. It is further assumed that multilingual proficiency depends to a high degree on the amount of effort that the individual speaker is prepared to invest in the maintenance of the individual language system(s) concerned. In the model this effort is referred to as general language effort, and is seen as the sum of (a) the effort put into the learning of a language and (b) the effort put into the maintenance of a particular level of proficiency once achieved by the speaker.

The maintenance of two or more language systems at a similar proficiency level can be seen as more than twice as strenuous as the maintenance of a monolingual system because the multilingual brain is constantly involved in processes of matching and differentiation of two or more language systems. Maintenance work in multilinguals also involves metalinguistic and monitoring processes in order to reduce interference as a processing phenomenon and to ensure a certain speed of recall of information among other aspects. Psycholinguistic systems containing two or more language systems can therefore be seen as less stable than monolingual ones, and repair or reactivation procedures are constantly required to maintain the system in a steady state. The result of lack of general language effort (or lack of motivation, or both, for instance) will be that the

speaker will return to a monolingual norm, and her/his linguistic information will be reorganised accordingly. In other words, the speaker will
undergo transition from the use of two languages to the use of one, and this
will result in systems displacement, which can be part of multilingual
development as illustrated in Herdina and Jessner (2002: 124).

## The Relationship between Language Attrition and Language Acquisition

In DMM it is therefore assumed that neither language acquisition nor
language attrition can adequately be understood if they are discussed as
processes in isolation, as known from current literature. The two processes
have to be seen as an integrated part of an evolving dynamic system, in
other words language attrition is a function of language acquisition. This
supports the view that positive and negative growth are not linear but
dynamic and that they show a high degree of interdependence.

According to the dynamic systems approach, the process of language
acquisition is modelled as mirrored in the process of language attrition (see
also De Bot & Weltens, 1991). The ideal-typical sine curve is inverted
because lack of maintenance leads to the onset of language attrition
expressed by scatter (as mentioned above) and to a phase of steep decline,
finally evening out when maintenance is reduced to a minimum. Based on
current theory of language acquisition, the rate of decay is assumed to
depend on, amongst other things, the age of acquisition of the various
language systems (Singleton & Lengyel, 1995), the duration of language
maintenance of a certain level of proficiency (De Bot & Clyne, 1989), the
competition between the language systems, and the limitations with
regard to available linguistic resources. The role played by age in language
attrition in adults (i.e. whether attrition in elderly people works faster than
in younger adults), also seems to present an interesting issue. The effect
that the natural cognitive phenomenon of forgetting, which increases with
age, exerts on language use in general has to be put in relation to language
attrition processes in healthy elderly bilingual and multilingual respon-
dents. This scarce kind of research has so far been concentrated on by De
Bot and Lintsen (1986) and De Bot and Clyne (1994), but certainly needs
more investigation.

In the interplay between language acquisition and language attrition,
language maintenance has a key role in the stability of a language system
(and the psycholinguistic system) and is thus a desired goal. It can be stated
that the equilibrium of the system is dependent on the requirements of

language maintenance: the system is bound to erode if insufficient energy and time is invested in maintaining its stability.

As already mentioned, a further significant element in DMM is that, within the psycholinguistic model, language systems are seen as inter-dependent and not as autonomous systems – the way they are still perceived in many studies on transfer and code-switching research. The behaviour of each individual language system in a multilingual system largely depends on the behaviour of previous and subsequent systems, and it would therefore not make sense to discuss the systems in terms of isolated development.

In DMM we assume subject-specific parameters that determine both the complexity and the variability of the system. At the same time, the given systems are influenced in both their development and structure by cross-linguistic effects. This dynamic systems framework also contributes to our understanding of the processes resulting in what is termed 'cross-linguistic interaction' in DMM in an attempt to adopt cross-linguistic influence as proposed by Kellerman and Sharwood Smith (1986) for dynamic multi-lingual systems theory. This way cross-linguistic interaction refers to all the known phenomena, such as transfer and interference phenomena (as defined in DMM) including code-switching and borrowing (Jessner & Herdina, 1996) as well as other transfer phenomena such as non-predictable dynamic effects that determine the development of the systems themselves and are particularly observable in multilingualism. Such interactional influences can be interpreted as synergetic and interferential, and thus cross-linguistic interaction (CLIN) does not present a category that needs to be added to the existing transfer phenomena, but is intended to shed new light on the discussion of transfer phenomena by focusing on the dynamic aspects of multilingual development, including language attrition.

## Implications for Future Research

For further investigations, it should therefore be kept in mind that language acquisition is not based on linear language growth, and language attrition and language maintenance must be integrated in a discussion of multilingual systems development. In dynamic systems terms, apart from negative and positive growth models, the balance between the systems is also an issue to be considered in multilingualism research. The dynamics of developing multilingual systems will become even more apparent and a challenging aspect in psycholinguistic research if we include in the discus-sion issues such as reemergence and reacquisition, which have been discussed as reversing language shift on the societal level.

## Acknowledgement

I am most grateful to Kees de Bot for his comments on an earlier version of this paper.

## References

Belcher, D. and Connor, U. (eds) (2001) *Reflections on Multiliterate Lives*. Clevedon: Multilingual Matters.

Briggs, J. and Peat, F.D. (1989) *Turbulent Mirror: An Illustrated Guide to Chaos Theory and The Science of Wholeness*. New York: Harper and Row.

Cenoz, J., Hufeisen, B. and Jessner, U. (eds) (2001) *Cross-linguistic Influence in Third Language Acquisition: Psycholinguistic Perspectives*. Clevedon: Multilingual Matters.

Cohen, A. (1986) Forgetting foreign-language vocabulary. In B. Weltens, K. de Bot and T. van Els (eds) *Language Attrition in Progress* (pp. 143–58). Dordrecht: Foris Publications.

Cohen, A. (1989) Attrition in the productive lexicon of two Portuguese third language speakers. *Studies in Second Language Acquisition* 11, 135–49.

Cook, V.J. (1991) The poverty-of-the-stimulus argument and multi-competence. *Second Language Research* 7 (2), 103–17.

Cook, V.J. (1993) Wholistic multi-competence: Jeu d'esprit or paradigm shift? In B. Kettemann and W. Wieden (eds) *Current Issues in European Second Language Acquisition Research* (pp. 3–9). Tübingen: Narr.

Cook, V.J. (1996) Competence and multi-competence. In G. Brown, K. Malmkjaer and J. Williams (eds) *Performance and Competence in Second Language Acquisition* (pp. 57–69). Cambridge: Cambridge University Press.

Cook, V.J. (1999) Going beyond the native speaker in language teaching. *TESOL Quarterly* 33 (2), 185–209.

Cummins, J. (1991) Language learning and bilingualism. *Sophia Linguistica* 29, 1–194.

De Bot, K. (1996) Language loss. In H. Goebl, P. Nelde, Z. Stáry and W. Wölck (eds) *Kontaktlinguistik: Ein internationales Handbuch zeitgenössischer Forschung* (Vol.1, 579–85). Berlin: De Gruyter.

De Bot, K. (1998) The psycholinguistics of language loss. In G. Extra and L. Verhoeven (eds) *Bilingualism and Migration* (pp. 345–61). Berlin: De Gruyter.

De Bot, K. and Clyne, M. (1989) Language reversion revisited. *Studies in Second Language Acquisition* 11, 167–77.

De Bot, K. and Clyne, M. (1994) A 16-year longitudinal study of language attrition in Dutch immigrants in Australia. *Journal of Multilingual and Multicultural Development* 15 (1), 17–28.

De Bot, K. and Lintsen, T. (1986) Foreign-language proficiency in the elderly. In B. Weltens, K. de Bot and T. van Els (eds) *Language Attrition in Progress* (pp. 131–41). Dordrecht: Foris Publications.

De Bot, K. and Weltens, B. (1991) Recapitulation, regression, and language loss. In H. Seliger and R. Vago (eds) *First Language Attrition* (pp. 31–51). Cambridge: Cambridge University Press.

Ellis, R. (1994) *The Study of Second Language Acquisition*. Oxford: Oxford University Press.

Elman, J., Bates, E., Johnson, M., Karmiloff-Smith, A., Parisi, D. and Plunkett, K. (1996) *Rethinking Innateness. A Connectionist Perspective on Development*. Cambridge, MA: MIT Press.

Faingold, E. (1999) The re-emergence of Spanish and Hebrew in a multilingual adolescent. *International Journal of Bilingual Education and Bilingualism* 2, 283–95.

Fishman, J. (1991) *Reversing Language Shift*. Clevedon: Multilingual Matters.

Fishman, J. (ed.) (2001) *Can Threatened Languages Be Saved? Reversing Language Shift Revisited: A 21st Century Perspective*. Clevedon: Multilingual Matters.

Gal, S. (1978) Peasant men can't get wives: Language change and sex role in a bilingual community. *Language in Society* 7, 1–16.

Gass, S., Madden, C., Preston, D. and Selinker, L. (eds) (1989) *Variation in Second Language Acquisition: Psycholinguistic Issues*. Clevedon: Multilingual Matters.

Gleick, J. (1987) *Chaos: Making a New Science*. New York: Viking.

Grosjean, F. (1982) *Life with Two Languages*. Cambridge, MA: Harvard University Press.

Grosjean, F. (1992) Another view of bilingualism. In R. Harris (ed.) *Cognitive Processing in Bilinguals* (pp. 51–62). Amsterdam: North Holland.

Grosjean, F. (2001) The bilingual's language modes. In J. Nicol (ed.) *One Mind, Two Languages: Bilingual Language Processing* (pp. 1–25). Oxford: Blackwell.

Grosjean, F. and Py, B. (1991) La restructuration d'une première langue: l'intégration de variantes de contact dans la compétence de migrants bilingues. *La Linguistique* 27, 35–60.

Hakuta, K. (1986) *Mirror of Language: The Debate on Bilingualism*. New York: Basic Books.

Hammarberg, B. (2001) Roles of L1 and L2 in L3 production and acquisition. J. Cenoz, B. Hufeisen and U. Jessner (eds) *Cross-linguistic Influence in Third Language Acquisition: Psycholinguistic Perspectives*. Clevedon: Multilingual Matters.

Harley, B. (1994) Maintaining French as a second language in adulthood. *The Canadian Modern Language Review* 50 (4), 688–713.

Herdina, P. and Jessner, U. (2000) Multilingualism as an ecological system: The case for language maintenance. In B. Kettemann and H. Penz (eds) *ECOnstructing Language, Nature and Society. The Ecolinguistic Project Revisited. Festschrift für Alwin Fill* (pp. 131–44). Tübingen: Stauffenburg.

Herdina, P. and Jessner, U. (2002) *A Dynamic Model of Multilingualism: Perspectives of Change in Psycholinguistics*. Clevedon: Multilingual Matters.

Hoffman, E. (1989) *Lost in Translation. A Life in a New Language*. New York: Dutton.

Hufeisen, B. (2000a) How do foreign language learners evaluate various aspects of their multilingualism? In S. Dentler, B. Hufeisen and B. Lindemann (eds) *Tertiär- und Drittsprachen: Projekte und empirische Untersuchungen* (pp. 23–9). Tübingen: Stauffenburg.

Hufeisen, B. (2000b) A European perspective: Tertiary languages with a focus on German as L3. In J. Rosenthal (ed.) *Handbook of Undergraduate Second Language Education* (pp. 209–29). Mahwah, NJ: Lawrence Erlbaum.

Hyltenstam, K. and Obler, L. (eds) (1989) *Bilingualism Across the Lifespan. Aspects of Acquisition, Maturity and Loss*. Cambridge: Cambridge University Press.

Hyltenstam, K. and Stroud, C. (1996) Language maintenance. In H. Goebl, P. Nelde, Z. Stáry and W. Wölck (eds) *Kontaktlinguistik. Ein internationales Handbuch zeitgenössischer Forschung* (Vol. 1, pp. 567–78). Berlin: De Gruyter.

Hyltenstam, K. and Viberg, A. (eds) (1993) *Progression and Regression in Language. Sociocultural, Neuropsychological and Linguistic Perspectives*. New York: Academic Press.

Jakobson, R. (1941) *Kindersprache, Aphasie und allgemeine Lautgetze*. Uppsala: Almqvist and Wiksell.

Jessner, U. and Herdina, P. (1996) Interaktionsphänomene im multilingualen Menschen: Erklärungsmöglichkeiten durch einen systemtheoretischen Ansatz. In A. Fill (ed.) *Sprachökologie und Ökolinguistik* (pp. 217–30). Tübingen: Stauffenburg.

Kallenbach, C. (1996) *Subjektive Theorien: Was Schüler und Schülerinnen über Fremdsprachenlernen denken.* Tübingen: Narr.

Kecskes, I. and Papp, T. (2000) *Foreign Language and Mother Tongue.* Mahwah, NJ: Lawrence Erlbaum.

Kellerman, E. and Sharwood-Smith, M. (eds) (1986) *Crosslinguistic Influence in Second Language Acquisition.* Oxford: Pergamon Press.

Lambert. W. and Moore, S. (1986) Problem areas in the study of language attrition. In B. Weltens, K. de Bot and T. van Els (eds) *Language Attrition in Progress* (pp. 177–86). Dordrecht: Foris Publications.

MacWhinney, B. (ed.) (1999) *The Emergence of Language.* Mahwah, NJ: Lawrence Erlbaum.

Meara, P. (1999) Self organisation in bilingual lexicons. In P. Broeder and J. Muure (eds) *Language and Thought in Development* (pp. 127–44). Tübingen: Narr.

Morris, P. and Gruneberg, M. (1994) *Theoretical Aspects of Memory.* London: Routledge.

Nemser, W. (1971) Approximative systems of foreign language learners. *IRAL 9,* 115–23.

Olshtain, E. (1986) The attrition of English as a second language with speakers of Hebrew. In B. Weltens, K. de Bot and T. van Els (eds) *Language Attrition in Progress* (pp. 187–204). Dordrecht: Foris Publications.

Paulston, C.B. (1994) *Linguistic Minorities in Multilingual Settings.* Amsterdam: Benjamins.

Phillips, D. (1992) *The Social Scientist's Bestiary. A Guide to Fabled Threats to, and Defences of, Naturalistic Social Science.* Oxford: Pergamon Press.

Schmid, M. (2001) First language attrition: Methodological frameworks and empirical evidence. Paper presented at Third International Symposium on Bilingualism, Bristol, April.

Seliger, H. (1996) Primary language attrition in the context of bilingualism. In W. Ritchie and T. Bathia (eds) *Handbook of Second Language Acquisition* (pp. 605–27). New York: Academic Press.

Seliger, H. and Vago, R. (eds) (1991) *First Language Attrition.* Cambridge: Cambridge University Press.

Selinker, L. (1972) Interlanguage. *IRAL 10* (3), 209–31.

Sharwood-Smith, M. and van Buren, P. (1991) First language attrition and the parameter setting model. In H. Seliger and R. Vago (eds) *First Language Attrition* (pp. 18–30). Cambridge: Cambridge University Press.

Singleton, D. and Lengyel, Z. (eds) (1995) *The Age Factor in Second Language Acquisition.* Clevedon: Multilingual Matters.

Van Geert, P. (1990) *Dynamic Systems of Development: Change between Complexity and Chaos.* New York: Harvester Wheatsheaf.

Weltens, B. (1988) *The Attrition of French as a Foreign Language.* Dordrecht: Foris.

Weltens, B. and Grendel, M. (1993) Attrition of vocabulary knowledge. In R. Schreuder and B. Weltens (eds) *The Bilingual Lexicon* (pp. 135–56). Amsterdam: Benjamins.

Weltens, B., De Bot, K. and van Els, T. (eds) (1986) *Language Attrition in Progress.* Dordrecht: Foris Publications.

## Chapter 13

# How to Demonstrate the Conceptual Effect of L2 on L1? Methods and Techniques

ISTVAN KECSKES AND TUNDE PAPP

## Objectives

This chapter discusses the L2→L1 effect in an environment where the main source of foreign language (FL) is classroom instruction and the target language culture is not directly present. In earlier works we argued that the L2 influence in these circumstances is only a potential and not a necessity (Kecskes, 1998; Kecskes & Papp, 2000a). When L2 proficiency reaches a hypothetical threshold, the conceptual system is affected by the new language. It is, however, very difficult to demonstrate that this influence exists, because it is conceptual rather than linguistic. Consequently, it affects the use of L1 as a whole. If we want to demonstrate the L2→L1 effect in a foreign language environment, we need to discuss the nature of this phenomenon, describe the factors that bring about the effect, and develop a special measurement system to show that it exists. In the first part of the chapter we will discuss proficiency and transfer as the two most important factors shaping the L2→L1 relation after the hypothetical threshold is reached. In the second part, concrete procedures and measurements are recommended for detecting the L2 effect in L1 production.

## Nature of L2→L1 Effect

Depending on the social context of the language contact situation, the nature of the L2 →L1 effect can vary in the following ways:

(1) L2 or FL serves as lingua franca, for instance, in countries such as Nigeria (English) or Senegal (French);
(2) pidgin and creole;
(3) immigrants studying the language of their new L2 community, which affects the use of their L1 significantly;

(4) bilingual L1 acquisition: the child is exposed to two languages from birth, e.g. De Houwer (1990);
(5) both languages are present in the same country or community, but one of them is dominant (Swedish/Finnish in Finland or English/Gaelic in Ireland);
(6) instructed foreign language in a relatively homogeneous language community.

Several cases on the list are addressed in this volume. Our chapter, however, focuses only on the last case: (6) *when the target is a foreign language in a relatively homogeneous language community*. The foreign language is learned through instruction in a classroom setting, and students usually do not have direct access to the target language culture. There have been a few efforts (Cunningham & Graham, 2000; Kecskes & Papp, 1995; Kecskes, 1998; Kecskes & Papp, 2000a; 2000b; Papp, 1991) to demonstrate that the emerging FL influences the use of the L1 in the foreign language environment, and that this process may lead to the development of multi-competence (Cook, 1991; 1992). As a result of those studies, it was argued that not only bilingual development but also intensive foreign language learning may lead to the emergence of a Common Underlying Conceptual Base (CUCB) that is responsible for the operation of two language channels. Investigation in this issue is important because it may give us an insight into the conceptual development of bilingual and multilingual persons. Kecskes (1998) and Kecskes and Papp (2000a) claimed that the L2→L1 effect in a foreign language environment is conceptual rather than linguistic. However, very little is known about how this influence occurs in L1 production. Extensive research is needed to explain the nature of the L2→L1 effect in these special circumstances. One of the first steps is to develop an adequate system of measurement to describe how the L1 is affected by intensive FL learning and use. Before such a system can be developed, we need to discuss several theoretical issues concerning L1 performance *affected by the development of another linguistic system* (L2) when exposure to the target language is intensive but is not supported by the constant presence of the target language culture.

## Factors shaping L2→L1 influence

Two interacting factors play a decisive role in shaping the L2→L1 influence:

(1) level of proficiency and the development of a Common Underlying Conceptual Base;
(2) nature of transfer.

## Level of proficiency

The level of proficiency in the L2 is one obvious factor. A person who has taken first year university Spanish will hardly develop a separate system for Spanish. De Bot (1992) argued that the L1 is usually flexible enough to add the emerging foreign language as an additional register to those already in existence. We claimed (Kecskes, 1998; Kecskes & Papp, 2000a) that intensive exposure to and regular use of the foreign or/and second language may lead to the emergence of a Common Underlying Conceptual Base (CUCB) that is responsible for the operation of the two or more languages. However, the development of the CUCB is dependent on proficiency in the L2, which has to reach a certain hypothetical threshold. Up to that proficiency level, foreign language learning is likely to be no more than a kind of educational enhancement that may only slightly affect cognitive development and may not necessarily result in the emergence of a CUCB. If the exposure to the foreign language is not intensive enough, the L1 conceptual base may remain practically unaffected because students usually learn only new labels for existing concepts. The emerging FL is incorporated into the classification system already available in the first language, and its operation relies on the previously developed conceptual system. In order for a Dual Language System (DLS) to develop, the conceptual structure needs to change from an L1-Conceptual Base into a Common Underlying Conceptual Base. We conceptualise the CUCB as the basis and originator of all bilingual or multilingual linguistic actions, a 'container' that includes everything but the language system itself (rules plus lexicon). It is in the CUCB that the socio-cultural heritage and previous knowledge of the learner are confronted with the new information entering the CUCB through both language channels, and real-world knowledge mixes with academic knowledge and develops into something that is frequently referred to as 'socio-cultural background knowledge' (Adamson, 1993; Kecskes, 1994; Kecskes & Papp, 2000a). It is in the *CUCB* that thoughts originate, and then are mapped onto linguistic signs to reach the surface through either of the language channels. Thanks to the CUCB, information processing skills and educational attainment may be developed through two languages as well as through one language. Cognitive functioning and school achievement may be fed either through one language or through two languages if both are well developed. In contrast to a one-language-governed conceptual base and one language channel of monolinguals, bilinguals/multilinguals have a CUCB that is a common knowledge base for both languages, and two language channels that are usually operational in both directions. *The existence of the CUCB as well as the constant interaction* of the two language channels make bi- and multilingual development and language use unique, and this is why neither of the participating languages can be compared with the monolingual system.

Exactly when the learner reaches the threshold in L2 proficiency that triggers the emergence of the CUCB is crucial for bilingual development. If we want to learn more about this hypothetical threshold that is crucial for the L2→L1 effect, we need to discuss what happens when adult foreign language learners start to learn new words in the target language. It is conceivable that they will relate a word in the FL to its translation equivalent in the L1, and will do so by constructing a lexical link between these two words. When encountering a new word in the foreign language, the learner tries to reach into the conceptual base to find the concept that the word in the target language stands for. Since the conceptual system of the learner is L1-based, the closest concept can be reached through a word that denotes the concept in the L1. Consequently, at that stage of development, there can hardly be any direct route between the FL word and the concept. The obvious way for the FL learner to reach the concept is through the L1 translation equivalent. This is called the 'Word Association Model' by Kroll and Stewart (1994) and, most recently, 'the first language (L1) lemma mediation stage' by Nan Jiang (2000: 47). For instance:

| FL word | → | L1 translation equivalent | → | L1 concept |
|---------|---|---------------------------|---|------------|
| 'comida' | | 'lunch' (English) | | [LUNCH] |
| 'tapa' | | 'zakuska' (Russian) | | [ZAKUSKA] |

The strength of connections between the FL word and the conceptual system varies as a function of relative fluency in the FL and relative language dominance (Kroll, 1993: 70). The greater the fluency in the foreign language, the less the learner has to rely on L1 word association because *the growth of foreign language proficiency brings about changes in the conceptual system, which starts to accommodate* knowledge and concepts gained through the foreign language. Consequently, it gradually ceases to be an L1 conceptual base and changes into a CUCB, which is responsible for the operation of two language channels. The emerging CUCB makes it possible to establish a direct connection between the foreign language word and the appropriate concept in the CUCB.

The Kroll–Stewart model suggests that in the bilingual system there are both lexical and conceptual connections between the two languages, but the strength of these links differs. With increase in fluency in the foreign language, there comes a reliance on conceptual mediation between the two languages, although lexical connections will remain active all the time. *If we want to demonstrate the FL→L1 influence, we need to look for signs in the L1 production that reveal conceptual change.* In our opinion these signs must primarily be sought in L1 vocabulary use and sentence building.

## Nature of transfer

The L2→L1 effect depends significantly on the changing nature of transfer. We have argued that transfer in multilingual development is a dynamic process that can result in positive or negative effects (Kecskes, 1998; Kecskes & Papp, 2000a). In our understanding, transfer is any kind of movement and/or influence of concepts, knowledge, skills or linguistic elements (structures, forms), in either direction, between the L1 and the subsequent language(s). In the language development of a bilingual or multilingual person, transfer is always present, and keeps changing all the time. It is more or less intensive, either positive or negative, its direction changes from L1 to L2 or vice versa, and it either occurs between the language channels or affects conceptual fields. This dynamic nature of transfer has recently been supported by other researchers such as Jessner (2002) and Francis (2000).

The changing nature of transfer usually leads to structural and lexical difficulties *in the first phase of multilingual development* that is dominated by unidirectional (L1→L2) processes. In this period of development, transfer in the opposite direction (L2→L1) is not significant, and seems to be a matter of interaction of the language channels rather than the conceptual system. That is why this transfer is usually considered as a negative phenomenon that is generally the sign of lack of some kind of linguistic knowledge and takes the form of grammatical and/or lexical mistakes and errors. The more proficient the learner becomes in the L2, and the more firmly the CUCB is established in the mind, the more positive the content of transfer may become. *This positive transfer is predominantly neither structural nor lexical but pragmatic, knowledge and skill transfer* that is bidirectional and has a serious bearing on the language behaviour and discourse organisation of the multilingual speaker because it is a phenomenon of CUCB rather than language channel (Kecskes & Papp, 2000a). Some researchers questioned the use of the term 'transfer' for this type of cross-linguistic influence (e.g. Cook, 2000; Francis, 2000; Kellermann, 1995). We have kept the term because not all knowledge and skills are language-neutral: a part of them is language-specific, and is 'transferred', that is to say, becomes usable within the CUCB.

It is important to note that if the environment and language use change, and the L2 is used less frequently, there may be a return to the phase of language channel transfer that is characterised by syntactic and lexical errors. Depending on this up-and-down movement on the multilingual developmental continuum and the dynamic change in transfer phenomena, *the effect of L2 on L1 can be more or less significant.* Low proficiency and relatively rare use of the FL result in linguistic transfer from the L1 to the L2, as has been described in the relevant literature several times. High proficiency in the FL, however, results in conceptual rather than linguistic transfer, and the strengthening of the L2→L1 influence. The changing nature of transfer requires a distinction between two types of transfer:

(1) *Transfer as a linguistic systems phenomenon*: when the interaction of the two or more language systems, and the L1-dominated Conceptual Base results in the transfer of a sound pattern, lexical item or structure from one language system to another.
(2) *Transfer as a CUCB phenomenon*: when knowledge or skills acquired through one language system become ready to be used through the other language channel(s).

The L2→L1 effect in a foreign-language environment can be explained as a CUCB phenomenon rather than a linguistic systems phenomenon because this influence occurs only if the learner's L2 proficiency has reached the threshold required for the CUCB to emerge. In our previous studies we developed three procedures to demonstrate the influence of L2 on L1 production. The first two procedures focused on (1) structural well-formedness, and (2) the use of linguistic memory vs. visual memory in written production (Kecskes & Papp, 1995, 2000a; Papp, 1991). The third procedure (3) measured the metaphorical density of texts produced by the participants of the Hungarian experiment (Kecskes & Papp, 2000b). These measurements helped us demonstrate that students who had gone through an intensive FL training or had the foreign language as a medium of instruction used their L1 differently from those who did not have access to those types of training. The difference was represented in a more sophisticated and elaborated use of the L1. The emergence of a Dual Language System (DLS) *resulted in a conceptual fluency* that significantly differed from the conceptual fluency of a monolingual speaker.

## Conceptual Fluency in Bilinguals

*Conceptual fluency* refers to the extent that bilingual speakers are able to understand and use concepts, knowledge and skills acquired through the channel of either language, and means the level of free access to vocabulary in both languages. It presupposes that the conceptual–semantic interface works properly and, as a result, depending on the level of conceptual fluency, the bilingual person has greater or lesser difficulty finding the right words to express his/her ideas through the channel of either language.

Concepts in the CUCB are either relatively neutral or culture-specific in their content, and language-specific through the lexical items that denote them (Kecskes & Papp, 2000a). Conceptual fluency is not an issue in L1 development because each learner goes through the same developmental processes and is exposed to the same language and culture. So conceptual fluency, just like Chomsky's 'competence' is a *collective* rather than an individual phenomenon. In the tradition of monolingual Chomskian linguistics, concepts are the same for everyone and the language learners' task is to identify the right label for the right concept. In multilingual development, however, each learner has an individual route of development. In other words each learner is exposed to each language and culture in a different way for a different period of time. Consequently, there is no 'ideal' bilingual speaker in the Chomskian sense of the word. Therefore, it is not the linguistic system of the bilingual that is of primary importance for researchers investigating multilingual development, but the conceptual system that is responsible for the operation of both the L1 and L2 (or L$x$).

If we want to demonstrate the L2→L1 influence, we need to focus on the *change in conceptual fluency*: How does the conceptual fluency of a monolingual speaker relate to the conceptual fluency of a bilingual speaker? How will the conceptual system change under the influence of the L2? How can this change be demonstrated in the L1 production? From what perspectives does L1 production need to be analysed? What elements of language production will give information on the conceptual change? In order to answer these questions, we suggest that the focus should be on the following features of bilingual L1 production in a foreign language environment:

(1)  structural well-formedness: sentence building and manipulation;
(2)  lexical quality;
(3)  cognitive functioning.

## Why Exactly These Features?

How do measuring structural well-formedness, lexical quality and cognitive functioning fit into our theoretical framework? Is there not a contradiction between what was claimed earlier about the nature of transfer and the features expected to demonstrate change in conceptual fluency? How can findings based on structural well-formedness or lexical quality support the claim that the L2→L1 transfer is primarily knowledge and skill transfer? These are all legitimate questions. In order to give an adequate response, we need to direct attention to some important issues concerning transfer and change in language use. First of all, we cannot expect L2→L1 transfer to be the same as L1→L2 transfer. The L2 effect will not necessarily result in any errors in L1 use. The problem is that the L2 influence is sometimes hardly 'visible' at all in the literal sense of the word. This effect cannot be expected to occur in the form of some sort of structure or vocabulary transfer (although there may be such examples), rather, it will influence the way in which L1 is used. For example it will result in a more sophisticated use of the L1, which may occur in the form of a positive change in literacy skills, text developing and manipulating skills, sentence-construction, and a more selective use of the vocabulary. When examining case (5) at the beginning of this chapter (two languages in the same country, but one dominant), Francis found that literacy skills learned through the dominant language (Spanish) can be applied to literacy tasks in another language (Náhuatl) that children understand, but in which they have not had the opportunity to practice reading and writing (Francis, 2000). Francis argued that this was possible because literacy skills are accessed from a Common Underlying Proficiency. Although Francis's research scenario significantly differs from that of ours, his results also support the existence of a CUCB that makes conceptual transfer possible in either direction.

As emphasised earlier, we cannot look for a direct effect of the L2 on the L1 because there hardly seems to be anything like this. What we look for is a *positive qualitative change* in the use of the L1 that is quantifiable. Positive qualitative change can be manifested in the form of improving literacy skills, text developing and manipulating skills, sentence-construction, and a more selective use of the vocabulary. So the main issue is: how can any positive change be demonstrated quantitatively? If quantitative proof is needed, it is essential to turn to concrete linguistic elements that are used in language production: structures and words. It may now be clear why we need to focus on structural well-formedness and lexical quality of texts when we attempt to demonstrate the positive change in the use of the L1 under the influence of the L2. Therefore our research question should be 'in what direction will the L1 use develop if learners have foreign language training, or use a foreign language as the medium of instruction?' rather than 'are there any structures or lexical items that are transferred from the L2 to the L1?'. Is there any difference in the L1 use of those students who are exposed to a foreign language in different ways, such as being taught content area through a foreign language, studying a foreign language intensively or taking foreign language classes just as an educational requirement or enhancement? Our claim is that, if there is a demonstrable difference in the quality of L1 use of various types of foreign language learners in comparison to their own L1 production when not (or before being) exposed to FL, and to that of monolingual L1 users, then that difference is likely to have been brought about as a result of a more or less intensive use of one or more foreign languages.

We will now describe procedures and measurements that can be incorporated into tests and surveys aiming to demonstrate the conceptual nature of the L2→L1 influence in a foreign language environment. It must be underlined, however, that these indices do not make too much sense if we use them separately. As mentioned before, it is change in conceptual fluency that we look for when we want to tap the L2→L1 effect. This change is identifiable only if at least two comparisons are made:

(1)  actual L1 production is compared with the L1 production of an earlier period when foreign language was not introduced yet, or exposure to the FL was less extensive;
(2)  the indices below are compared to each other in both surveys.

### Structural Well-Formedness

Linguists investigating child language acquisition have argued that the complexity and nature of clause organisation and dependence is an important sign of how thought is developed (Clark & Clark, 1977; Limber, 1973; Papp, 1991; Slobin, 1973). A sign of positive change in conceptual fluency can be an elaborated use of subordinations and variety of conjunctions. The following indices may reveal this change:

### Sentence complexity ratio (S/C)

This is the total number of sentences divided by the number of subordinate clauses (Wolfe-Quintero *et al.*, 1998). Using sentences as a production unit captures the ways that learners coordinate, subordinate, and reduce their thoughts within a single unit that has psychological reality for them. A positive change is when the small gap between the numerator and the denominator increases or (if the gap was originally too wide) decreases. Both an increase and decrease can be a positive sign of conceptual change.

### Loban index

$$\frac{B, C, D}{A, B, C, D}$$

In this index, A (1 point) is a subordinate clause that is directly dependent upon a main clause; B (2 points) is a dependent clause modifying or placed within another dependent clause; C (2 points) is a dependent clause containing a verbal construction (i.e. infinitive, gerund, participle); and D

(3 points) is a dependent clause modifying or placed within another dependent clause that in turn, is within or modifying another dependent clause.

The Loban Weighted Index of Subordination (Loban 1954; 1963) was successfully used in our experiment with Hungarian learners of several foreign languages (Kecskes, 1998; Kecskes & Papp, 2000a). It focuses on the use of complex sentences with particular emphasis on the frequency and types of subordinations therein, and relates the number of more complex subordinations to the total number of subordinations. When this index is high, it means that well-constructed sentences can be found in the text.

### Conjunction index (TC/NC)

In this index, the number of types of conjunction is divided by the total number of conjunctions. A high ratio here demonstrates the proper use of the potential of the language and an increasing level of conceptual fluency. One of the main problems in language production is the proper and varied use of conjunctions. The introduction of a foreign language requires the conceptualisation of new conjunctions and the reconceptualisation of the existing ones. This process may have a positive effect on the use of conjunctions in the L1 because it requires the rethinking of the functions of existing conjunctions that may clarify conceptual mechanisms responsible for subordinations. When making a comparison between the functions of the English conjunction *although* and its possible Hungarian equivalents (*bá, habár, jóllehet*) an English/Hungarian bilingual may discover new potentials of a conjunction that s/he used only occasionally earlier.

The Loban Index alone cannot give an adequate picture of language use because learners may use the same or similar types of complex subordination again and again. However, the comparison of the Loban Index and the Conjunction Index will help us identify a real positive tendency in the L1 production. If both indices are high, there is little doubt about the sophisticated use of language means.

### Lexical Quality

Lexical Quality is concerned, not with how many words are present in the production, but with how varied and sophisticated the words or word types are. Lexical variation and sophistication are related to language development. Learners who have more productive vocabulary items available to them are able to vary their word choices more freely. Consequently, a larger ratio on variation and sophistication measures should reveal greater lexical proficiency that is, in our view, one possible indicator of conceptual fluency. Confidence in vocabulary use is directly connected to conceptual development because fully developed concepts result in proper use of their labels (Corson, 1997; Kecskes & Papp, 2000a).

How can the L2→L1 influence be detected in lexical quality? The increase and change in the content of certain concepts, reconceptualisation and concept modification brought about in the CUCB by the emergence of L2 may result in the activation of L1 words that earlier belonged to the passive vocabulary of the speaker. It may also result in a more elaborated and frequent use of L1 words related to the new vocabulary and metaphorical system developed through the L2 channel. So what we expect here is not borrowings from the L2, but L1 words that are indirectly activated by the new language.

### Variation ratio (LWT/W)

This is the number of lexical word types (LWT) divided by the total number of words. LWT refers to the number of content words represented in the text. We count all possible morphological representations of the same word only once. Cumming and Mellow (1996) investigated this measure with Japanese and French learners of English. As lexical word types (content words) usually denote concepts, this ratio demonstrates how rich a student's vocabulary is, and what concepts (concrete or abstract) students feel comfortable with.

### Sophistication ratio (SWT/LWT)

This is the number of sophisticated word types divided by the number of lexical word types. The definition of sophisticated word types changes study by study. The term usually refers to lexical word types that are generally parts of the Graeco-Latin word stock of English, denote abstract concepts and belong to the group of less frequently used words in the Birmingham Corpus. These words are available in the lexicon of several languages of Indo-European, Finno-Ugric or other origin. This index might be a good indicator of the effect of English on the L1 of students because the occurrence of these words in languages other than English or Neo-Latin languages (such as Italian, French and Spanish) is not as frequent as in English, even in the scientific literature.

### Synonymy ratio (S/LWT)

This is the number of applied synonyms per number of lexical word types. The knowledge of a foreign language is expected to open up new lexical routes to one and the same concept in the CUCB. This might direct language users' attention to aspects of a concept that earlier they did not notice. The variety of lexical routes to one and the same concept is expected to raise the need in the user to look for lexical items that can express and/or denote a concept and/or thought in the most adequate way. This ratio can be applied in the summaries that will be described below.

## Cognitive Functioning

Bilingual memory differs from monolingual memory to a great extent (see, for example, Paradis, 1997; Pavlenko, 1999). We argue that bilingual memory is the CUCB where mental representations of two languages coexist and interact. The result is a kind of cognitive functioning that is not the same as that of monolingual speakers. This difference is reflected not only in the use of concrete linguistic elements such as structures and words, but also in cultural values, text comprehension and discourse organisation of bilingual speakers. Each language used as an L1 of a community has a system of expectations and traditions. 'Performance' (even in the Chomskian sense of the word), pragmatics and language use have their own rules. Bilinguals with a CUCB may not apply these rules in the usual and/or expected way because their language production is operated by a conceptual system that includes the mental representation of not one but two languages. It is possible that, for instance, a speaker whose L1 is Russian under the influence of English as an L2 will use politeness formulas in his L1 differently from monolingual speakers of Russian. Kasper and Blum-Kulka (1993) spoke about 'intercultural style', which refers to a unique development of the CUCB when speakers fully competent in two languages may create a unique style of speaking that is both related to and distinct from the styles prevalent in the two substrata. They rely on this style regardless of the language being used. Although the existence of intercultural style is supported by studies that focus on immigrants only, we claimed (Kecskes & Papp, 2000a) that intensive foreign language learning can also bring about this language behaviour, which can be demonstrated especially well in the L1 production of foreign language learners. The indices described below may give us some insight into this unique part of the conceptual system of bilinguals.

### Modality index (ME/C)

This is the number of modality expressions per number of subordinate clauses. An important feature of conceptual fluency is how confident students are in the use of modality. Hinkel (1995) demonstrated how cultural values are reflected in the use of modal verbs in the language production of non-native speakers of English. Modality is expressed differently in configurational (CON) and non-configurational (NON-CON) languages, so we must be careful in the use of this index. Configurational languages (such as, for example, English or French) have bound/fixed word order governed by grammatical rules (White, 1989). Phrase structure configurations encode the grammatical functions, and logical relations can be computed only at a virtual level of representation. For instance:

Peter likes dogs.

No other permutation of this sentence is allowed: *Likes Peter dogs, Dogs Peter likes, Likes dogs Peter,* etc. are all incorrect.

In contrast to configurational languages, non-configurational languages (such as Russian or Hungarian) have complex morphology and a word order that is governed by pragmatic rather than grammatical rules (Kiss, 1987). For instance, the sentence *Peter likes dogs* can have several equivalents in Hungarian such as, for instance:

Peter szereti a kutyakat. ('Peter likes dogs.')

A kutyakat Peter szereti. ('Dogs Peter likes.')

Szereti Peter a kutyakat. ('Likes Peter dogs.')

The difference between these sentences is in emphasis: which element of the sentence is emphasised by the speaker. These permutations are made possible by the suffixes and endings, which make clear how the words in the sentence are connected grammatically.

In a CON language such as English, modality is usually expressed by modal verbs used in different configurations while in a NON-CON language such as Catalan, Nepalese or Hungarian special suffixes are used to denote modality. For instance:

English: You *would need* to leave.

Hungarian: El *kellene* menned. ( kell-ene)

The modality index relates the number of modality expressions (with either modal verbs or modality suffixes) to the number of subordinate clauses in the text, which basically shows how many of the clauses contain expressions referring to modality. The higher this number, the more confident the speaker appears to be in the use of modality.

## Metaphorical density (MET/TS)

This is the number of metaphorical expressions divided by the number of sentences. Metaphor underlies the representation of a considerable proportion of our common concepts (Lakoff & Johnson, 1980). If a new language is added to the L1, with increasing proficiency the L1-based conceptual system is restructured and develops into a CUCB. Based on this change, we can hypothesise that the new conceptual mechanisms and structures may result in new metaphors in the use of L1. Our research findings pointed to that possible tendency (Kecskes & Papp, 2000b). Danesi (1992) suggested that metaphorical competence (MC) is as important as grammatical and communicative competence because it is closely linked to the ways in which a culture organises its world conceptually. Not only thinking and acting are based on this conceptual system, but in large part communication as well. Therefore, language is an important source of evidence of what that system is like. MC is a basic feature of native-speaker speech production because native speakers usually program discourse in metaphorical ways. Can the use of metaphors in the L1 be influenced by intensive foreign language learning? Is this index an adequate means of demonstrating the L1→L1 effect? The answer is 'yes'; however, we must look not only at the numbers but also at the kind of metaphors the speaker uses. With the emergence of the CUCB, the number and nature of metaphors in L1 language production is expected to change, because bilingual speakers may rely on a vocabulary that is supported by mental representations from two languages.

Some unusual metaphors are also expected to appear in the L1 language production under the influence of L2 conceptual structures.

An index of metaphorical density (MD) should be computed for each written production (test or survey). This measures the number of metaphorical expressions as a percentage of the total number of sentences written. If, for instance, a text consisting of 9 sentences contains 3 metaphorical expressions, the MD index is $3/9 = 0.33 = 33\%$. It is irrelevant for this count whether metaphorical expressions occurred in only one sentence or in several sentences.

## Summary Writing

Summary writing may be a good way to check whether a student has already reached the hypothetical threshold that results in the emergence of the CUCB. How does this relate to the L2→L1 effect? As claimed earlier, the first and most important condition for L2→L1 influence is the existence of the CUCB. Before that, the conceptual system of L1 is basically unaffected by the development of the new language. Consequently, if the CUCB already exists, the L2→L1 effect is a potential that may or may not occur.

It is interesting to compare how students write summaries in their L1 and their L2. They are expected to do a summary in their L1 conceptually. By 'conceptual summary' we mean a summary that focuses on the content rather than on the repetition of words and expressions found in the original text. In the L2, however, conceptual summary is expected only if the CUCB already exists. Otherwise students are supposed to rely on lexical rather than conceptual means. It has to be emphasised, however, that the difference between conceptual and lexical summary is a potentiality rather than a necessity. This means that *NOT all native speakers will do conceptual summaries, nor will all L2 learners with a CUCB. In the case of non-native speakers, when a summary is written in the L2, and it is a conceptual rather than a lexical summary, we can almost be sure that the given person has passed the hypothetical threshold and developed a CUCB.*

## How to analyse summaries

The following word-types must be distinguished in the original text and its summary:

*Key-words*

These refer to the most important information in the text. These words must be included in the summary otherwise the original content of the text cannot be preserved.

*Content-words*

These carry the content of the text but can be substituted by synonyms without changing the original story. The use of these words is crucial for the final outcome of the analysis because if the student clings to the words that are in the text and does not try to use synonymous words or expressions (in the summary) that can express the same or similar ideas, the result is usually a lexical summary that is basically a short repetition of the original text.

*Fill-in-words*

These are mainly function words and very frequently used lexical words (*think, reason, ask, find,* etc.) that serve to ensure the coherence of the text. An example for analysis can be the following text:

## Example

### Traffic Stop Leads Officer to His Long-Lost Father

*Los Angeles (AP)*

Paul Benitez thought the policeman was staring into his eyes to see if he was drunk, but there was another reason: Officer Kelly Benitez realised that he had found his long-lost father.

'Were you ever married to a woman named Debra?' Officer Benitez asked the man in the beat-up Ford Thunderbird he had just pulled over for driving with an expired registration tag.

'No', he said, but he had dated a woman with that name about 30 years ago. Then he noticed the officer's nametag.

'Are you Kelly?' he asked.

The officer nodded.

'Oh my God. I'm your dad,' the driver said.

'The Mr. Cop role stopped right there, ' said the 29-year-old officer.

The two embraced, prompting several cars to pull over at what they thought was a policeman being assaulted. Kelly held onto his father and waved the cars into traffic with a free hand.

### Word-types in the text:

*Key-words:* long-lost father; expired registration tag; nametag

*Content-words:* stare into; drunk; realise; married; beat-up; pull over; date a woman; dad; cop role; embrace; prompt; assault; hold onto; wave; free hand; etc.

*Fill-in-words:* think, ask, find, be, etc.

### Data collection methods

The following methods are recommended for data collection:

*Picture series*
   *Task:* Write a text (or story) based on a series of pictures (30 minutes).

*Composition*
   *Task:* Write a composition titled 'My Plans for the Future' in L1 (30 minutes)

*Summary*
   *Task:* Summarise the content of an article in no more than 8–10 sentences.

## Conclusions

Our goal with this chapter is to support those researchers who plan to analyse the effect of L2 on L1 in a foreign language environment. The procedures and measurements described above may contribute to the design of experiments or surveys aiming to investigate conceptual development and changes in bilingual memory. Multilingual development is not a linear process. It is a constant interaction between two or more languages, with its ups and downs. In this process an individual variability is present all the time, and there are points and phases on the developmental continuum where one aspect of development may progress at the expense of another. Consequently, we are not interested in defining or identifying some kind of developmental level with the measurements described above, rather we focus on the state of the Dual Language System of each individual student at two given points of time:

(1)  when there is no foreign language instruction, or instruction is not intensive enough to result in the development of a CUCB;
(2)  after a period of intensive foreign language learning which is expected to have resulted in the emergence of a CUCB.

Based on the indices described above, L1 production in the first and second period should be compared, and changes registered and analysed. The results of this analysis can give researchers information on the differences between monolingual and bilingual memory, the nature of the L2→L1 effect, and the change in conceptual fluency as a result of multilingual development.

Foreign language environment, however, is only one of the possible scenarios for L2→L1 influence. Although the procedures and measurements discussed in this chapter were developed for this particular case, some of them may be used with success in other cases of bilingual or multilingual development.

## References

Adamson, H.D. (1993) *Academic Competence*. New York, Longman.

Clark, H.H. and Clark, E.V. (1977) *Psychology and Language*. New York: Harcourt Brace Jovanovich.

Cook, V.J. (1991) The poverty-of-the-stimulus argument and multi-competence. *Second Language Research* 7 (2), 103–117.

Cook, V.J. (1992) Evidence for multi-competence. *Language Learning* 42 (4), 557–591.

Cook, V.J. (2000) Is transfer the right word? Paper presented at the 7th International Pragmatics Conference, Budapest, July. Available online at: privatewww.essex.ac.uk/~vcook/OBS8.htm.

Corson, D. (1997) The learning and use of academic English words. *Language Learning* (47) 4, 671–718.

Cumming, A. and Mellow, D. (1996) An investigation into the validity of written indicators of second language proficiency. In A. Cumming and R. Berwick (eds) *Validation in Language Testing* (pp. 72–93). Clevedon: Multilingual Matters.

Cunningham, T.H. and Graham, C.R. (2000) Increasing native English vocabulary recognition through Spanish immersion: Cognate transfer from foreign to first language. *Journal of Educational Psychology* 92 (1), 37–49.

Danesi, M. (1992) Metaphorical competence in second language acquisition and second language teaching: The neglected dimension. In J.E. Alatis (ed.) *Georgetown University Round Table on Languages and Linguistics* (pp. 489–500). Washington, DC: Georgetown University Press.

De Bot, K. (1992) A bilingual production model: Levelt's 'speaking' model adapted. *Applied Linguistics* 13 (1), 1–24.

De Houwer, A. (1990) *The Acquisition of Two Languages from Birth: A Base Study.* Cambridge: Cambridge University Press.

Francis, N. (2000) The shared conceptual system and language processing in bilingual children: Findings from literacy assessment in Spanish and Nahuatl. *Applied Linguistics* 21 (2), 170–204.

Hinkel, E. (1995) The use of modal verbs as a reflection of cultural values. *TESOL Quarterly* 29 ( 2), 325–243.

Jessner, U. (2002) *The Dynamic Model of Multilingualism.* Clevedon: Multilingual Matters.

Jiang, Nan (2000) Lexical representation and development in a second language. *Applied Linguistics* 21 (1), 47–77.

Kasper, G. and Blum-Kulka, S. (eds) (1993) *Interlanguage Pragmatics.* Oxford: Oxford University Press.

Kecskes, I. (1994) Conceptualization in foreign language learning. *Hands on Language* 6, 55–64.

Kecskes, I. (1998) The state of L1 knowledge in foreign language learners. *Word* 49 (3), 321–340.

Kecskes, I. and Papp, T. (1995) The linguistic effect of foreign language learning on the development of mother tongue skills. In M. Haggstrom, L. Morgan and J. Wieczorek (eds) *The Foreign Language Classroom: Bridging Theory and Practice* (pp. 163–181). New York and London: Garland.

Kecskes, I. and Papp, T. (2000a) *Foreign Language and Mother Tongue.* Hillsdale, NJ: Lawrence Erlbaum.

Kecskes, I. and Papp, T. (2000b) Metaphorical competence in trilingual language production. In J. Cenoz and U. Jessner (eds) *Acquisition of English as a Third Language* (p. 99–120). Clevedon: Multilingual Matters.

Kellerman, E. (1995) Crosslinguistic influence: Transfer to nowhere. *Annual Review of Applied Linguistics* 15, 125–150.

Kiss, K.E. (1987) *Configurationality in Hungarian.* Dordrecht: Reidel.

Kroll, J. (1993) Accessing conceptual representations. In R. Schreuder and B. Weltens (eds) *The Bilingual Lexicon* (pp. 53–83). Amsterdam/Philadelphia: John Benjamins.

Kroll, J. and Stewart, E. (1994) Category interference in translation and picture naming: Evidence for asymmetric connections between bilingual memory representations. *Journal of Memory and Language* 33, 149–174.

Lakoff, G. and Johnson, M. (1980) *Metaphors We Live By*. Chicago: University of Chicago Press.

Limber, J. (1973) The genesis of complex sentences. In T.E. Moore (ed.) *Cognitive Development and the Acquisition of Language*. New York: Academic Press.

Loban, W. (1954) *Literature and Social Sensitivity*. Champaign, IL: National Council of Teachers of English.

Loban, W. (1963) *The Language of Elementary School Children*. NCTE Research Report No.1. Champaign, IL: NCTE.

Papp, T. (1991) *Az anyanyelvi tudás és az eredményes idegennyelv tanulás összefüggései egy többszint?* longitudinális vizsgálat alapján ('The study of the interrelation of the mother tongue development and foreign language learning in a multi-level longitudinal experiment'). Unpublished dissertation for the candidate degree of the Hungarian Academy of Sciences. Budapest.

Paradis, M. (1997) The cognitive neuropsychology of bilingualism. In A. de Groot and J. Kroll (eds) *Tutorials in Bilingualism. Psycholinguistic Perspectives* (pp. 331–335). Mahwah, NJ: Lawrence Erlbaum:

Pavlenko, A. (1999) New approaches in concepts in bilingual memory. *Bilingualism: Language and Cognition* 2 (3), 209–230.

Slobin, D.I. (1973) Cognitive prerequisites for the development of grammar. In C.A. Ferguson and D.I. Slobin (eds) *Studies of Child Language Development*. New York: Holt, Rinehart and Winston.

White, L. (1989) *Universal Grammar and Second Language Acquisition*. Amsterdam and Philadelphia: John Benjamins.

Wolfe-Quintero, K., Inagaki, S. and Hae-Young, K (1998) *Second Language Development in Writing: Measures of Fluency, Accuracy and Complexity*. Second Language Teaching and Curriculum Center: The University of Hawaii at Manoa.

# Index